Janáček Studies

This volume of essays constitutes the first major study of the music of Janáček, now widely considered one of the most important composers of the early twentieth century. The essays deal with a broad range of topics relating to opera, symphonic poem, instrumental music, cultural context and reception. Some topics, such as the sources of Janáček's musical expressivity, questions of narrative, Janáček as musical analyst and Janáček as realist, have hitherto received little attention, whilst other more conventional topics, such as 'speech melody' and Janáček's ethnographic activities, are reappraised. A transcription of Janáček's analytical study of 'Jeux de vagues' from Debussy's *La mer* is published for the first time, and this document is considered in the light of Janáček's theory of music as a whole and of the reception of *La mer*.

Paul Wingfield is a Fellow of Trinity College, Cambridge, and is author of the Cambridge Music Handbook *Janáček: Glagolitic Mass*.

Janáček Studies

EDITED BY PAUL WINGFIELD

 CAMBRIDGE
UNIVERSITY PRESS

PUBLISHED BY THE PRESS SYNDICATE OF THE UNIVERSITY OF CAMBRIDGE
The Pitt Building, Trumpington Street, Cambridge CB2 1RP, United Kingdom

CAMBRIDGE UNIVERSITY PRESS
The Edinburgh Building, Cambridge CB2 2RU, UK   http://www.cup.cam.ac.uk
40 West 20th Street, New York, NY 10011–4211, USA   http://www.cup.org
10 Stamford Road, Oakleigh, Melbourne 3166, Australia

© Cambridge University Press 1999

First published 1999

Printed in the United Kingdom at the University Press, Cambridge

Typeset in Adobe Minion 10.25/14pt, using QuarkXpress™ [SE]

A catalogue record for this book is available from the British Library

Library of Congress cataloguing in publication data

Wingfield, Paul.
Janáček studies / edited by Paul Wingfield.
    p.   cm.
Includes index.
Contents: Expressive sources and resources in Janáček's musical
language / Robin Holloway – 'Nothing but pranks and puns': Janáček's
solo piano music / Thomas Adès – Narrative in Janáček's symphonic
poems / Hugh Macdonald – Evasive realism: narrative construction
in Dostoyevsky's and Janáček's *From the House of the Dead* / Geoffrey
Chew and Robert Vilain – Direct discourse and speech melody in
Janáček's operas / Miloš Štědroň – Kundera's eternal present and
Janáček's ancient gypsy / Michael Beckerman – Janáček's folk
settings and the *Vixen* / Zdeněk Skoumal – Janáček's operas in
Australia and New Zealand: a performance history / Adrienne Simpson
– Janáček's Moravian publishers / Nigel Simeone – Janáček, musical
analysis, and Debussy's 'Jeux de vagues' / Paul Wingfield.
ISBN 0 521 57357 2
1. Janáček, Leoš, 1854–1928 – Criticism and interpretation.
2. Janáček, Leoš, 1854–1928 – Contributions in music theory.
3. Debussy, Claude, 1862–1918. La Mer.   I. Title.
ML410.J18W57   1999
780′.92–dc21   98–38096   CIP

ISBN 0 521 57357 2 hardback

Contents

v

Preface

Robin Holloway writes on p. 11 below of this volume: '[Janáček's] reception is both ardent and on-target; he is not misunderstood, and no longer a cause. The next steps, alas, are academic appropriation and universal establishmentarianism.' Holloway is surely right to suggest that Janáček's works are now viewed widely and enthusiastically as core repertory – particularly the operas, which are performed more regularly than those of almost any other twentieth-century composer. And, of course, the devotion of a 'Studies' volume to a composer's music is the seal of 'academic appropriation' *par excellence*. Nevertheless, I hope this volume might be excused on the grounds that very little has yet been published about Janáček's music, even if, as Hanns Eisler once famously remarked, he is perhaps this century's most innovative composer in terms of musical 'expression'. In fact, the Janáček literature is still so overwhelmingly dominated by popular biography that a 'Studies' book could be regarded as long overdue, or at least as a valuable corrective.

The essays are not themed: the weighting towards opera, for example, reflects Janáček's apportioning of his energies rather than a scholarly agenda. Two authors essentially share Eisler's view of Janáček as the ultimate creator of musical expression. Holloway takes on both the entire oeuvre (centred on opera) and Janáček the man, seeking to discover how music 'can be reconciled with an aesthetic of unmitigated expression grounded in human utterance'. Tom Adès confines himself to a single 'underestimated' medium (solo piano), arguing that conventional analytical approaches are powerless when confronted by a composer who can transform a simple enharmonic shift into the most potent of signifiers.

A notable feature of Janáček research hitherto has been an avoidance of the concerns of modern musicology in the broader sense. This is certainly not true of the chapter by Geoffrey Chew and Robert Vilain, who, by exposing tensions between the music of *From the House of the Dead* and the work's literary model, raise important questions about the nature of operatic realism. Similarly, Hugh Macdonald's essay, which investigates the fractures between Janáček's symphonic poems and their programmes, has significant implications for the study of musical narrativity in general. Michael Beckerman's essay invites us to contemplate nothing less than the 'critical' differences between musical and dramatic time.

Not that familiar Janáček topics are excluded. Miloš Štědroň tackles the most frequently debated subject of all, 'speech melody', arguing that, contrary to received opinion, Janáček's deployment in his operas of vocal motives based on the rhythms and inflections of spoken Czech is a relatively rare, if powerful, compositional device. Zdeněk Skoumal offers a new approach to another mainstream topic: the interconnections between Janáček's activities as composer and ethnographer. Two further essays have a historical orientation. Nigel Simeone provides details about the provincial musical marketplace within which Janáček operated for most of his career. Adrienne Simpson reminds us that major developments in the reception of Janáček's music have not been limited to Europe and the United States.

One recurring motive in the book is the vital relationship for Janáček between music theory and composition. My own chapter thus grants the final word to Janáček the theorist and analyst, offering a transcription of his unpublished 1921 analytical study of 'Jeux de vagues' from Debussy's *La mer*, and considering this document in the light of Janáček's theory of music as a whole and of the reception of *La mer*.

I should like to take this opportunity to record some personal debts. First, to all my contributors, for their conscientious scholarship and their good-natured forbearance in the face of my editorial interference and constant requests for clarification. Also, I am grateful to Dimitra Stamogiannou for practical assistance. David Gascoigne provided invaluable advice concerning translation of the French texts quoted in my article. Inevitably, the period of a book's preparation is one of great trial to those close to the editor or author, and I would like to acknowledge my profound indebtedness to Anne, Jack, Alison, Pam, Christine and David, who have in different ways suffered and given their unqualified support over the last year or so. Finally, just as Debussy's *La mer* was written at a time of personal crisis for the composer, so the completion of this volume coincided with a turbulent phase in my own life. Penny Souster has borne the resulting delays and ditherings with considerable patience and understanding.

1 Expressive sources and resources in Janáček's musical language

ROBIN HOLLOWAY

Broadly speaking either composers want primarily to make shapes, patterns, forms, journeys, buildings, tables, gardens, mud-pies, or they want primarily to utter what wells up from within themselves, or from what is suggested within themselves by the impact of things from around them. If Haydn is the ultimate instance of the 'pure' composer writing 'music about music' (though manifestly not deficient in humanity), Janáček can surely be seen as the ultimate composer of *Affekt* in whom music becomes the medium for expression so immediate as to transcend the linguistic metaphor to become in itself the thing that feels and moves.

Suppose, when traversing the back routes of his loved and hated native land by coach or train a vast pang of inarticulate emotion swells up around the composer's heart – 'my country'; suppose, thinking of his parents, his earliest memories, impressions, motivations, sensations, thoughts – 'my childhood'; suppose, reliving the deepest, tenderest, most painful intimacies, their mixture of harsh and delicate, tender and cruel, guilty and carefree, blighted and flowering, dampened and burning – 'my life'; suppose, then, the composer would seek to 'express' these feelings, to capture the unutterable, as music purportedly can, in a chord-sequence, in a turn of phrase, a rhythmic gesture, a timbral combination, how would he do so? *What* chords, intervals, rhythms, timbres? They would need to be precise, notated without ambiguity (let alone mistakes) as performance-instructions to players; also accurate containers of the complex of emotions and sensations, to be conveyed to the listeners so that they understand aright. It would be Janáček above all, and in some respects Janáček alone, who would be able to show how such things might be done.

But only if the means were sonorous – utterance, articulate or

1

inarticulate, though not necessarily verbal. His *raison d'être* for writing music, and his main source of material with which to, is the sound of a human being in a condition of body and soul that compels such utterance. The human sound, whether heard or imagined wrung from the depths, or casually observed in, as it might be, the vocal intonations of two girls chatting as they wait for a man who doesn't turn up. Here with something concrete to start from, Janáček speculates about their characters, their lives, their futures; notates their converse as if collecting a folk-song, finds the clue to its rhythmicisation and pitching; and eventually from these, the harmony and coloration that will realise its latent musical life:

> Perhaps it was like this, strange as it seemed, that whenever someone spoke to me, I may [not have] grasped the words, but I grasped the rise and fall of the notes! I knew what the person was like: I knew now he or she felt, whether he or she was lying, whether he or or she was upset. As the person talked to me in a conventional conversation, I knew, I *heard* that, inside himself, the person wept ... I have been collecting speech melodies since 1879; I have an enormous collection. You see, these speech melodies are windows into people's souls – and what I would like to emphasize is this: for *dramatic music* they are of great importance.[1]

The same eager appetite to record is applied to birds, beasts, the mosquitoes of Venice, even the waves on the seashore at Vlissingen: there he is, notebook in hand, pencil poised, ears pricked.[2] One feels he could have understood the language of 'rocks and stones and trees' and give contour to 'what the wild flowers tell me', so long as they spoke in noises not signs.

Thus far it could almost be the attitude of an ethnologist, a naturalist, even a speech-therapist. But not quite. Janáček, in being after all a composer, can take the idea further: 'Identical ripples of emotion compel rhythms of tone which accord with rhythms of colours and touch. This is the secret of the conception of a musical composition, an unconscious

---

[1] Janáček in an interview (8 March 1928) for the Prague literary fortnightly *Literární svět*, translated in Mirka Zemanová, ed. and trans., *Janáček's Uncollected Essays on Music* (London and New York: Marion Boyars, 1989), pp. 120–4 (pp. 121–2).

[2] See Zemanová, *Janáček's Uncollected Essays*, Plate 8 – a reproduction of a photograph of Janáček on the seashore at Vlissingen, Holland, taken around 8–10 May 1926.

[3] From Janáček's feuilleton 'Sedm havranů' [Seven Rooks], first published in the Brno daily *Lidové noviny* (30 November 1922), and translated in Vilem and

spontaneous compilation in the mind.'[3] After conception, however, the problems begin: continuation, for a start, then continuity into whatever forms and organisations such material will suggest and be able to sustain. The empirical approach – 'successive minute touches linked together by instinctive clairvoyance' as Debussy in characterising Musorgsky also characterised himself – is all very well, but there has to be coherence and direction however spontaneous, and logic, even grammar, however wayward or erratic. Janáček of course knew all this, and here too his solution is typically extreme. Strange though it is to think of him as a theorist of music, he attacked aesthetic and linguistic problems with all his wonted assiduity, fervour and oddness for most of his life, alongside the composing or, more usually, in unconscious prophecy of it. The almost impossibly elusive current of utterance mooted above, equally with the prosaic chit-chat of daily life, and every shade of feeling in between, as it emanates in sound, were for him deliberated theoretical goals as well as artistic starting points of tingling immediacy. He wished by his notions of 'percolation', 'interpenetration' etc.,[4] to elaborate a thoroughgoing quasi-scientific dossier of affective usage wholly congruent with, indeed inseparable from, his 'enormous collection' of human and animal sounds. Old Janáček hearsay – 'a chord that bleeds', 'a chord that makes you wring your hands' and so forth – can now be substantiated from what amounts to a composing-kit, however sketchy and in some obvious ways absurd. For Janáček even the most ordinary chord-connections contain an explosive emotional potential. Thus the $\frac{6}{4}$ is 'like the swallow flying which almost touches the ground, and by that refreshing, lifts into the heights', and the 4–3 'ruffles' the V^7–I cadence 'as a breeze ruffles the surface of a fishpond'.[5] If these bedrocks of tonal cliché can evoke such fantasy, the idea that more complex

---

Margaret Tausky, eds., *Leoš Janáček: Leaves from his Life* (London: Kahn and Averill, 1982), pp. 101–4 (p. 103).

[4] These terms are both attempts to render into English different connotations of Janáček's concept of 'prolínání'; further details can be found in Michael Beckerman, *Janáček as Theorist* (Stuyvesant, NY: Pendragon Press, 1994), pp. 72–9. [ed.]

[5] See Beckerman, *Janáček as Theorist*, p. 115. '4–3' refers here to the intervals formed in a perfect cadence by the seventh of chord V^7 and the third of chord I in relation to the tonic (e.g. F–C and E–C in C major). Janáček's theory of harmony in fact rests on the hypothesis that in chord progressions all the notes in both chords relate to the bass note of the second chord. [ed.]

dissonances can cut, or be cut into, with a knife, like a knife,[6] suddenly ceases to be so preposterous.

The aim is for music to achieve its purpose, the intense utterance of feeling, via the startling physicality of its every sonorous constituent. Together, they reach the auditor direct, circumventing formalist routines and play of conventions. Music's innermost meaning lies 'above', 'behind', 'beyond' the working-relationships of its notes that make its intrinsic, non-referential grammar.

This sense of what music can legitimately and naturally do leads inevitably to claims still more ambitious. Janáček would, one senses, have endorsed with enthusiasm these questions from the Shostakovich/Volkov *Testimony* that resounds with his own Slav urgency:

> Meaning in music – that must sound very strange for most people. Particularly in the West. It's here in Russia that the question is usually posed: What was the composer trying to say, after all, with this musical work? What was he trying to make clear? The questions are naive, of course, but despite their naiveté and crudity, they definitely merit being asked. And I would add to them, for instance, Can music attack evil? Can it make a man stop and think? Can it cry out, and thereby draw man's attention to various vile acts to which he has grown accustomed? To the things he passes without any interest?[7]

'All these questions began for me with Mussorgsky', Shostakovich continues. They are equally germane for Janáček. The problem is, how with such views of music as essentially a humanistic moral agent, can it be composed as an art, disinterested, uncommitted, as organisation into grammar and form of pitches and durations and timbres?

Composers who put the *cri expressif* before all else usually have an internal music-machine to turn the wheels, which flows, courses, surges, spins; a force they can drive or be driven by – Schubert, Wagner, Tchaikovsky, Mahler. But when the utterance-type lacks this inner stream, or cannot reach it easily, cannot swim, or finds it dammed, choked, frozen –

---

6   See Janáček's employment of the term 'zářez' (incision) in relation to certain types of voice-leading: Beckerman, *Janáček as Theorist*, pp. 66–7.

7   Solomon Volkov, ed., *Testimony: The Memoirs of Dimitri Shostakovich*, trans. Antonina Bouis (London: Faber, 1979), p. 181.

Schumann, Brahms, Berg are instances – schemes and artifices are needed; games, codes, constructivistic manipulations of material not 'naively' born from music in its primeval state. Though their eventuality appears spontaneous, its making has been contrived, even arbitrary. And when the utterer by instinct is by technique a stutterer – whether because the need for scaffolding or gameplaying denies in its defiance of naturalness the utterer's 'from the life' directness, or through sheer lack of musical skill, or even talent, to match the sensitivity of the vibrations and the intensity of the vision – then there are radical problems for which only radical solutions will suffice. Examples of this are Musorgsky again, and Janáček, and indeed Shostakovich too, were it not for his being cursed, contrariwise, with one of the most facile music-machines ever seen. (Instances of vision outweighing skill or talent would include very obviously a Gurney or a Satie, rather controversially a Delius or an Ives.) What all these composers have in common, however different and mutually incomparable, is the primacy of expression. Each has his unique 'letter to the world', or, as Wordsworth said of the poet, he 'rejoices more than other men in the spirit of life that is in him'; he has a message and will burst if it is not delivered. They all stand at the polar opposite from the Stravinskian position which objects in sheer self-defence to music's capacity to say anything whatsoever outside itself.

It is not immediately clear how Janáček relates to these fellow-utterers. To Musorgsky for passionate commitment to naturalism, the expression of emotional truth via truth to human speech. But Musorgsky's manifest deficiencies in compositional technique and miraculous capture, in a handful of songs and some moments of opera, of exactly what he was after – exquisite musical precision in the teeth of incompetence – are like Janáček only in the upshot. For Musorgsky despised learning and training, whereas the youthful Janáček could not get enough. His bottomless craving for discipline is touchingly evoked in the early pages of Michael Beckerman's *Janáček as Theorist*.[8] Then came the revealing moment (possibly apocryphal) when his youthful work was deemed 'too correct'; a judgment inconceivable *chez* Musorgsky, notoriously 'corrected' by an overseer who mistook empirical genius for ignorant ineptitude or wanton perversity. (The truth being in Musorgsky's case a bit of all three.) The mature Janáček offers a comparable

---

8   Beckerman, *Janáček as Theorist*, pp. 1–14.

mix, again involving well-meant and sometimes well-made improvements to scores wherein brilliance and clumsiness are often juxtaposed and sometimes combined. He was determined, clearly, that his music could never again incur the same charge!

The middle category can be discounted. Janáček did not need scaffolding or schemes to unbind utterance. He is, rather, the most urgent of all composers. Once he found himself, in late middle life, the sheer impetuosity precludes Schumannish letter-and-word-play as much as Brahmsian note-play, let alone the sedulous ramifications and sophistries of a Berg. What he shares with this composer-type is a more personal trait, the obsessive fixation upon an unattainable muse to whom every aspect of his art is referred. Yet while his mature musical speech is nothing if not obsessional, the two fixations do not go hand in hand. He would never chain in codes the fetishistic initials or names or events: blurting directness, not swathed secrecy, is his intonation. But neither does he contain a mighty machine like Schubert, nor the infinite interweave of Wagner's leitmotivic procedures, nor the melodic fertility (and sequential shamelessness) of Tchaikovsky, nor the improvisational splurge of Mahler. The native endowment is song-and-dance length, Dvořák as prototype, manifested in modest, blameless Slav-nationalist successes like the *Lašské tance* (Lachian Dances; 1893) or the faded lyricism of the *Idylla* (Idyll; 1878) and the Suite (1877). When he gets into being himself the lengths remain brief and the units become tiny, but the shapes are large, and the powers of driving continuity inexhaustible.

The problem is to discover just how music as such can be reconciled with an aesthetic of unmitigated expression grounded in human utterance and guided by such peculiar theories (however well they worked for him in practice). His getting into being himself is a matter first of finding the right genre to take these overriding preoccupations – opera; then of finding what can be done with opera that squares with them, what can be put in and left out, what it can, when radically deconventionalised, astonishingly turn out to be able to do. The crucial leap, precipitated by the harrowing illness and early death of Olga, comes between *Jenůfa* (1894–1903; rev. 1906–7) and *Osud* (Fate; 1903–5; rev. 1906, 1907), the first a masterpiece in a received mould (Smetana not so far behind, except in stature), the second a Confession, of the utmost artistic oddity, an apparently unworkable maverick which, as it happened, prognosticates his late flowering into total idiosyncrasy. Once opera could be made wholly odd, other genres followed: song cycle, string quartet, piano sonata and lyric (here alone are precedents, for this is what the small piano lyric had always been for), all the way to 'Concerto' (the two bizarre works of 1925–6), 'Symphony' (*Sinfonietta*, 1926) and 'Mass' (*Glagolitic*, 1926; rev. 1927).

'Unmitigated expression': Janáček places a higher premium upon this dangerous weapon than any composer before or since. Not that music before him had lacked the desire or the means not just to be freely expressive but to encapsulate emotion within a sonorous image so fully that one has to say that this music means, or says, this thing. Its pre-romantic history lies in tropes from madrigals and lute songs, onomatopoeia and charged-up rhetoric from Monteverdi to Purcell, Charpentier, Rameau, the entire charter of baroque *Affekt* and its individual intensification in the hands of J. S. Bach. Nietzsche's notion of a 'lexicon' in Wagner of the most intimate, decadently perfumed, *telling* fragments, the miniaturist in him who palpitates with expressive life whereas the colossal remains stillborn, simply brings into the open what had been achieved with consummate success in countless unflawed gems of Schubert, Schumann, Chopin, and was to flower further in Brahms, Fauré, Wolf, Webern.

As this latter list shows, it is a gift that lies at the opposite end of music's spectrum from opera. The phrase that speaks low, bearing a secret caress or a private message, is a creature of small spaces and small forces – song, solo piano, music for the chamber. Opera is, obviously, a collective genre that needs to raise its voice to cross footlights and be heard in the upper circle. The illusion of intimacy is one of its resources. That it can whisper was well known to such professional masters of the caress as Puccini or Massenet; their desired reaction is corporate, a unison 'oooh!' throughout the house. At the other extreme, the most famous whisper in all opera, the declaration of love in *Pelléas*, is overheard not shared. Janáček's intimacy is guiltless as Debussy of titillation, but otherwise resembles neither extreme. He is doing something else. Each individual within an attentive audience must feel that this music's utterance is directed to them alone. Even in communal scenes this tendency can be sensed; in the monologues it is undisguised. In Wagner's monologues or duologues the audience is witness to a situation and its participants – this Wotan or Sachs, these two lovers, or two squabbling brothers, or two contrasted sisters (and so on). The presentation is detached, indeed objective, for all the nudging commentary in the orchestra's tissue of leitmotives and the heated immediacy of the musical language in general. Whereas Janáček compels every hearer to identify with the single figure – the Forester, say – and with every person in a group as their turn comes – the circle of regulars at the village inn, or badger, vixen and dogfox, owl, in the forest. Nothing could be further from the various ways in which opera usually proceeds; different though they already are, Janáček is in contradistinction to them all; he makes verismo and Wagnerismo seem as stylised as aria and cabaletta. Music in Janáček's operas is his means of dissolving the distances and boundaries of convention, not of establishing them. And inasmuch as the same goes for his concert-music, thus far does he differ from all other composers.

Auden declared that in *Pelléas* Debussy flattered the audience, meaning (presumably) that, being given so little in the way of the usual vocal delights, their only compensation is the glow of cultural refinement their sacrifice has won them. Yet *Pelléas* is for the most part lovely to hear, if a little washy and deficient in dramatic momentum. These particular criticisms clearly do not apply to Janáček! But he is still more deficient than Debussy in grateful voice-centred lyricism, and can often be harsh, insistent, obsessive, tedious; even his brevity can seem aggressive because so foreshortened and brusque. Whole stretches and one or two whole works could fairly be called repellent for all his growth straight out of Dvořák and Smetana, and his non-relation to any of the commonly hated veins of 'ugliness' in twentieth-century music. He neither 'flatters' the specialised susceptibilities of the refined, nor wows his audience *all'italiana* to bring down the house. In this genre of music more posited than any other on pleasing, he does not try to please. More often, he stings, shocks, burns. His music to go with the whipcracks and chain-bearing in *Z mrtvého domu* (From the House of the Dead; 1927–8) renders physical pain that makes the hearer wince; crueller still is rendition in sound of mental and spiritual anguish. Compare the lashing in *Elektra*, the crushing in *Salome*, the torture in *Tosca*, or even such deeper expressions of psychological distress as the Kiss and its outcome in *Parsifal*, or Tristan's delirium. The audience writhes in its plush-covered seats with a groan of satisfaction. These places are protected, and distanced, by music, as surely as the padding and plush separate the soft body from the hard frame. Only such exceptional moments as Boris with the vision of the murdered boy, Golaud twisting Mélisande by her hair, Katerina Ismailova's song about the black lake, the music for the hanging of Billy Budd, dare go so naked as Janáček does by habit. While *Wozzeck*, enthusiastically hailed in the last year of his life ('a dramatist of astonishing importance, of deep truth ... each of his notes has been dipped in blood'),[9] can seem altogether too well-dressed, in interesting, absorbing, intricate, richly inventive *music*. And in *Lulu* the discrepancies between its gorgeous sonic opulence, its intellectual fascination and the moral then physical degradation of its characters can often be hard to bridge.

Be it unbearable physical pain or mental torture; or quivers, ecstasies, visions, desires, delusions; or merely some equivalent of the two girls waiting for the man to arrive (like the tiny cameo for the engineer and the young widow in *Fate* Act I) Janáček's unique grip upon utterance, from mind and spirit, in the body, via the voice, produces this 'intimate letter' from individual to individual that, so far from pleasing – flattering, wooing – his audience, is an exposure of them as much as of his characters. He strips the warm clothing of protective safety to reach naked empathy. To get 'into the skin' of, say, Káťa's religio-erotic outpourings or Emilia Marty's 337-year-old weariness, he puts every auditor there too, singly – there is no plural.

Also there is no space between the state of being and his rendition of it, whether it be just a flock of silly hens or the repartee of visitors at a summer spa – but it might equally be the farmer's decent son suffused with desire and shame, excitement and compunction – and correspondingly, no space between the music and its recipient. The only thing he does not express is *himself*; the absence of romantic egotistic self-projection is remarkable. As, also, the complete avoidance of preachiness; no judgements are made, no moral is drawn. The incentive is generous but by no means soft. Hard, if anything. Also aggressive: shocking in rawness; rude, embarrassing, button-holing, speaking too close in your face in public places; as excruciating, or as boring, as it would be in reality – the mad mother's accusations and leap from the balcony, the breakdown at the piano, the night of illicit romance and the subsequent admission wrested from guilt by the

---

9 Janáček in his 1928 interview for *Literární svět*, translated in Zemanová, *Janáček's Uncollected Essays*, p. 123. [Chew and Vilain quote the whole of this passage about *Wozzeck* on p. 64 below of this volume. (ed.)]

conniving elements, the night of icy sex in exchange for a much-desired document, the three prisoners' successive slow motion monomaniac monologues for the first yet umpteenth time. 'Realism' – not so much an art-historical term, as something the dog brings in, mangled and disgusting, a tribute yet also a victim, for its unwilling owner to share – see, feel, smell, taste, with its own keen senses; added to which, the wholly human sense of what everything *means*.

Yet it is not so much an appeal to pious *Family of Man* humanity ('from the heart, let it go to the heart' as its facile motto), still less a compassionate weepie of emotive blackmail anticipating tendencies all-too-familiar nowadays. 'Janáček is, if anything, hard.' He presents documentation of people observed, caught, notated, collected. The truest alignment lies with the photo-document, akin to the work of August Sander, who plonked a specimen of 'businessman', 'architect', 'composer', 'peasant', 'artiste', before his camera, squeezed the bulb, and gave the world the dispassionate image that makes the viewer weep. It's worth remembering that Janáček too began as a 'human naturalist' in observations from the 'field' that claimed quasi-scientific objectivity. For him this employment is without retirement. The humanity is boundless; the attitude towards its all-too-human manifestations is ardently unsentimental, most of all in its refusal to stereotype.

To achieve all this his actual music itself, if not exiguous, ought at any rate not to be given first place. In the old operatic debate *prima la musica, poi le parole*, Janáček would award the *pomo d'oro* to expression, rendered by natural human utterance. Which would imply that music as such must be thinned out – the Monteverdi/Musorgsky/*Pelléas* aesthetic rather than the Mozart/Wagner/*Wozzeck*. In fact it is anything but: rather, it is vehement, assertive, busy, gesticulatory, frantic, emotive, and sometimes violently unrestrained. Simply on the practical level the orchestra has often to be curbed in order that the sensitive *parlante* of the voices that it ostensibly supports can be heard properly. Another kind of convention is at work, surprising but necessary, in this recasting of the genre that throws formality to the winds; for music undoubtedly comes first, possibly in spite of Janáček's wishes. He is in the end a composer, odd though this sometimes seems, and the composer in him cannot be prevented. It's not simply that the music is every bit as close-up as the life it renders – this is the first characteristic to strike every newcomer. It is something about his music itself. It can often be insufficient as such, yet it is the only medium that can carry his 'enormous collection' of human intonations, so spontaneously affixed to subjects and characters that it seems he might have collected these, too, at the bus stop or in the fishmongers. It is the medium for his simultaneous detachment from and involvement with them all, and for his urgent concern to confront each single recipient in a physical encounter with what he has apprehended so acutely. It is the medium through which his recourse to the 'exotic and irrational' genre of opera (though his recasting of it is just as bizarre) can be rationalised and used, and its artificialities made real. It is the medium through which he can utter human speech. As this, it becomes great music like any other – albeit unlike any other in its premises and procedures.

Because Anglo-Saxon culture came quite late to Janáček, some potentially prohibitive problems of interpretation, in every sense, have been largely avoided. From pioneering productions, mainly by the old Sadler's Wells, the operas have become standard repertory in the other principal companies. Our chamber musicians play the chamber works, our tenors sing *Zápisník zmizelého* (The Diary of One Who Disappeared; 1917–19; rev. 1920) in Czech, our orchestras pitch bravely into the orchestra pieces and our choirs into the *Mass*. And with the benefit of outstanding scholarship both historical and textual (its first fruit lies in the series of superlative recordings under Mackerras) the chaos over 'versions' that stood so long in the way of authentic Musorgsky, and can still bug authentic Bruckner, has been obviated. Thus the Anglo-Saxon embrace of this initially so localised music has given a picture true enough to need little or no exegesis. What we hear and admire is exactly what there is. His strangeness and extremity have become normative, his obliqueness direct, his foreignness native.

This makes him difficult to write about further. His reception is both ardent and on-target; he is not misunderstood, and no longer a cause. The next steps, alas, are academic appropriation and universal establishmentarianism. That he remains resistant to analysis one discovers when banging one's head against his music in vain. He lays his materials and his processes, however eccentric, so squarely and clearly that there is nothing that cannot be followed, and description or unknitting seems more than usually futile. Monumentalising him is more attractive and more damaging. He has become the unlikely but perfect candidate in an epoch of fragmentative, alienating experiment, deliberate renunciation, even spurning, of liberal-humane themes, for music's continued concern with and expression of them without recourse to the bankrupt debris of late-romantic *espressivo*. He is in his own freaky way a Modern, who retained pre-modernist values while driven to 'make it new' in idiosyncrasy and isolation.

Such is human nature that the moment anything revolutionary shows signs of settling into marble, an impulse of reaction sets in. Perhaps an attempt to work it out can help towards further definition of this strange and wonderful figure. The qualms begin with the element of wilfulness, deliberate mannerism, even affectation – the perversity, cussedness, going-against-the-grain, in all that he does. It is provocative – he seems to be saying 'look how peculiar I can be'. Which is of course inseparable from his genuine strangeness whose authenticity and ardour cannot be mistaken. The choice of way-out subjects goes with the choice of way-out instrumental registers, voicing and spacing, odd habits of momentum and eccentric notations both of pitch and rhythm. It is as if burning sincerity *depended* upon being peculiar. When it works, his idiosyncratic vision carries music's empire into territory hitherto unsuspected. When it does not work, the result is merely eccentric without illumination.

And there is no difference. His manner is so all-pervasive that the stretches where he is tedious are indistinguishable from the stretches where he is electrically inspired. The pressure is as consistent as if he wrote always in *italics* or CAPS. Thus, initially at least, discrimination is disarmed. Recognition of the co-existence of inferior material indistinguishable from superior material, with plenty of infill between the two, is compounded by the unfamiliarity of the idiom as well as its gestural consistency. And that all of it is equally aimed at the utterance of burning human intensity makes it still more difficult. When everything depends upon the throb of committed subject-matter, making secondary the calibre of the materials and their workmanship, then tendentiousness looms. Because Janáček is manifestly as artist and as exalted spirit far above any low emotional blackmail, it seems mean to hold artistic scruples concerning the protagonists of a Makropulos affair or amidst the denizens of a prison-house. Like holding one's nose; like denying that in every living creature is a spark of God. But one has to acknowledge that, in taking on such subjects and treating them with such all-out sincerity, Janáček has deprived his listeners of their options.

Fate near the start of his maturity, *Věc Makropulos* (The Makropulos Affair; 1923–5) and *From the House of the Dead* at its end show the difficulty most clearly. Between them comes the bulk of his mature achievement with its exact match of idiosyncratic music to the subject it sets, from the most intimate – *The Diary of One Who Disappeared* and the two programmatic string quartets (1923, 1928) drawn respectively from fiction and from life with equal immediacy – to the most public and ceremonial – *Sinfonietta* and *Glagolitic Mass*; not forgetting such joyous divertimenti as *Mládí* (Youth; 1924) and the *Říkadla* (Nursery Rhymes; 1925; rev. 1926). But the triumphant vindication of theory and practice alike, in all their peculiarity, comes in the two central operas, *Káťa Kabanová* (1920–1) and *Příhody Lišky Bystroušky* (The Adventures of the Vixen Bystrouška; 1922–3). Their greatness silences reservations; the human tragedy with its blight upon happiness, tenderness and ardour crushed beneath the pitiless tyranny of propriety, and the animal comedy with its ecstatic cycle of endless renewal circumventing the vicious circle of ageing and death, are manifest high peaks of the century's artistic endeavour, good deeds in wicked times, vindicating humane themes in an epoch of cynicism and mechanisation.

So too are the three more awkward pieces, where greatness is flawed by his peculiarities outstretching their limitations, the inescapable obverse of his chosen manner. In all of them situations of extreme boldness are matched in music that appears to be on the point of fraying through sheer stress of wear. Sonorous images of unforgettable originality and intensity lie alongside stuff that sounds as if it was the first thing that came into his head in his tearing haste to get it down on paper.[10]

In some ways *Fate* is musically the most satisfying. It shines with unforced surprise at what the new techniques can release, above all the way that the speech-intonation of the voices grows into instrumental texture and thence into a continuity which can shape a whole act. Both in the 'photographic' rapportage of its places – the sunny day at the animated spa, the storm raging while the apprehensive students gather round the piano to rehearse their master's opera – and in the 'reports' from a terrain of private

---

[10] This observation applies equally to the early drafts of the Second Quartet, where some passages (removed before Janáček compiled his final score) are astonishingly humdrum. [ed.]

anguish shot through with twisted disturbed states of being – Janáček is pushing to the ultimate from two opposing yet fused positions, the avid theorising and the lacerating poignancy of his daughter's words notated as she lay dying.

Yet the artistic catalyst was Charpentier's *Louise*, that talentfree piece of cheap tat! Like many a child of its time, something in it, lost to later comers, sufficed to fertilise a work that completely transcends it. But *Fate*'s deeper kinship is rather with such adjacent theatrical adventure as Strindberg (for the painfully private pushed into public exhibition), Pirandello (for its extraordinary games of life *vis-à-vis* art in the work's own workings), Chekhov (for acute human observation, told by implication and ellipsis), and Maeterlinck (poetic suggestiveness in meshes of repetition and echo). Of course it is in such company vitiated by its amateurishness – the inept stage mechanics, the arty language, the inartistic ambiguities as opposed to those that function. Livid, red-hot content, clumsily handled, into which sensitive production can breathe the convincing theatrical life given it by the music, every page of which is infused with the passion that forced it into being. *Fate* is the first opera ever in the difficult new area, set up by Janáček, where the music, though vehemently present, could not exist as such without the pressure of what has caused it, without which it would simply disintegrate. Which is more of a tribute than a qualm.

And *From the House of the Dead* is the last. (It is worth remembering that he neither saw nor even heard either work.) Every discovery so fresh and vivid in *Fate* – speech-intonation filling out the entire instrumental fabric, violent foreshortening, quasi-cinematic flashback, intercutting, montage – here reaches the end of its tether. The three acts are articulated through sonorous imagery of unforgettable simplicity, sometimes sweet, sometimes exalted, more often naked, gawky, awkward, and frequently pulverising in its ferocity. The simplest and most memorable idea of all, the *Urklang* that, like the *Tristan*-chord brings the whole work before one's eyes in a flash, is a chord of only three pitches but so spaced and voiced as to verge upon the physical pain it depicts.

This sound dominates Act I in an orchestra of squeals, squawks, shrieks up high, and growls, lurches and scrabbling down below, presenting a claustrophobic *huis clos* of oppression, lashings, privation, that makes *Billy Budd* seem snug as a captain's cabin. Between piercing acridness and

14

menacing snarl the 'stuffing' – the orchestra's middle range of warmth and support – has been kicked away, replaced only by the clash of chains and the furious orders of a military drum. The shafts of ardent tenderness in the course of Luka's Lujza-narrative provide pain of a different kind. In Act II the bare start – a *Bohème* Act III, with chains – then the brilliant success in the risky endeavour of presenting bell-sounds by real bells as well as their instrumental imitation, then the unwonted gentleness of Skuratov's monologue, all yield to the riot of crazy energy discharged into the holiday double-bill – cheeky, coarse, vulgar, parodistic, cubist Dvořák crossed with X-ray instrumentation *à la Renard* (the nearest comparison in burlesque folkloric puppet-theatre), littered with 'the right wrong notes', real 1920s impertinence but entirely his own, all the more remarkable within an idiom that however stretched remains fundamentally euphonious and Czech.[11]

The first part of Act III presents in the piteous tale told by Shishkov a perfect instance of Janáček's 'manners' as distinct from his mannerisms. Its villain/hero, unrecognised, is nearby, dying. Coughs, spasms, death-gasps, are rendered, but not the actual moment of death – not a nudge, let alone a symphonic elegy, simply a stage direction at an arbitrary turn of the narration, which itself is equally non-expressionistic. The agonising tenderness of the scenes with Akulina, so long ago, so immediately relived, is not exuded by the haunting beauty of the accompanying string-phrase but contained within it – the ultimate example of Janáček's 'concordance' (so to speak) hurting more, wringing more from its hearers, than the most excruciating of dissonances or the most swooning *espressivo*. Yet it is during the later stages of this same monologue that inspiration flags and monotony sets in which is not intended and does not contribute to the artistic impact. Instead, it is accidental: the music, going on just as before, goes off the boil to become not the suggestive minimum that permits a closer proximity to

---

[11] Like all great originals he was anxious to appear unbeholden, but he has to wear borrowed garments boldly because the personality within is incapable of disguise. Strauss and Debussy, as well as Puccini, figure unmistakably yet wholly translated. The remarkable parallels with Sibelius are presumably the result of affinity rather than knowledge (some of the most striking, the 'Janáček' in the *Kullervo Symphony* written when Janáček himself was still writing 'Dvořák', he couldn't possibly have heard or seen since the work lay withdrawn and unpublished after its first performance in 1892 till well after Sibelius's death).

emotional truth, but merely, actually, scrappy. A dividing line that cannot be drawn has nevertheless been passed. Once discerned, it can never be ignored.

And thus the closing stretches stir up contrary reactions into a profoundly disturbing ambiguity. A wild priapic character infuses this music; it is 'possessed' in Dostoyevskyian fashion, driven by demons, written in speed and chaos, faster than it can be composed, written as if 'each of its notes has been dipped in blood'. This churning brew of simultaneous upsurge and downtread produces extraordinary emotional turbulence. A clear comparison again comes from *Billy Budd*, where the fomenting mutiny after Billy's execution is drilled backed into order (Janáček provides the visceral thrust, Britten the fudge). A longer shot might be to find it akin to the feelings of the elect, among the audience revelling in the Hymn to the Leader, who share the unspeakable secret that by this music Stalin is excoriated. But in sheer musical calibre – and what else is there? – the ideas cannot take the strain. The power, incontrovertible and in its way beyond compare, comes from everything else. This is great *something* – Electricity, Intensity, Strangeness, Compassion, Uplift, Humanity – the actual notes are second to whatever in Janáček's version of the operatic equation comes *prima*.

The Makropulos Affair shows such worries more plainly. The electricity and shock inherent in story and situation go without saying. They produce awed astonishment at the boldness of treatment and breadth of understanding. But cavilling cannot be sopped. One is aghast at the really poor musical ideas upon which so much depends, especially the big primal melodic gesture manifestly intended to be the clue to the opera's dizzying subject; most of all when it is given in the fullest blaze of his orchestral heat an apotheosis that it cannot bear. Not even recourse to wordless off-stage voices (unforgettable for the seduction in the *Diary*, wonderfully atmospheric as soul of the Volga in *Kát'a* or the spirit of the forest in *Vixen*) can save the scene of Elena's rejuvenescence and disintegration which, by virtue of its extreme singularity, leaves the listener aghast anyway. The chorus in the third act of *From the House of the Dead* falls just the right side of emotional manipulation to be heartstopping, but it's a near thing. Its use in *Makropulos* is not so much manipulative as by rote, an 'effect', synchronised with the surreal lighting, disconcerting in a composer who, unlike Wagner, would seem to have no truck with such old tricks.[12] Elsewhere, *Makropulos* surpasses all his other stage works for variety, quiddity and unexpected wit – the 'Spanish' vignettes, for instance, which encompass a tiny world of quaint, touching vulnerability; though it also has, overall, the highest proportion of routine, humdrum, and (dare one say) note-spinning. Often one wishes he had never happened upon the whole-tone scale or the ostinato. In really bad moments one can even regret the whole doctrine of speech-inflection upon which his art is based.

Such qualms, reservations, scrupulous attempts to sift chaff from grain, attempts to pinpoint the weakness within the greatness, are all very well. Then one hears Janáček again and falls to one's knees. He pulls and pulls your ears till you scream with the pain. Your art and your life fly about you in demented fragments; you are 337 years old and life has dried within you; you have murdered an officer, and a man who came between you and your girl, and then your sweetheart herself. You are exposed in all your human baseness. Yet you are not just told about the spark of God in every creature, you are made to feel its actual presence. You rejoice not with the stoical wriggle of the cut worm who forgives the plough but with the soaring flight of the freed eagle. Janáček, musical theorist, human ethnographer and composer, has brought all this about. There has never been anything like it, with or without music. 'What's music to do with it anyway?' Though, more often than not, the music is fully up to the insistent demands he makes upon it.

[12] It's true, as the editor pointed out to me, that Janáček wanted the *Diary* to be performed in a ghostly 'half-dark' lighting; but the work does not *depend* upon such an adventitious effect: here, as always when at his best, he's got the emotion into the notes.

2 'Nothing but pranks and puns': Janáček's solo piano music

THOMAS ADÈS

The growing recognition of Janáček as a true radical, rather than a crank, has two primary bases: the technical daring of his orchestration, and the dramatic works' uniquely intense relationship between linguistic and musical motivic expression.[1] Innovations are, therefore, far less frequently identified in his solo piano music, whether because its instrumental sonority appears closer to convention than is the case with the orchestral work, or because Janáček's single most far-reaching quality, seen at its purest in these pieces, is still generally underestimated: the redefinition of structural tonality through an unprecedented concentration on ambiguous, and particularly enharmonic, key relationships.

Volatility of texture and economy of material combine in the mature Janáček to give a relationship between harmonic colour and underlying tonality more highly-charged than in any other composer. *Na památku* (In memoriam), thought to date from 1886–7, sows the seeds of all the major piano works to come (Example 2.1).[2]

Each of the three paragraphs is underpinned by a perfect-fifth pedal, giving an apparent **ABA** tonal structure of A♭ – V of E – A♭; yet it makes no sense to describe these pedals as functions of a tonal scheme. The low B_1/F♯ dyad of bb. 9–15 is not resolved at any stage; neither in b. 16, nor in b. 17, with its extraordinary second inversion, nor even in the closing bars of the piece. The sense of resolution in the last four bars is far from merely rhetorical; but *tonality* is only tangentially involved. To speak of the second paragraph of

---

[1] Janáček remarked about the Capriccio (1926) in a 1928 interview: 'je to rozmarné, samé schválnosti a vtipy' (it is capricious, nothing but pranks and puns); see Adolf Veselý, 'Poslední rozhovor s Leošem Janáčkem' [A Last Interview with Leoš Janáček], *Hudební rozhledy* (Brno), 4 (1928).

[2] This edition of *Na památku* is by Paul Wingfield.

Example 2.1   Janáček, *In memoriam*

Example 2.2   Janáček, *In memoriam*, bb. 15–16: summary

the piece as 'an excursion to E major', as the appearance of the score might suggest, gives no clue as to its true role within the structure. For that, it is necessary to isolate the cadence in bb. 15–16 (Example 2.2). D♯ translates into E♭, C♯ retrospectively into D♭. That this, rather than any modulation, is the defining event of the piece already has an index in the 'orchestration' of b. 9: a significant *subito* dynamic increase, the dramatic introduction of a new register; and, crucially, an accent distinguishing the central $d\sharp^1$ from the melodic $e\flat^2/e\flat^1$ of bb. 1–8. This coloration is sustained in b. 10, raising the $d\flat^1$ of bb. 1–8 into the new context as a $c\sharp^1$. The independence of this stratum of the texture is emphasised by its being suspended for the succeeding three bars, an absence made palpable by the rich d♯ of b. 11, the stretched spacing of b. 12, and the contrast between the voice-specific accent of b. 9 and the bare *sforzando* of b. 13. Its resumption in b. 14 is gently, though still unequivocally, pointed by an unconventionally spread chord. Furthermore, the control of this enharmonic shift over the cadence into b. 16 is sealed by its assuming the rhythmic personality of the principal melodic voice, thereby revealing a latent identity with the germinal idea of the piece (Example 2.3).

The other enharmonically translated note involved in this cadence has an equally strong structural weight: the d♯ on the final semiquaver of b. 11, evident from its textural and rhythmic position as a coinage from the e♭ of the first seven bars. This note too is confirmed as an independent event by the bar which follows, in which the otherwise consistent triplet figure at the end of every bar is slowed down threefold, placing an answering e♮ on the final semiquaver of b. 12, which is in turn resolved, on the final semiquaver of b. 15, in the cadence of Example 2.2.

It is these two threads in the texture which alone determine the strategy by which Janáček unifies *Na památku*. The *forte* D♭ chord (from '*ppp*') of b. 27 owes its great conclusiveness to the melodic voice in the left hand, describing a curve of a tone in either direction from b. 25 to the end: up

Example 2.3   Janáček, *In memoriam*, bb. 1–2 and 14–15

from the e♭ on the final semiquaver of b. 25 through an e♭ exactly a bar later –
a restaging of bb. 11–12 – then reclaiming that e♭ for the tonality of the third
paragraph and of the piece with the climactic f♮ of b. 27. The melodic curve
is completed by the f♭ of the penultimate bar, also on the final semiquaver,
providing a synthesis with the e♮ on the final semiquaver of b. 12, its forebear
in deceleration.

Though ostensibly an early work, *Na památku* offers all the essentials
of the profoundly new approach to the materials of composition which
Janáček was to develop in his maturity. A traditional tonal structure (the
ABA solo piano miniature) is motivated not by the received imperatives of a
tonal system, but by texturally and melodically defined enharmonic shifts.
Apparently germane terms such as 'dominant' or 'flattened submediant' are
in fact quite useless to any meaningful account of the piece; the structural
event is an enharmonic progression, acting as a caesura in the structure, a
problem solved by a closure of the enharmonic circle (Example 2.4). The
subservience of merely tonal functions in the piece is discreetly but unambiguously demonstrated by the inimitable second inversion at b. 17, gently
defusing any possible finality in the return to the tonic, and preparing the
more truly conclusive D♭ of b. 27, which serves not as a functioning sub-
dominant but as ancillary coloration of the long-range enharmonic shift
described by Example 2.4.

The inclination towards a structure defined by a harmonic bifurcation is, in fact, already evident in the *Thema con variazioni (Zdenčiny*

Example 2.4   Janáček, *In memoriam*: summary

variace) (Zdenka Variations), 'Op. 1' (1880), a student effort with a theme shared almost equally between G minor and B♭ major. Many characteristic flourishes notwithstanding, the work fails to convince precisely because Janáček's tendencies towards economical closures of the kind so powerfully achieved in *Na památku* are frustrated by the schematically augmentative nature of the theme-and-variations genre, and by the fact that the relationship between the two harmonic areas concerned is a convention of tonality, rather than a succinct and potent progression in its own right (cf. Example 2.2). After *Na památku*, however, Janáček's control of enharmonic devices becomes ever more profound. The fourteen completed pieces collected under the title *Po zarostlém chodníčku* (On an Overgrown Path; 1900–11) – an unfinished fifteenth, in E♭ major, appears in a barely satisfactory performing version in František Schäfer's edition – are highly sophisticated reinventions of binary or ternary structure, exhibiting long-range events which rely on potent relationships between individual harmonic/coloristic objects almost to the exclusion of conventions of tonal 'logic'.[3] As we have

---

[3]   The genesis of *On an Overgrown Path* is convoluted: Janáček originally wrote seven pieces for harmonium, five of which (now nos. 1, 2, 4, 7 and 10 of Series I) were published in *Slovanské melodie* in 1901–2; in 1908–11 he then wrote five more pieces, adding them to the five previously published ones and issuing all ten as Series I, now for piano (1911); in addition, at some point in the period 1908–11 he began writing a second series for piano, completing only two pieces (the first of which was published in the Brno daily *Lidové noviny* on 30 September 1911) and leaving a further one unfinished – its manuscript comprises a sketchy initial ink draft with partial pencil revisions. (Publication details of all three editions mentioned above are given in the appendix to Nigel Simeone's article in this volume, on pp. 180–1 below.) Considerable confusion has been caused by František Schäfer's posthumous edition of 'Series II' (Prague: Hudební matice, plate no. H. M. 832; 1942), which includes the two early unpublished harmonium pieces, the two completed numbers actually intended for a second piano series, and a

seen in *Na památku,* the importance of 'orchestration' in establishing these objects cannot be exaggerated: the exact spacing of a chord, the weighting of its individual elements, the dynamic context, the precise register at which the pitch occurs; furthermore, 'orchestration' more generally applied to the musical clothing of the enharmonic skeleton, for example long-term rhythmic rhymes (as between bb. 12 and 27 of *Na památku*). Bald identification of 'tonal areas' or of decontextualised pitches in analysing Janáček is absolute impotence.

The most economical illustration of Janáček's structural practice at the time of *On an Overgrown Path* is provided by the third number of the cycle, 'Pojd'te s námi!' (Come With Us!; Example 2.5).[4] The numinous, gratuitous 'C♯ major' chord in b. 4 is the germinal enharmonic event of the piece: the **B** section (bb. 14–32), identical with the opening until the last quaver of b. 17, expands the passing quirk of coloration into a dramatic digression 'in D♭'. The striking g♯–g♯^{1} octave in b. 6 underpins the whole of this section (bb. 17–24), the lower note as a pedal, the upper as a persistent final anchor for the stretching melodic line, the two unified and absorbed by the answering inner voice of b. 24. The enharmonic ghosting of the **A** section of the piece continues past b. 17 into b. 19, of which the melodic span a♭^{1}–g♭^{2} is identical to that of b. 6. The true correspondence is, however, between bb. 6–13 and 25–32, which close the enharmonic gap with a gesture of the greatest imaginable simplicity, yet technically so elliptical as virtually to make nonsense of any conventional tonal account (Example 2.6).

The longest of the pieces, an untitled movement for harmonium in C minor,[5] sees a relaxation of the essentially binary structure so generous as to point towards the achievement of the first movement of the Sonata

---

particularly unfortunate edition of the unfinished piano piece, which conflates the ink and pencil texts, even though in many instances the pencil insertions constitute alternatives rather than additions to certain passages of the ink draft. [ed.]

4 Example 2.5 has been edited by Dimitra Stamogiannou and Paul Wingfield.

5 This is one of the two harmonium pieces not published in 1901–2; Schäfer's 1942 edition, although far from ideal, will be of more use to the reader than the relevant volume of the Complete Critical Edition of Janáček's works, which makes extensive unauthorised changes, including enharmonic respelling (Ludvík Kundera and Jarmil Burghauser, eds., *Leoš Janáček: souborné kritické vydání; řada F/svazek 1; klavírní skladby* [Leoš Janáček: Complete Critical Edition; Series F/Volume 1; Piano Works] (Prague and Kassel: Supraphon and Bärenreiter, 1978), pp. 77–83). [ed.]

Example 2.5   Janáček, 'Come With Us!', from *On an Overgrown Path*, Series 1

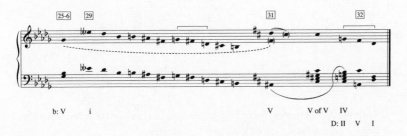

Example 2.6 Janáček, 'Come With Us!', bb. 25–32: summary

1.X.1905 (1905): an ingenious expansion of these microcosmic forms into an idiosyncratic but exact sonata allegro. Without yet embarking on any true developmental process, as will *1.X.1905*, this piece exploits a web of enharmonic relations deftly enough to suggest tonal functions associated with sonata form, allowing access to the structural rhetoric associated with it. The 'second subject' is arrived at in the conventional relative major, in this instance E♭; yet the relationship between the two keys is given an entirely original tension by the prestidigitatory enharmonic twists which precede it (Example 2.7). This is an E♭ minor so strongly inflected with G♭ major that enormous distances from the opening C minor seem already to have been travelled. The perfect cadence into E♭ minor (bb. 51–3) would be the expected end of the first part of the binary structure, leaving enharmonic tensions to be resolved in economical ways analogous to those we have seen in 'Come With Us!'; perhaps an elegant equation between the F♯ minor of bb. 13–24 and the mournful mediant G♭ major of bb. 32–47. Here, however, the epic Janáček, latent even in the picturesque miniatures, emerges at the centre of the stage. The 'second subject' material is played entire for a *third* time, with the balance between its major and minor characters reversed: in place of an E♭ minor touched with G♭ major comes E♭ major haunted with a C minor heard as utterly remote from that of the opening. This is, of course, the relative major that one would have expected for the first appearance of this music, approached in such a way that one could effect a *segue* from b. 28 to b. 57 without any disruption to the strict binary form; and yet the intervening music, far from structurally redundant, affects the balance of the form so deeply as to demand one of Janáček's most overwhelming turns: an hermetic *Adagio* bridge passage (bb. 112–35),

Example 2.7   Janáček, Piece for harmonium in C minor (rejected from *On an Overgrown Path*, Series 1), bb. 1–32: summary

in an E♭ minor darkened to the degree of touching on A♭ minor/C♭ major, then clearing, in a 'surprise' modulation which never loses any of the power of its first hearing, to a C major of unearthly calm. Although this is the fifth time that the surging 'second subject' melody appears, it here possess such a light of renewal that one has the sense of having arrived at the coda of an intensely developed sonata movement, whereas this is in the strictest terms but the natural conclusion of a binary miniature.

It is not rhetoric alone, nonetheless, which marks out the first movement ('Předtucha' (Premonition)) of *1.X.1905* as an essay in true sonata development.[6] Janáček's appropriation of sonata form in this piece is remarkable for its rigour, yet it is not the politics of tonality but the intense structural focus on particularities of texture and specific harmonic details which act as the major agents in the projection of this form. The second-subject group of the exposition maps on to that of the recapitulation with preter-classical exactness; all the melodic material returns on the identical pitches, merely substituting A♭ major (bb. 92–5) for G major (bb. 24–7). Between b. 96 and b. 107, only the lower part of the texture provides any empirical distinction from bb. 28–39; the melodic material is presented effectively untouched. Nonetheless, there is in this recapitulation every sense of violence undergone, and this can be traced to the devastatingly economical enharmonic alteration of the preparatory bridge passage: bb. 88–9 are as bb. 22–3 but for a single accidental, G♯, translated at a stroke into the A♭ of a dominant seventh in the tonic for the only two additional bars of the recapitulation, then breathtakingly endowed with illusory tonal status for the start of the second-subject group (b. 92), placing the greatest tug of

---

[6]   There is no satisfactory published edition of *1.X.1905*. The original Hudební matice print (Prague: plate no. H. M. 339; 1924) is, however, infinitely preferable to that on pp. 25–35 of the Complete Critical Edition of the piano works. [ed.]

26

Example 2.8   Janáček, Piano Sonata *1.X.1905*, 'Premonition', b. 111

irrevocable experience on the very note which marks the beginning of literal melodic congruence with the exposition: the $c\flat^1$–$c\flat^2$ octave of b. 96.

This is a defining event in the history of developing structures, irreducibly of its time and of its author. Here as in every bar he wrote, economy of means, structural, harmonic and textural, is the result, and not the substance, of Janáček's originality, regardless of the medium. Eccentricity has nothing to do with it. For example, the inimitable spacing of the movement's final chord (Example 2.8) honours the three registral layers which define the orchestration of the entire movement: the persistent ache of the $g\flat^2$ of bb. 1, 11, 33, 77, 101, 103 etc., together with its heightening to $g\natural^2$ at the development (beginning in b. 41); the violas' $g\flat^1$, reached by step in b. 8 and always thereafter preceding a fall (e.g. bb. 32, 34, 36, 71, 73, 96, 100, 102 and 104); and the decisive low $E\flat_1$, promised since the end of the exposition and sealing the tragic end of the development in b. 77.

For the second movement ('Smrt' (Death)) of *1.X.1905*, Janáček coins an obsessively monothematic sonata structure; once again, the monumental power of its harmonic story can be ascribed to the tiniest enharmonic inflection in the melody. This direct descendant of the caesura identified in earlier pieces operates now more with the depth of an open wound in the tonal surface, a wound healed (one might say posthumously in the case of 'Death') by the closure of the enharmonic equation. A skeleton of the harmonic structure reveals the influence of the $A\natural$/$B\flat\flat$ in the momentous second-time cadence (Example 2.9). Speaking as for the second time, the exposed $A\natural$ of b. 9 casts a baleful light over the already attenuated $G\flat$ major of b. 10, its fragile orchestration weighting every subsequent bar more and more towards the bass $d\flat$, which is to underpin the next eighteen bars of music (bb. 9–28 are summarised in Example 2.10). The note disappears from the register for bb. 29–34; after its decisive reinstatement in b. 35 it remains as a pedal (internal from b. 39) until the last possible moment,

Example 2.9   Janáček, Piano Sonata *1.X.1905*, 'Death', bb. 1–19: summary

Example 2.10   Janáček, Piano Sonata *1.X.1905*, 'Death', bb. 9–28: summary

the return of B♭-as-dominant, exiled since the second-time b. 7 by this fatal d♭/c♯. Even the six bars of the entire development free of this specific pitch (bb. 29–34) are stamped with its influence (see Example 2.11, which summarises bb. 26–36): the figure introduced at b. 26, awkwardly straddling both a hopeful dominant of A major and the inexorable obstructive pedal two octaves beneath, is transferred down an octave, in enharmonic translation, to the ('tutti', surely, where b. 28 is 'solo') internal voice of b. 29, at which more ominous pitch it resurges in b. 35, shrivelled by a demisemiquaver during its five bars in the cold, to dominate the texture, now motivically, until the first silence on a first beat (b. 46) since the seminal *low* d♭ reappeared, also in b. 35 (Example 2.11).

   Has such devastatingly consistent use of a silent first beat ever been made in a sonata movement? Indeed, could one imagine a silence more solidly *fortissimo* than that of b. 45? The few bars of the piece of which the first beat is actually sounded tell their own story (Example 2.12). The catalytic chord from b. 9 is the last sound on a first beat (b. 54); the superb *mezzo-forte* marked at b. 55 signals the inevitability of its ultimate resolution, the enharmonic change of b. 60 weakened now both structurally and rhythmically, as too the last dominant at b. 62, and further still the final, shattered tonic. In fact, b. 45 goes so far in its conquest of silence with

Example 2.11 Janáček, Piano Sonata *1.X.1905*, 'Death', bb. 26–36: summary

Example 2.12 Janáček, Piano Sonata *1.X.1905*, 'Death', bb. 4–54: chords struck on the first beat of the bar

significance as to elevate the semiquaver rest to the status of a sort of secondary tonic, its sway firmer with each silently passing barline.

As a statement about death – specifically, about the death of a joiner called František Pavlík during demonstrations in Brno demanding the founding of a Czech university – *1.X.1905* is a document of passionate clarity: death is violent, silent and final. It is, in fact, rather the public gesture that one might expect from a political comment on unnecessary tragedy; yet its author was set to produce in his three final operas the most subtle and various expositions of the subject of death any composer has ever achieved. The way to this ultimate overview, or profound eschewal of one, lay – setting to one side for a moment the relatively conventional *Kát'a Kabanová* (1920–1) – through a work about the inaccessibility of any form of Utopia: *Výlety páně Broučkovy* (The Excursions of Mr Brouček;

1908–17). The drunken Everyman Brouček stumbles into a moonscape of idealists and poets, lovers and vegetarians; tumbles into Czech national history and encounters not storybook heroics but ignominious near-death in a barrel. Whatever the overriding meaning of the work, long in gestation and resistant to summary as it is, it represents a decade of massive broadening and deepening within Janáček's musical constituency: there is no place for the mere, the predictable, the second-hand; or for the picturesque, the ideological, the stock. Characters are limned more realistically than in any verismo piece, but they inhabit a world without certainties. It is hardly necessary to point out that this was the exact decade (1908–17) of the most convulsive overhaul in history of the apparatus of composition, from the perspective of three or four figures for whom standard technique became the focus of sustained assault; on this highest level of technical engagement, however, no composer was better prepared for the liquidities of modern psychology than Janáček, and of this it is *V mlhách* (In the Mists; 1912) that gives the first measure.[7]

Although all four movements of *In the Mists* retain features of binary structure to the extent of operating with two very clearly distinguishable groups of material, each embodies quite different deployments of these groups, to the extent that no one aspect of the structure of any of the movements is predictable, or, as it were, 'formal'. The first movement appears from the key-signature to be in D♭ major; of its seventy bars of A material, fifty contain a pedal d♭/c♯; it ends quite firmly and with unexpected inevitability in that key; and yet from the very first bar, any hope of *hearing* D♭ major as such before the final bars is utterly abandoned. Here as in the other three movements it is as if some invisible meteorological pressure is clouding the tonic major with flats, irresistibly darkening the sky into the

---

[7] The editorial history of *In the Mists* is particularly problematic. The first edition (1913) was published by the *Klub přátel umění* (Friends of Art Club) in Brno (plate no. 1 – see Simeone's appendix on p. 181 below); a second edition – revised extensively by Václav Štěpán largely without the composer's knowledge – was published by Hudební matice (H. M. 704) in 1924 and then reissued with further modifications by Štěpán in 1938. Moreover, the edition by Kundera and Burghauser on pp. 89–108 of the Complete Critical Edition of the piano works not only accepts Štěpán's changes without question but also corrupts the text further, and Radoslav Kvapil (Prague: Bärenreiter Editio Supraphon, 1993; plate no. H 6070/5) simply tinkers with Kundera and Burghauser's version. [ed.]

Example 2.13 Janáček, *In the Mists,* first movement, bb. 104–16

minor mood. The only extended passage in the piece of which D♭ is not the immediate tonal centre (bb. 71–80) moves no further than an obviously transitional dominant. The effect when the **B** section returns for the $V^{♭6-5}_{4-3}$–I cadence at the end is thus very strongly one of the revelation of a fact fully present from the outset; the daring economy of the cadential moment lies in the identity of the particular d♭^{1} on which the resolution takes place with the tolling internal pedal coloured from the start by virtually every harmonic shade other than the tonic of which it is the root (Example 2.13 shows bb. 104–16 – note Janáček's original dynamics for this passage, erroneously standardised to its previous appearance in Ludvík Kundera's and Jarmil Burghauser's edition).[8]

This tonal strategy is replayed very similarly in the second movement, with still greater boldness in that D♭ is unambiguously presented as a caden-

---

[8]   Example 2.13 has been edited by Paul Wingfield.

tial root many times before showing through the flattening mists as a clear tonic in the benediction of the last four bars. The play of binary functions in this movement gives a structure characteristic of *In the Mists* in expressing profound ambiguities with total clarity. The **A** and **B** motivic groups both appear in a slow and a fast personality (shown here by 'A' and 'B' for slow, and 'a' and 'b' for fast), within an exactly-balanced form of severe tonal economy:

Motivic groups   **A**   **a**   **A**   /   a+b   **A**   **a**   **B**   /   a+**B**   **A**   **a**   **B**
Harmony   I   V   I   V   I   I   I   I   V   V   I

Here as in the first movement, the surface of D♭ major is smoked with E♮s throughout the opening section, after which 'I' stands for the tonic *minor* until the last four bars cast their ray of assuagement. Rhythmically, too, the movement is unforgivingly consistent: the silent first beat of the opening tune, more sophisticatedly than that of 'Death', serves to weaken every subsequent downbeat to the extent that the melody appears to contain no stronger stress than the initial silence. This dislocation is retained throughout the movement: there are no strong downbeats in any of the melodic material, greatly raising the stakes for the performer during the *presto* sections. (Janáček's ligature must be scrupulously considered, especially in such places as the downbeats of bb. 39 and 74, and by implication b. 63, where the halving of note-values on the barline makes the accustomed notation impossible, and where Václav Štěpán imposes a crass downbeat *sforzando*, moving Janáček's *pianissimo* to the second note, ruinously for both the rhythmic and the tonal narratives of the piece.)[9]

The opening of the third movement, albeit tentative, seems for one four-bar phrase in G♭ major to promise more clement conditions, perhaps an answering four-bar phrase closing the tonic–dominant–tonic circle; but a vapour of B minor (Janáček's spelling) dampens the dynamic to '***ppp***' and obscures the path to the end of the paragraph, as if blotting an eighth bar from view. The **A** section continues with the longest clear stretch of development in the work, warming to an exultant *forte* at b. 19 where Janáček shifts the spelling to give A♭ major, falling to a D♭ inflected with a flattened F. Here the sharps return for four bars, three in E major, then one in C♯, enharmonically translated in b. 27 (sic) to D♭ major (again the original orthogra-

---

[9] See Štěpán's 1924 edition, full details of which are in note 7. [ed.]
[10] Kundera and Burghauser respell in sharps bb. 27–9 of this movement. [ed.]

Example 2.14   Janáček, *In the Mists*, third movement, bb. 37–57: summary

phy).[10] Bar 30 clouds this to a dominant seventh, with a chill flattened supertonic to lead to the opening seven bars, the hesitation of the final bar now augmented to three beats. This B minor qualm is the pivotal moment of *In the Mists*. The **B** section (bb. 37–75) opens by driving an enharmonic wedge into the crack of doubt, whereon a storm of harmonic tensions from the foregoing movements rages past (bb. 37–57 are shown in Example 2.14). After this, the return of the opening (bb. 69–75) is too abashed to proceed beyond the now insuperable hiatus. Janáček's instructions as to the repeat of this section are unresolved: he allegedly sanctioned both a complete repeat of **B** and one of just the second half (with or without a crotchet's rest). However, the initial intention seems most likely to have been for no repeat to be given, reflecting the unrepeated development section of **A**, but by the same measure deepening the unease with which the movement breaks off, the fever of **B** untreated.

The imbalance created by holding the repeat of the **B** section of the third movement in abeyance is mitigated by its cataclysmic invasions of the finale, with the force of an unhealed wound bursting apart, a dormant infection breaking out. The structural violence is extraordinary. In the following summary of the finale, '**A**' represents the opening antecedent–consequent paragraph, identical at every appearance, but for dynamics, and outlining in essence a simple V–I in D♭ minor (Example 2.15); '**A¹**' etc. describe episodes derived from the tune of '**A**'; the '**B**' sections (from which '**B¹**' is derived) begin in D♭ minor over an a♭/f♭¹ pedal, the first of them incorporating a central *fortissimo* on the dominant of A♭ major, retaining the clinging F♭:

A A¹ A A² A / B B¹ / A A³ / Third movement (tonality of B¹) / B / A

Within this barely adorned **ABABA** structure (bb. 1–55, 56–94, 95–120, 121–49, 150–9), the intrusion in bb. 121–30 of the **B** section of the third

Example 2.15   Janáček, *In the Mists*, fourth movement, bb. 1–9: summary

movement is integrated in two ways: harmonically, by association with the central paragraph (bb. 77–91) of the first **B** section, of which its G♯ minor (original spelling, shifting to flats for bb. 125–30) is the enharmonic dark twin; and motivically, by the binding interjections of the five-note descending figure which flashes through the **B** material. This passage (bb. 121–30) sees the most serious of many errors of taste and of editorial discretion in Václav Štěpán's edition of *In the Mists*: by conventionalising Janáček's motivic strokes of lightning into a stock pianism, he shows a complete absence of the slightest appreciation of the composer's aesthetic. In Janáček, not a note, not a gesture is rhetorical, is inertly for its own sake; every detail is to play for; every slightest instrumental or harmonic colour fires its particular charge into the structure. After the unequivocal *sforzando* of b. 131 on a three-octave A♭, nothing is left to hope for; no harmonic chink remains in the restricted tonal space of all four movements to provide an escape from the black *fortissimo* D♭ minor of the close.

The greatness of *In the Mists* lies in its very claustrophobia, an austerity of means affecting every aspect of the music. The solo piano becomes a narrow space with four solid walls. Janáček was to go no further in this direction; the next instrumental work involving a solo piano, the Concertino (1925), surrounds the instrument with an instrumental ensemble that grows larger with each movement, as though a community of friendly animals were emerging from its interior. The work certainly belongs to the enchanted world of *Příhody Lišky Bystroušky* (The Adventures of the Vixen Bystrouška; 1922–3); indeed, Janáček associated the opening horn solo with the behaviour of a hedgehog residing at that point in his garden.[11] Similarly, the Capriccio, 'Vzdor' (Defiance; 1926), for

---

[11]   Leoš Janáček, 'Concertino', *Pult und Taktstock*, 4 (1927), pp. 63–4; English translation in Mirka Zemanová, ed. and trans., *Janáček's Uncollected Essays on Music* (London: Marion Boyars, 1989), pp. 108–10.

piano left-hand finds a group of woodwind and brass as if within the gleaming resonances of the tessitura of the keyboard which it exploits.

There is however, a coda: *Vzpomínka* (Souvenir; 1928), an irreducibly simple telling of an untranslatable aphorism about mediant relationships.[12] Thirds inform the piece at every level; the paradox transcends negotiability in the 'Un poco più mosso' (bb. 13–16), its D♯/F♯ in the right hand irreconcilable with the D♯/F✕ in the left; the abrupt return of the opening, far from a formality, far from the bleakly inevitable recapitulations of *In the Mists*, *speaks* to the opened void in the harmony, in the structure, through its responsive *ritardandi*. This micro-drama contains within its tiny frame the immense truths of Janáček's three final operas. Characters may be able to hold no communication, may be essentially alone; but they are all of the same species. Death and difference do not answer appeals; otherness is persistent, a fact, as is failure; but a C♯ can become a D♭, and that is what is meant by humanity.

---

[12] The original edition of *Vzpomínka* was published in the Serbian periodical *Muzika* (Belgrade, 1928). In line with Janáček's late compositional practice, this score has no key-signatures: accidentals are simply used where necessary. A minimally emended edition (by Jan Trojan) of this version was issued by Supraphon in 1975 (plate no. H. 5781). The edition by Kundera and Burghauser (on pp. 111–12 of their complete edition of the piano works) is all that many readers will be able to find; unfortunately, this as usual recasts the piece by adding key-signatures, respellings etc. [ed.]

3 Narrative in Janáček's symphonic poems

HUGH MACDONALD

To claim that Janáček is unorthodox in his artistic procedures never provokes surprise, since almost all the techniques and attitudes of his mature music went against the grain of convention to some extent. His word-setting, his orchestration, his treatment of large-scale and small-scale structure, his views on harmony, theory and language, his style of notation and his methods of work, even his unforeseen late flowering – all these betray a mind which was never inclined to follow a worn groove. He was not an iconoclast simply in order to be rebellious; he preferred always to devise his own methods and pursue his instincts wherever they might lead.

In the case of the three symphonic poems – *Šumařovo dítě* (The Fiddler's Child; 1912–13; rev. 1914), *Taras Bulba* (1915–18) and *Ballada blanická* (The Ballad of Blaník; 1919) – his instincts led to an additional unorthodoxy that is scarcely to be found in his other music. This arises from the fact that all three are based on narrative literary sources and purport to convey the content of those works, as all symphonic poems do, without recourse to words. So Janáček's celebrated concern for the 'melodic curves of speech' (*nápěvky mluvy*) has no actual words to build on. He had composed plenty of instrumental music before he embarked on symphonic poems, but none of it has the same precise literary framework as these three works, not even the *Pohádka* (Fairy Tale; 1910; rev. 1912, 1913, 1923) for cello and piano, which claimed at one stage to represent Zhukovsky's epic poem *A Tale of Tsar Berendei*. On the other hand the almost complete lack of discernible connections between Zhukovsky's poem and the three short movements of *Pohádka* should prepare us for a similar mismatch of music and literary source that characterises all three of Janáček's symphonic poems. Whereas in his choral music and his operas the vocal text binds the music closely to its dramatic and poetic function, no such obligation exists

36

in the symphonic poems. Janáček seized the opportunity to compose music designed to further a larger, more idealistic artistic purpose than the mere illustration of a literary text.

The Fiddler's Child, probably begun in late 1912, was composed mainly at the beginning of 1913 and was rehearsed, though not performed, in 1914. A score published in that year by the Brno Friends of Art Club contains the full text of Svatopluk Čech's poem on which it is based, as did a second edition, published by Hudební matice of Prague in 1924. Janáček also wrote a note about the programme which identifies a number of themes and explains his faith in instrumental timbre as an essential part of the poetic conception.[1] *The Fiddler's Child* is, or purports to be, a narrative symphonic poem of a type familiar from the works of Fibich and Dvořák. Čech's poem, first published in 1873, has nineteen short verses recounting the story of the old village fiddler who dies leaving a child to be cared for by the village. An old woman is charged with the child's care and the fiddle is hung up on the wall. One night, when the old woman has dropped asleep, she is awakened by a vision of the fiddler who sings to his child with images of the happy life above the clouds. The old woman makes a sign of the cross and falls asleep again. In the morning the child is found to be dead and the fiddle gone:

THE FIDDLER'S CHILD

1   The old fiddler died
     And the parish inherited his goods.
     On the peg hung his fiddle,
     In the cradle lay his child.

2   Under the law
     Everything was taken away.
     An old woman with glasses
     Was given care of the child.

---

[1] It was published in the Brno *Hudební revue*, 7, nos. 4–5 (1914), pp. 203–5, and is reprinted in Jarmil Burghauser and Radomil Eliška, eds., *Leoš Janáček: souborné kritické vydání; řada D/svazek 6; Šumařovo dítě* [Leoš Janáček: Complete Critical Edition; Series D/ Vol. 6; The Fiddler's Child] (Prague and Kassel: Supraphon and Bärenreiter, 1984), pp. 82–3; there is an English translation in Mirka Zemanová, *Janáček's Uncollected Essays on Music* (London: Marion Boyars, 1989), pp. 80–3.

3   On the red cradle
    A pentacle is drawn.
    But a safer shield
    Is the Lord!

4   The kind old lady
    Watched over him,
    Her glasses slipped,
    Her eyelids drooped.

5   Around midnight
    She suddenly rubbed her eyes.
    The room was filled
    With silvery moonlight.

6   And there over the cradle –
    She could hardly believe her eyes –
    Stood the old withered fiddler
    Looming like a ghost.

7   With the fiddle in his hand
    He leaned over the child.
    From the tangled strings
    A soft song sounded:

8   'Sweet angel,
    Lidunko has gold,
    Awake, unclasp your hands,
    And cry "Papa!"

9   'Come into these loving arms,
    I'll not leave you here
    For the child to die,
    Like his father, of hunger!

10   'If he were driven by a storm
    To a cheerless hearth,
    In the frost of people's hearts
    He would soon wither.

11   'If you were gilded
    From head to foot,
    You would only be paying
    With your soul.

12 'Come, my dear child,
  We will fly aloft
  Over meadows and forests,
  Over earthly gloom.

13 'I will take the fiddle
  And play it there,
  Rocking for ever
  In the golden clouds.

14 'Beautiful dreams
  Encircle your head
  With golden stars
  And throngs of angels!'

15 The fiddler kissed
  The sleeping child on the mouth.
  Suddenly the old woman
  Made the sign of the cross all around.

16 Moonlight pours through the window,
  The trees murmur outside.
  The guardian fell asleep again
  As old women do.

17 And when the magistrate came
  Soon after breakfast,
  She was busily rocking
  A dead infant.

18 The fiddle was gone,
  To the villagers' sorrow.
  But toward the guardian
  Their recrimination was severe.

19 But I believe the old woman –
  'Tis proof of the saying
  That the world would be boring
  If no tales were told.

This poem can be divided into three parts: (1) the death of the fiddler and the old woman's taking charge of the child; (2) the midnight appearance of the fiddler and his 'song' to the child; and (3) the old woman's exorcism of the vision and the discovery of the dead child in the morning.

It would not be unreasonable to assume, as Hans Hollander and most brief accounts of the work do, that the music attempts to narrate the poem and that the three parts of the poem can be discerned in three divisions of the music.[2] The poem could clearly have made a lucid narrative in orchestral form if Janáček had chosen to do so. A standard approach to this story from any composer of c. 1900 would identify the fiddler with a solo violin, suggest his death in some way, depict the caring old woman who drops asleep, introduce the fiddler's ghost and his rhapsodical 'song', with a climax when the old woman wakes and makes the sign of the cross. The closing section might introduce a more solemn note with the finding of the dead child and the recrimination of the villagers, perhaps with a smiling epilogue to echo Čech's humorous moral in the manner of Strauss's *Till Eulenspiegel*.

Almost none of this is found in Janáček's composition. The only one of these elements he retains is the fiddler, represented, as one would expect, by a solo violin, as we know from his own notes. Specifically, the melody at b. 3 represents the dying fiddler. At b. 67 he is a happy fiddler – presumably the dying fiddler's recollections of happier days. At b. 358 he is luring his child and at b. 383 he is offering golden dreams, as suggested in verses 13 and 14 of the poem.[3]

But there is no depiction of the old woman, no climactic moment when she awakes and makes the sign of the cross, no solemn judgment from the village, and no smiling epilogue. Janáček chose instead to focus on two other elements, merely hinted at in the poem. One is the suffering peasanthood, vividly and touchingly portrayed by the violas in four parts, first heard in b. 11 and often throughout the piece. Janáček's comment is: 'If the "soul" of those people who eke out their harsh lives in peasants' huts in our villages had found its musical expression in the motive on *four violas*, surely the growth and development of a motive of such character could not be *transferred* to other instruments' (Example 3.1).[4]

[2] Hans Hollander, *Leoš Janáček: His Life and Work*, trans. Paul Hamburger (London: Calder, 1963), pp. 180–1; see also Jiří Vysloužil's introductory essay in Burghauser and Eliška, eds., *The Fiddler's Child*, pp. ix–xi (there is an abridged English version on pp. xiv–xv).

[3] Bar numbers are those of Burghauser's and Eliška's edition.

[4] Janáček wrote his note on *The Fiddler's Child* before he revised the work; consequently the rhythmic cast of Example 3.1 differs from that of the published version of these bars. [ed.]

(Con moto)

Example 3.1   Janáček, *The Fiddler's Child*, violas, bb. 11–12

(Allegro)

Example 3.2   Janáček, *The Fiddler's Child*, cellos and double basses, b. 173

(Adagio)

Example 3.3   Janáček, *The Fiddler's Child*, bb. 139–41

The other prominent feature in Janáček's presentation is the magistrate, whom he defines as follows: 'The *magistrate* is all-powerful. He is omnipresent in the community; wherever he looks all bow to his will. While the cellos and basses measure his steps, the *bass clarinet* with the same motive expresses the fear he inspires, and the harshness of his judgment is heard on the *trombones*. The hut trembles at his approach, and his motive floods the whole orchestra' (Example 3.2). The prominence and menace of this motive are strong from its entry in the woodwind in b. 171 onward (Janáček actually quotes the motive as it appears in the cellos and basses in b. 173). It may also shape the three-note woodwind phrase that he added at the very beginning of the piece before the entry of the solo violin, perhaps an oblique reference to the magistrate's motive, still shadowy. But what about the violent three-note phrase that cuts off the solo violin in b. 9 and then becomes much more threatening in the passage leading up to the 'Vivo' in b. 67? This is either a suggestion of violence in the community, or, more probably, death itself.

The 'Adagio' section in C♯ minor at b. 137 and its plaintive modal theme (Example 3.3) are without any explanation in Janáček's note and without any obvious relation to Čech's poem. Scored mostly for oboe, it should probably be interpreted as a depiction of the child, although Vogel claims that it indicates 'rather disjointedly' that the fiddler is dead.[5] Drawing also on Janáček's letter to Otakar Ostrčil of 6 November 1917[6] for an interpretation of the passage for viola (not strictly a solo, though usually performed that way) at b. 279, we may piece together a narrative from the music as follows:

Bars	Narrative
1–52	The fiddler is dying (bb. 3, 19, 31). Suggestions of violence, perhaps death (bb. 9, 25). The desperate plight of the peasants (bb. 11, 27). The menace of the magistrate (b. 15).
53–66	An irruption of violence, perhaps death.
67–116	The fiddler's joy remembered.
117–36	The fiddler is dying (b. 136). The child moans (bb. 128, 136). The peasants suffer (b. 129).
137–70	The child's plight.
171–4	The magistrate approaches.
175–9	Suggestions of former happiness.
180–258	The peasants' distress under the magistrate's oppression.
259–308	Peasants (violas) falling asleep. The old woman's sleeping may be intended.
309–42	Further reference to the child (oboe) – plaintive as before.
343–424	The appearance of the fiddler, now a ghost. His allurements (b. 358), his promise of golden dreams (b. 383).
425–67	The entry of the magistrate. His harsh judgment (b. 437), his all-powerful presence (b. 445).
468–503	A return to the peasants' harsh life under the shadow of authority.

Not only does this sequence of events bear little resemblance to Čech's poem, its internal balance is very curious since the one section of the music that can be related to the poem, the fiddler's promise of golden dreams in bb. 343–424, comes quite late in the piece. The first two thirds of the composition, up to b. 342, seem to be a non-narrative sequence of motives mag-

---

[5] Jaroslav Vogel, *Leoš Janáček: A Biography*, trans. Geraldine Thomsen-Muchová, rev. 2nd edn (London: Orbis, 1981), p. 192.

[6] Vogel, *Leoš Janáček*, p. 192.

nifying the abstract opposition of the peasants' hardship and the magistrate's authority, neither of which have any real presence in Čech's poem. With considerable effrontery Janáček has told a quite different tale, which can be summarised as follows:

> An old fiddler lives in oppression and poverty with his child. An all-powerful magistrate tyrannises the villagers. The child cries out in distress. Despite the magistrate's threats the fiddler appears to the child in a vision with allurements of gold and wealth. The magistrate intervenes and has the last word. The peasants continue to suffer under his authority.

Despite the non-performance of *The Fiddler's Child* in 1914, Janáček embarked on another symphonic poem the following year. The composition of the 'symphonic rhapsody' *Taras Bulba* belongs to the year 1915. Based on Gogol's long story of 1842 set in fifteenth-century Russia, Janáček made a three-movement composition out of the deaths of the hero Taras Bulba and his two sons. Gogol's story is unremittingly vivid and violent, and the character of Bulba himself is painted in the strongest colours as a Cossack warrior committed to a life of brutal activity, hostile to leisure, laziness, women, Jews and Poles. Antipathy to the Poles was widely shared by Gogol's readers, while the eternal solidity of the Orthodox Church is also loudly proclaimed. The Cossacks' military prowess and their scorn of the value of life, whether their enemies' or their own, are central themes of the story. Despite some humorous touches it is hard not to see Gogol's evocation of a relentlessly barbarous world as a cynical mockery of the soldier's debased ethics. Since Taras Bulba, his two sons and many of the Cossack warriors, not to mention countless Poles, suffer an endless variety of unpleasant deaths, there is little glory or rejoicing left at the end. 'There are no fires, no tortures in the world, no force indeed that can break the Russian spirit!', Gogol may proclaim in the last lines of the story, but there is little hope or happiness for the few survivors.

The story starts with lengthy descriptions of the Cossacks in camp and on the march. Taras Bulba, impatient with inaction, decides to lay siege to the city of Dubno. His younger son Andrei has fallen in love with a beautiful girl who turns out to be a Polish princess. On learning that she is trapped within the city of Dubno, Andrei finds a secret entrance to the city and joins his beloved who is surviving amid desperate scenes of starvation and horror. At the news that his son has gone over to the enemy, Taras Bulba prepares for battle. The Poles eventually emerge from the city, driven by hunger and by the belief that the Cossacks were preparing to lift the siege and pursue the Tartars, who were also harassing them. At the head of the Polish cavalry rides Andrei. In a bitter battle the Cossacks overpower him. His father drags him from his horse and with barely a word of reproach shoots him dead.

But in the battle the Cossacks are routed and Taras Bulba's elder son Ostap is captured by the Poles and taken to Warsaw. With the help of some Jews Taras Bulba secretly enters Warsaw where he witnesses his son's elaborate execution, a deed of such barbarity that Gogol cannot bring himself to describe it. Taras Bulba returns to his men and systematically lays waste to Polish villages, burning churches and indiscriminately slaughtering men, women and infants. He is finally overpowered by some Poles and tied to a tree. As they kindle the flames beneath him he defiantly curses the Poles and with his last breath promises a time when a Russian, with the Orthodox faith behind him, will rule all nations.

The deaths of Andrei, Ostap and Taras Bulba stand out at the end of the story from the swirl of slaughter and battle all around. By basing his three movements on these three events Janáček seems to place his focus on the unremitting flow of blood rather than on the broader circumstances of Cossack glory in Russia's early history. But as with many pieces of this kind, a composer's purpose can combine the depiction of particular events with a larger concept more general than narrative. Janáček composed the work, as he himself explained,[7] to illustrate Gogol's closing patriotic words, quoted above. But there are also some narrative elements which tie the music to the story. In the first movement ('Smrt Andrijova' (Andrei's Death)), for example, we have a portrait of the beautiful princess and of Andrei's passion, mingled with anxiety and remorse. This at least is the interpretation offered by Vogel on the basis of a conversation with the composer.[8] The organ passages illustrate the prayers of the besieged citizens of Dubno. The Adagio in B major, beginning at b. 100, provides a ravishing love scene with

[7] Quoted in ibid., p. 240.
[8] Ibid., pp. 240–2; all subsequent quotations from Vogel's interpretation of *Taras Bulba* are taken from pp. 240–4 of this book.

Example 3.4   Janáček, *Taras Bulba*, 'Ostap's Death', b. 2

Example 3.5   Janáček, *Taras Bulba*, 'Ostap's Death', bb. 12–13

oboe and cellos prominent. From b. 200 to the end, though, the violence is unremitting, with a brief memory of love, perhaps in the mind of the dying Andrei, in bb. 259–70. Unless it is a record of Janáček's own words faithfully transmitted, Vogel's interpretation of the closing section seems more detailed than the music itself warrants:

> A battle follows . . . in which at first the faithless son fights valiantly against his own people. However, when he comes face to face with his father, he lowers his gaze in shame, and on his order dismounts and accepts death at his father's hand. As he dies he once more remembers his love while the relentless Taras gallops away into battle.

There is still the puzzling detail of two rapid cymbal clashes which intrude in bb. 129–30, and then come back as a distant memory in bb. 263–4. There is no rifle shot (an effect which Tchaikovsky admirably conveyed in his symphonic poem *The Voyevoda*), no suggestion of Polish colour, or any appeal to Russian national spirit. If Andrei and his princess are touchingly represented, Taras Bulba himself is no more than an intrusive force that has, as yet, no marked identity.

The second movement ('Smrt Ostapova' (Ostap's Death)) purports to depict Ostap's gory dismemberment and death. That part is plain enough in the anguished passage near the end (at b. 176) where the E♭ clarinet screams out over muted flutter-tongued trumpet chords. The dramatic tension here is strung tight. But what of earlier passages of the movement? The first seventy bars alternate two principal ideas, a group of six stabbed notes in the strings, and a strongly rhythmic pattern at a faster tempo

Example 3.6 Janáček, *Taras Bulba*, 'Andrei's Death', bb. 19–20

(Examples 3.4 and 3.5). Vogel calls the second of these, plausibly, a cavalry battle (although he does not explain why it continues to be heard after Ostap's capture), while the first remains unidentified, perhaps a picture of Ostap's fighting spirit. The desolate melody in sixths (b. 73) may depict his capture, while the mazurka rhythm at b. 126 undoubtedly represents the Poles' triumphant dance of joy. But where is Taras Bulba himself, whose hidden presence at the execution is such a poignant part of Gogol's account? Vogel sees him 'larger than life' in the triplet figure recalled from b. 19 of the first movement (Example 3.6), but since he previously identified that as Andrei's music this can hardly be right. In any case that theme is not heard at this point, nor anything much like it. The brevity and concentration of this movement, as well as its suggestion of violence and heroism, make it one of Janáček's most powerful movements.

Taras Bulba himself is the subject of the last and longest movement, which, according to its title ('Proroctví a smrt Tarase Bulby' (The Prophecy and Death of Taras Bulba)), encompasses his prophecy of the glorious future of Russia as well as his death. There is no problem identifying the prophecy in the grand coda, beginning at b. 166, where the full orchestra, including the organ, offers a gloriously diatonic vision of Russia's greatness. It is unmistakably the close of the full work, not of just a single movement, like the ending of a symphony.[9]

The first half of the movement is less easy to interpret. It shows us Taras Bulba, certainly. It is mostly based on a four-note figure (Example 3.7) which takes many different forms and is scored for a variety of instruments. There is something of Bulba's fury here, as he lays waste the Polish countryside. At b. 44 there is a moment of serenity, interrupted by a wild Polish dance at b. 52 which also uses Bulba's theme, although if this represents his

---

[9] Janáček's 'gloriously diatonic vision' at the end of *Taras* is – in terms of orchestral sonority, structural function and programmatic context – a candid intertextual reference to the grandiose diatonic climax of the finale of Tchaikovsky's 'Manfred' Symphony (1885). [ed.]

Example 3.7   Janáček, *Taras Bulba*, 'The Prophecy and Death of Taras Bulba', b. 2

Example 3.8   Janáček, *Taras Bulba*, 'The Prophecy and Death of Taras Bulba', b. 84

captors, as it presumably does, they should scarcely borrow his motive. Finally the trombones break in with Example 3.8, the only motive to be heard in more than one movement of the work, a triplet figure at b. 84 taken from b. 200 of the first movement where Taras Bulba confronts his traitor son Andrei. Vogel thinks Bulba witnesses the daring feat of horsemanship – a leap into the river Dniestr – by which his warriors escaped their pursuers, but there is nothing in the score that can truly be read in this fashion. Instead we have a certain suggestion of the flames that encircle him and lead directly into the apotheosis. 'More deeply felt and more authentically national music than this can scarcely be imagined', writes Vogel. There is no doubting the depth of Janáček's feelings and his faith in Russia at a time when the movement for Czech liberation saw all its hopes embodied in the Russians' struggle against the Austrians; he had long been a committed admirer of Russian literature and culture. But *Taras Bulba* is not by any stretch of the imagination 'authentically national' music. It is Czech, certainly, by virtue of Janáček's roots in Czech music, but it is not Russian music, nor is there any hint of Russian music in it. The Russian Cossacks are characterised by Janáček's flexibly expressive style which he had developed from his study of the Czech language, not from Russian folk music or even from Orthodox chant. We know that the music is full of faith in Russian greatness, but only because Janáček said so and because Taras Bulba, in Gogol's story, stands for the defiant Russian spirit.

It is still odd, as John Tyrrell has pointed out, 'to see the agnostic Janáček celebrating the victory of Christ, and even odder that he could take the defeat of one Slavonic nation by another as "the victory of the Slavs".[10] *Taras Bulba* is not a good text for pan-Slavophiles, since the Poles are treated with unremitting contempt.[11] They are less barbarous, on the whole, than the Cossacks, but that does not win them any friends. These internecine struggles are no advertisement for the Slav fraternity in which Janáček had such faith. Could he not have found a story in which Slavs defeated Germans instead, as Smetana had in *The Brandenburgers in Bohemia*?

The Fiddler's Child was first performed in 1917 and *Taras Bulba* was considerably revised in 1918. Janáček's third symphonic poem, *The Ballad of Blaník*, followed soon after by the beginning of 1920, and, like *The Fiddler's Child*, seems to recall the national flavour of earlier Czech music. If *The Fiddler's Child* is an echo of Dvořák's Erben pieces, *The Ballad of Blaník* picks up a subject already treated by Smetana in the last ('Blaník') of the *Má Vlast* (My Country) cycle of symphonic poems (1874–9) and by Fibich in his opera *Blaník* (1874–7) first performed in 1881. In the light of the assured spirit of Czech national identity felt by all Czechs in 1919 following the establishment of an independent Czechoslovak state, Janáček's choice might be read as an expression of pride in the legend of the warriors who sleep in the heart of the Blaník mountain (a hill in southern Bohemia) waiting for the day when they will ride out to save the Czech nation in its hour of need. Janáček chose as his source a narrative poem by Jaroslav Vrchlický, published in his *Selské balady* (Peasant Ballads) of 1885:

THE BALLAD OF BLANÍK

Every year on Good Friday,
As the Passion is sung, Blaník opens up.
Woe, woe to him who sets foot there,
He must wait, wait for a full year to pass.
In truth he is fortunate
If he can endure the year's misery

---

[10] Quoted from Tyrrell's disc note to Simon Rattle's recording of the work (EMI CDS7542121, 1990).

[11] Disparagement of the Poles is commonplace not only in Russian nineteenth-century operas but also in Czech operas of the period, most notably in Dvořák's *Dimitrij* (1881–2; rev. 1883, 1885 and 1894–5). [ed.]

Until again on Good Friday,
As the Passion is sung, Blaník opens up.

Much worse is it for him on whose eyelids
Sleep heavily presses,
He must sleep there for a hundred years.
Oh, what woe dogs his errant steps!

One Good Friday was an unhappy day.
Good friend Jíra came out of his gate,
And instead of going to church where they were singing the Passion,
He turned towards the woods. The day was dark and gloomy,
How desolate were the trees, how sad their murmuring!

Jíra was, by common consent, a thinking man.
Gloomy woods held more for him than God's house.
Further and further on he goes, to the foot of Blaník.
Old stories swarmed in his brain,
He smiled. – Ah, this rock wall
Beneath the pine roots is enticingly open.
Jíra enters, lowering his head.
The distant Passion hymn echoes through the woods.

Before him is a long passage; at the end is a glimmer
Like a bright star, or a shining cloud.
Towards that light Jíra steps closer and closer
Till he comes suddenly upon a hall of stone.
Neatly around the wall stood rows of horses;
Some wore bells on their stirrups and harness;
Some shook their heads, some pawed the ground,
Raising echoes in the dark hollow passage.
Beside the horses, as told by legend,
Stood a band of dark-visaged knights
Clothed in stillness, arrayed in a circle,
As if plunged in deepest reverie.
At their feet shone mounds of weapons,
On their head flashed helmets like the stars,
Huge shields, their surfaces sparkling like silver,
Covered their whole body and the horses too,
Great swords, mightily sheathed,
Catapults and slings with volleys loaded,
Ball-and-chains, pikes and daggers,

Maces and spears. Marshalled in lines
God's troops stood clothed in stillness,
Ready to fight but plunged in sleep.

From the midst of that horde a banner arose
On which St Václav's eagles spread their wings.

Jíra looked close, anxious to understand.
Boulder doors closed with a terrible clang.
Through the desolate wood the Passion lament
Reverberated weakly here in the rock,
As when a bird with wounded wings rears up
And flutters in the empyrean, dying.

Suddenly Jíra felt a heaviness in his limbs.
He sinks down, thinking to take a rest.
He sinks and dozes in that living grave.

God knows how long he slept. When he awoke,
It was a time when Blaník was open.
Unaware, he looked around.
He rubbed his astonished eyes, and again took fright.
Neatly around the wall stood rows of horses;
Some wore bells on their stirrups and harness,
Some shook their heads, some pawed the ground,
Raising echoes in the dark hollow passage.
Beside the horses again stood a row of men,
Swaying like shadows that flicker in the trees,
Clothed in stillness, arrayed in a circle,
Still plunged in deepest reverie.
But at their feet the weapons were gone.
In place of huge shields like the moon
Shone ploughs, farrows in place of slings,
Instead of swords could be seen
Scythes, spades, flails, harrows,
Hoes and sickles newly forged.
From the midst of that horde a banner arose
On which St Václav's eagles spread their wings,
Fluttering with joy . . .

The dying sound
Of the Passion hymn is lost in the mountain.
Hola, Jíra, bestir yourself, go seek the woods,

Take the road home!
But look back! – The horses neighed,
Jíra breathlessly fled Blaník's rock.
God orders the passing of the years.
Jíra happened to lean over a stream
And trembled to see his flickering image,
His whole head now a colour of grey,
His pallid temples lined with wrinkles,
Like the man who has read many books of wisdom
Which God seldom gives us to read
And for whose deep understanding
There is only indifference – the rest are blind.

A bewildered Jíra came to his village.
They did not know him, and he too knew no one.
In the fields all were at work, the only sight to see,
And above the smiling country the joyful skylarks sang.

Vrchlický's poem had clear Utopian significance for those who longed for a world in which destructive weapons might give place to productive tools and swords might be transformed into ploughshares. There was no nationalist emphasis. The knights do not ride out to save their country, they are always asleep. But time effects a wonderful change on their power for good. Janáček found much in this message to admire, but the narrative is full of sound and incident, as he cannot have failed to notice. Within the conventions of the symphonic poem, this was highly suitable for musical treatment: there is the Passion Hymn sung on Good Friday, the murmuring of the forest as Jíra wanders out, the atmosphere of the dark mountain passage, the sudden revelation of the warriors and their horses in the heart of the mountain, their resplendent armour, the banner of St Václav, the clang of the rock door closing, Jíra falling asleep, the passing of time, the transformed vision of the warriors and their horses when he awakes, his breathless flight, the discovery of his ageing, and the song of the skylarks in the final line.

Yet although virtually every commentary and programme note emphasises the dependence of Janáček's music on Vrchlický's poem, there is very little connection between them. Some of the music can be interpreted to fit the poem, with a certain licence, but much remains obscure.

In formal terms the work has an exposition divided into first and

Example 3.9   Janáček, *The Ballad of Blaník*, bb. 1–2

Example 3.10   Janáček, *The Ballad of Blaník*, b. 10

second sections (bb. 1–75 and 76–157), development (bb. 158–260), and recapitulation (b. 261 to the end). The first part of the exposition can be related to the poem with some degree of success. The theme in b. 1 on clarinets and violas (Example 3.9) perhaps represents placid village life, while Jíra himself has the more forthright theme in b. 10 (Example 3.10). The distorted chorale in b. 28 may be the village passion hymn from which Jíra has escaped, the violent music at b. 46 representing his flight. The next hymn, at b. 54 (Example 3.11), is presumably a representation of the knights of St Václav.

Thus far the meaning of the music, as a rapid telescoped representation of the first part of the poem, is more or less intelligible. But hereafter there are problems. There is no crash of the rock door, although Vogel thinks it occurs at the end of the harp episode (b. 75) where the septuplets of the strings 'tumble downward without, however, reaching any emphatic conclusion'.[12] But tumbling strings do not convey a crashing rock, and the fact is that Janáček, for his own good reasons, did not represent this effect at all.

There follows a long lyrical passage, bb. 76–157, whose meaning is baffling. It is relaxed and melodious, in light 3/8 rhythm. It ought to represent Jíra falling asleep and the passing of many years, but it does neither of those things in a conventional way despite the marking 'un poco meno mosso' twice and 'dim. et rit.' once. We have to see it as Jíra falling asleep, although Vogel interprets it quite differently as Jíra's call for help and his

[12] Vogel, *Leoš Janáček*, p. 252.

Maestoso

Example 3.11   Janáček, *The Ballad of Blaník*, bb. 54–5

Example 3.12   Janáček, *The Ballad of Blaník*, bb. 170–4

running back and forth searching for a way out of the mountain. It is a con-
genial episode, free of stress and unrelated musically to anything heard so
far, comparable to a symphonic second group.

The next section, from b. 158 to the climax at b. 248 is involved and
developmental. It introduces a distorted version of Jíra's theme, a new
theme (Example 3.12), an echo of the Passion Hymn, a recapitulation of the
previous relaxed episode, a dramatic transformation of the opening pages,
a triumphant diatonic version of Jíra's theme and a *sforzando* climax.

In symphonic terms this is evidently development, but in narrative
terms it suggests Jíra's dramatic quandary, a new picture of the knights, the
sound of the village outside, more time passing, and an increase of tension
towards the climax. This is far from anything in Vrchlický's poem. In only
one respect does it fit: in the transformation of the knights' music at b. 178.
But as warriors the knights were presented with far greater nobility. As har-
bingers of peace they are dignified, but no more glorious or more optimistic
than they were before. If the twist in Vrchlický's poem is the pacifist interpretation of the Blaník legend, Janáček makes no special point of that at all.
The echo of the Passion hymn at b. 187 could fit the line of the poem 'The
dying sound of the Passion hymn is lost in the mountain', but why does the
relaxed 3/8 music recur immediately after, at b. 205? If it was a representa-

Example 3.13 Janáček, *The Ballad of Blaník*, bb. 251–3

tion of sleep or of time passing it has no place. Only if it were Jíra's search for escape would it belong here. Why does Jíra's theme then (at b. 233) become diatonic and triumphant, suggesting heroism and youth? Where is the picture of Jíra in extreme old age? Could it be the new theme (Example 3.13) at b. 251? If that is so, why is it a new theme, not a transformation of the first one?

Recapitulation occurs at b. 261, with a calm return to the opening, followed by the knights' music in its first warlike form, full of nostalgic longing with a big Mahlerian cadence in D♭ major, as if that was the true image of the Blaník warriors.

If it is relatively simple to interpret the first 75 bars in parallel with the poem, the remaining 200 or more bars have the most tenuous relationship with it, ignoring the opportunities for musical illustration they contain and making no attempt to underline the poem's message. Janáček has, in sum, merely taken the poem as his starting point and then gone on to write a symphonic movement rich in ideas and marvellously varied in texture but having nothing whatever to do with Vrchlický or Blaník.

Why, we may ask, did Janáček put up the effective smokescreen of naming the sources of his symphonic poems when their real expressive purpose was a different theme? Why did he not call the first poem 'Oppression', the second 'Patriotism', and the third 'Hope', in the manner of Suk's mysteriously general *Ripening*, Foerster's *Legend of Happiness*, Dvořák's *Nature*, or even his own *Žárlivost* (Jealousy; 1894–5; the original Prelude to *Jenůfa*)? The composer's licence to depart from his literary source is absolute, yet audiences were familiar with the conventions of symphonic programme music (as they still are) and could reasonably expect a basic correlation between specific literary material and the composition it inspired. In all three of Janáček's symphonic poems that expectation is denied by a wilful departure from the anticipated narrative. Yet he named the source in all three cases and printed the poems of the first and third works in the score. Gogol's story was well known. It was unreasonable to expect his audience to follow the narrative when it was either missing or different, yet most commentators still cling to the idea that the literary narrative parallels the music. Even Vogel, who went furthest in facing up to the challenge of matching one to the other, was unable to acknowledge that Janáček might have deliberately avoided the expected procedure and substituted a different mode of narrative without troubling to explain what that was to be.

The problem is made more acute by a comparison with Janáček's vocal works, where the words specify the function of the music and where one cannot question the integrity of music and meaning. By common consent the operas, in particular, display a vivid dramaturgy based on the realistic setting of words and an instinctive feeling for the sound and shape of language. In the symphonic poems that intimate connection between music and meaning seems to have been severed without any change in the style of the music. It ought to be possible to interpret the orchestral works as though they were operas without words, yet every attempt to do so, even with the literary sources as guides, leads to contradiction and confusion.

Whereas in Dvořák's Erben symphonic poems the narrative is essential for an understanding of the music, Janáček's symphonic poems are better understood if the narrative is ignored and only the most general verbal meaning is attached to them. But what should that meaning be? In *Taras Bulba* an answer is not hard to find, but in the other two we have no specific goals or themes to put in their place. None of these problems reflect on the quality of the music, of course. Its formal sequences are perhaps better understood in structural terms – with all the licence that allows – than as narrative, since our appetite for a good story or for a simple folk tale may blur our appreciation of Janáček's uniquely personal language and procedures. If he strayed from the true path of narrative programme music, in other words, we forgive him.[13]

---

[13] I am grateful to Judy Mabary, Jan Smaczny and Michael Beckerman for help with the translation of the Čech and Vrchlický poems.

4   Evasive realism: narrative construction in Dostoyevsky's and Janáček's *From the House of the Dead*

GEOFFREY CHEW AND ROBERT VILAIN

Tolstoy famously regarded *The House of the Dead* (1860–1) as Dostoyevsky's finest work; indeed, he elevated it to a supreme position among nineteenth-century books written by Russian authors:

> I have read *The House of the Dead* … I do not know a book better than this in all our literature, not even excepting Pushkin. Not its tone, but its point of view is admirable: sincere, natural and Christian. A good, instructive book.[1]

This verdict significantly makes no reference to *The House of the Dead* as a novel; and George Steiner has indeed suggested that it reflects the fact that the book is the least 'Tolstoyan' of all Dostoyevsky's works – not really a novel at all, but 'plainly an autobiography'.[2] In this he takes his cue from Tolstoy himself, for in a postscript to *War and Peace*, Tolstoy categorised both *The House of the Dead* and Gogol's *Dead Souls* as works that cannot properly be called novels.[3] The work's full title, *Notes from the House of the Dead*, itself in some respects confirms the work's distance from the novel genre, and in his massive biography of Dostoyevsky, Joseph Frank is,

---

[1] Letter to N. N. Strakhov of 1880; quoted by Jaromír Hrubý in the introduction to his edition of *The House of the Dead*, a copy of which Janáček owned (F. M. Dostoyevsky, *Zápisky z mrtvého domu: přeložil H. Jaroš*, Ottova ruská knihovna, vol. IX (Prague: Otto, 1891), p. 341): see Jaroslav Procházka, 'Z mrtvého domu: Janáčkův tvůrčí i lidský epilog a manifest' [*From the House of the Dead*: Janáček's Creative and Human Epilogue and Manifesto], *Hudební věda*, 3 (1966), pp. 218–43, 462–83 (p. 474).

[2] George Steiner, *Tolstoy or Dostoevsky*, rev. 2nd edn (London: Faber, 1967), pp. 293, 102.

[3] 'Some Words about *War and Peace*' (1868), in vol. XVI of the Soviet Academy's edition of the Complete Works; for an English translation of this text, see Henry Gifford, ed., *Leo Tolstoy: A Critical Anthology* (Harmondsworth: Penguin, 1971), pp. 39–40.

significantly, content to use *The House of the Dead* as a primary source for the sections on the author's imprisonment.[4] Thus, at the outset, there are some uncertainties attaching to *The House of the Dead*. These include the genre to which it belongs; the degree to which it agrees with, and depends on, the aesthetic and moral principles cited in Tolstoy's verdict, especially the 'sincere' and the 'natural'; and, implicit in these, the respective parts that are played in it by the 'realistic' and the 'fictive', in the various ways in which these categories might be defined. And, as we shall see, some of the same questions may be raised in relation to Janáček's reworking of Dostoyevsky's text, in the medium of opera. Janáček's work is a *Literaturoper*[5] – or in other words an opera created directly, in prose, from a literary original, rather than a setting of a generic libretto; even this genre, however, is arguably compromised, because the literary model is both highly compressed and manipulated in certain significant ways. And the manipulations have, once more, to do with constructions of truth and fiction, and their representation in terms of music theatre.

Dostoyevsky's *House of the Dead* is certainly heavily autobiographical, and is based on the author's exile at the age of twenty-eight to the *katorga* or prison camp at Omsk in Siberia between January 1850 and February 1854. He had been sentenced to hard labour, to be followed by a period in the Russian army as a private, for his part in the Petrashevist conspiracy. During a spell in the prison hospital, Dostoyevsky made notes on sheets of paper sewn together into a booklet, kept for him secretly by one of the medical officers and returned to him on his release. This 'Siberian Notebook', added to subsequently, eventually consisted of 522 jottings

---

4 Joseph Frank, *Dostoevsky: The Years of Ordeal, 1850–1859* (London: Robson Books; Princeton, NJ: Princeton University Press, 1983); see especially pp. 69ff.

5 Carl Dahlhaus, *Vom Musikdrama zur Literaturoper: Aufsatze zur neueren Operngeschichte* (Munich and Salzburg: Emil Katzbichler, 1983), pp. 46–7: 'The "Literaturoper" ... depends from a technical compositional point of view on the principle of "musical prose", which was recognised by Schoenberg in the essay "Brahms the Progressive" as one of the fundamental presuppositions of the New Music of the twentieth century: the regular, "foursquare" structure in periods, which formed the basis of operatic melody and the principal feature of popular singing style, was jettisoned and dissolved into fragments of unequal, irregular length, whose inner coherence was no longer guaranteed by the rhythmic correspondence of the syntactic units, but by motivic relationships or by the sense of the literary text.'

(songs, individual turns of phrase, folk-sayings and idioms) of which more than 300 were to find their way into the finished work.[6] Of the completed work, the introduction and the first chapter were originally published in *Russkiy Mir* on 1 September 1860, but publication was suspended until early 1861, when the introduction and the first four chapters were published in the same journal. The censors had publication suspended again, but the full text was first printed in *Vremya* in 1861, chapters 1 to 4 in April, the rest between September and December (with the exception of chapter 8 of Part II, which was suppressed).[7] The work was so powerful a human document, it was said, that the Emperor himself was moved to tears.

Such a response is not dependent on the degree of autobiographical veracity in the work, but the assumption that *The House of the Dead* is essentially a personal diary has led to its neglect in the standard works on Dostoyevsky's fiction.[8] Whether as novel or autobiography, very little attention is devoted to it in Steiner's book, for instance; yet *The House of the Dead* serves as one of the chronological cornerstones of Steiner's thesis, a thesis which complicates the generic uncertainty of the work still further. Steiner aims to show the incompatibility of Tolstoy's and Dostoyevsky's art, representing the two great Russian 'realists' as rationalist and visionary respectively, an opposition which he develops in terms, respectively, of the epic tradition headed by Homer, and the dramatic tradition headed by Shakespeare.[9]

---

[6] Cf. John Jones, *Dostoevsky* (Oxford: Oxford University Press, 1983), p. 137, where the figure is put at 306, disputing the total of nearer 200 quoted by the Soviet editors of the Complete Works. The 'Siberian Notebook' was first published in *Zven'ya*, 6 (1936), pp. 415–38.

[7] See Edward Wasiolek, *Dostoyevsky: The Major Fiction* (Cambridge, MA: MIT Press, 1964), pp. 201–2.

[8] With the exception of John Jones's highly coloured account of *The House of the Dead* in *Dostoevsky*.

[9] Steiner, *Tolstoy or Dostoevsky*, p. 131: 'Dostoevsky's relation to the dramatic is analogous, in centrality and ramifications, to Tolstoy's relationship to the epic. It characterized his particular genius as strongly as it contrasted it with Tolstoy's. Dostoevsky's habit of miming his characters as he wrote . . . was the outward gesture of a dramatist's temper. His mastery of the tragic mode, his "tragic philosophy", were the specific expressions of a sensibility which experienced and transmuted its material dramatically. This was true of Dostoevsky's whole life, from adolescence and the theatrical performance recounted in *The House of the Dead* to his deliberate and detailed use of *Hamlet* and Schiller's *Räuber* to control the dynamics of *The Brothers Karamazov*.'

A similar view of Dostoyevsky as 'visionary', 'epiphanic', is developed also by Thomas Mann, this time in terms particularly of the lyric:

> [Dostoyevsky's novels] are only apparently concerned with objective, quasi-clinical inquiry and analysis – in reality they are more concerned with psychological *lyric* in the broadest sense of the word, with confession (*Bekenntnis*) and terrible admission (*Gestehen*), with the unsparing revelation of the depths of his own criminal conscience.[10]

Mann is here using 'lyric' to point up the difference between the characteristic novelistic method and the typical lyric mode. The novel, or epic, is the genre of detail, narrated in the past, often with a third-person narrator gifted with some degree of insight into the workings of the protagonists' minds, dependent for its effect on time, in terms of sequence, simultaneity and consequence; it depicts, presents, explains, demonstrates and makes clear. The lyric voice, on the other hand, is that of epiphanic insight, most characteristically in the first person, without the need for a chronological framework, and presupposing for its full effect the existence of a sympathetic spirit in the reader. This is not to say that, according to this view, Dostoyevsky's novels would ideally all be first-person narratives. Rather, they are seen to possess a confessional dimension ('Bekenntnis', 'Gestehen'), whereby even events retold from the point of view of a third party are felt to be shared as the self-revelation of a common humanity.

For Janáček, the significant differences between Tolstoy and Dostoyevsky outlined above may very likely have seemed unimportant, as we shall note below, though we may note immediately that his method is allusive and 'lyrical', not rational. Both authors are included in the list of the sources on which Janáček drew for material for his works; he had developed an amateur's interest in their thought, well-known in Bohemia and Moravia in the second half of the nineteenth century, and he played an enthusiastic and active part (as chairman, he may personally have been responsible for drafting the telegram of condolence addressed by the circle

---

10 Thomas Mann, 'Dostojewski – mit Maßen', written as the introduction to an American edition of Dostoyevsky's stories, first published in *Die Neue Rundschau*, September 1946, then in *Neue Studien* (Stockholm: Bermann-Fischer, 1948), and quoted here from Thomas Mann, *Schriften und Reden zur Literatur, Kunst und Philosophie* (Frankfurt am Main: S. Fischer, 1960), pp. 7–20 (p. 17).

to Tolstoy's family in 1910).[11] It was the serious commitment of both writers to morality, humanity and truth that appealed to him; and it seems possible, through considering some of Janáček's remarks over the years, together with some aspects of the libretto and its musical setting, to arrive at some understanding of these elusive qualities, as the composer understood them.

As John Tyrrell has shown, there is no evidence that Janáček was working on *From the House of the Dead* at all before 1927;[12] and even in the well-known open letter to Max Brod quoted in this article on p. 64 below, which was published in February 1927, which makes specific reference to *The House of the Dead*, Janáček may not yet have formulated any clear plans for using the Dostoyevsky book as the basis for a new libretto. Nevertheless, by the second half of February he had made his choice and begun sketches; he possessed two copies of Dostoyevsky's novel, one in the original Russian and one in a Czech translation by 'H. Jaroš' (Jaromír Hrubý), though, from the evidence of the annotations, he hardly used the latter.[13]

Structurally, Janáček's principal task was obviously condensation; and the first stage in writing the libretto was to mark his choice of passages of dialogue and narrator's text in the Russian version, and extract them. He translated them into Czech as he went along, often very quickly (indeed the whole opera was written at extraordinary speed), sometimes merely transliterating rather than translating, and occasionally leaving Russian words in

[11] Procházka, 'Z mrtvého domu', p. 474.
[12] John Tyrrell, *Janáček's Operas: A Documentary Account* (London: Faber, 1992), pp. 327, 330–1. There is evidence of a violin concerto, called 'Putovaný dušičky' (The Pilgrimage of a Soul), on which Janáček worked in 1926, part of which is embedded in the overture to *From the House of the Dead*. For an argument strenuously championing this piece, see Miloš Štědroň and Leoš Faltus, 'Janáčkův houslový koncert: torzo nebo vrcholné dílo posledního údobí skladatele?' [Janáček's Violin Concerto: A Torso or a Crowning Work of the Composer's Last Period?], *Opus musicum*, 20 (1988), pp. 89–97; see also Jarmila Procházková, 'Duša v očarovaném kruhu' [A Soul in the Realm of Bliss], *Opus musicum*, 21 (1989), pp. 200–7.
[13] Janáček possessed a copy (preserved in the Janáček Museum in Brno) of a Russian edition of Dostoyevsky (Berlin, 1921), besides the Hrubý translation already noted; see Marina Melnikova, 'Interpretace Dostojevského textu v libretu poslední Janáčkovy opery' [The Interpretation of Dostoyevsky's Text in the Libretto of Janáček's Last Opera], *Hudební věda*, 23 (1986), pp. 43–55 (p. 45).

the Cyrillic alphabet. This was no doubt to give himself the freedom to maintain the differences in speech register which he had exploited much earlier in other works as a means of abrupt contrast, paralleling his musical techniques of sudden shifts à la Debussy from one tonal world to another – diatonic, modal in the folk style, highly chromatic, and so on. In *From the House of the Dead*, he uses dialect Czech at one end, and formal liturgical Old Slavonic at the other, of a wide spectrum of speech ranging from the most familiar to the most formal, archaic and 'poetic'; this spectrum here incorporates sections or fragments of Czech, Ukrainian, Russian, Church Slavonic, and text that is (whether by ignorance or design) macaronic and 'pan-Slav', precisely conforming to no 'national' rule.[14] By so doing, Janáček succeeds very conspicuously in adding a further level of variety to a work which, with its lack of female characters (with the exception of the small part for the Prostitute in Act II and the breeches role of Aljeja[15]), notoriously lacks the diversity of vocal type normally essential to the success of an opera.

The ordering of the libretto, in its final form, in fact corresponds fairly closely to that of Dostoyevsky's original. Marina Melnikova's study provides a diagram to illustrate Janáček's deployment of Dostoyevsky's material over the three acts of the opera, which (in view of its inaccessibility to most English-speaking readers) may perhaps usefully be reproduced here (Figure 4.1). She is concerned particularly to trace the ways in which Janáček sets about constructing direct speech when this is absent in his model, and the particular constraints under which Janáček was working in his threefold role as translator from a foreign language, librettist and composer.

Janáček supported this process of excerpting the model by drawing up 'scenarios', brief synopses for the sake of orientation, with lists of

---

14 For the purpose of representing Russian phrases realistically, according to his own principles of musical prosody, he had possessed his own 'Russian Notebook', from the time when he had made notes of the intonation of Russian speech as he had heard it travelling to St Petersburg decades earlier; cf. Melnikova, 'Interpretace Dostojevského textu v libretu posledního Janáčkovy opery', p. 54.

15 Note that all names of characters in the opera are given here in Czech spelling, and those in the novel in English transliteration of Russian, as a convenient means of distinguishing them from one another.

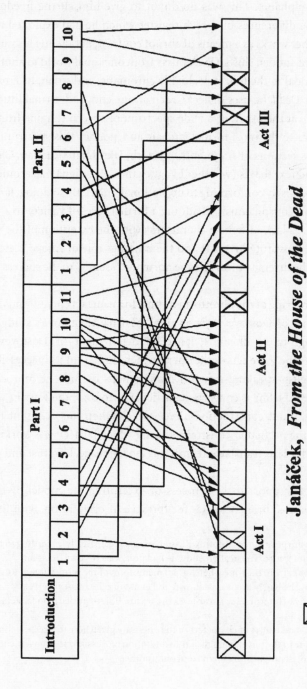

Figure 4.1   Janáček's deployment of Dostoyevsky's material in *From the House of the Dead*

principal characters, episodes, stage settings and so on, together with page references to his copy of his Russian model, which represented his selection of the material available to him in it. (The earliest dated synopsis of this sort was sketched in late February 1927.)[16] These synopses, as we shall argue, provide useful evidence for Janáček's interventions in the structure of his original. And they assisted him in a further aim: to arrive at an idiosyncratic style of dialogue, which is not merely in prose (the hallmark of the *Literaturoper* of the late nineteenth and early twentieth centuries) rather than traditional verse, but in a highly concentrated and laconic style, with many abrupt sentences often comprising only one or two words. In this manner he broke conspicuously free of the usual rhetorical style even of other *Literaturopern* of the time with prose librettos; his libretto is full of short, disjointed sentences, whose effect is sometimes familiarly colloquial, sometimes comic and sometimes threatening. (Janáček himself claimed to have been influenced in his prose style by that of Viktor Dyk, with whom he had previously collaborated.) The individual character of his prose emerges very clearly, for example, if one contrasts it with that of the libretto of the closest contemporary parallel to *From the House of the Dead*, Otakar Jeremiáš's setting of another Dostoyevsky text, *The Brothers Karamazov* (1922–7, premiered in 1928); a glance at its highly rhetorical prose style shows its distance from that of Janáček, even though parts of this opera illustrate brutal conflicts quite similar to some of those in *From the House of the Dead*.

Janáček's prose style supplies evidence of his desire increasingly (and particularly in this, his last opera) to strip away conventional rhetorical effects and replace them, or at least give the effect of replacing them, with a new kind of 'raw' rhetoric, based on lived experience. As early as 1918, he writes in a letter to František Procházka of his aim to turn the theatre stage into a 'stage of life'; and his commitment to 'truth' understood in this sense of social and human engagement was very clearly expressed in an open letter to Brod which was published in February 1927:

[16] These synopses were variously published by Leoš Firkušný, in 'Poslední Janáčkova opera Z mrtvého domu' [Janáček's Last Opera, *From the House of the Dead*], *Divadelní list*, 12 (1936–7), pp. 358–68, 386–400, and in Procházka, 'Z mrtvého domu'; for English translations see Tyrrell, *Janáček's Operas*, pp. 328–30.

In a similar case, if I were thinking in terms of composition, I would incline right to the truth, right to the harsh speech of the elements, and I would know how to advance a little by means of art. On this path I do not stop at Beethoven, nor at Debussy, nor at Dvořák, nor at Smetana, because I do not meet them there. I do not borrow from them, for it is now impossible to repay them. Here I am close to F. M. Dostoyevsky. In *The House of the Dead* he discovered a good human soul even in Baklushin, even in Petrov, even in Isay Fomich. 'Good man, Isay Fomich!' Dr Brod, you have observed supreme depth of expression there.[17]

A year later, when the second version of the opera had been completed, Janáček repeated very similar views on Dostoyevsky's *House of the Dead*, adding some comments positioning himself with regard to other contemporary opera; despite Janáček's usual disjointed prose, these again assist materially in arriving more precisely at his idea of 'truth':

> Wrong, wrong! Wrong is done to Wozzeck, wrong was seriously done to Berg. He is a dramatist of astonishing consequence, of deep truth. Have his say! Let him have his say! Today he is torn to pieces. He suffers. As if he had been cut short. Not a note. And every note of his was soaked in blood! Look, art in the street! The street produces art. *Jonny spielt auf* produces the houses! Boredom, sir, boredom![18]

Clearly, then, Janáček was prepared to overlook the formal, generic and technical aspects of operas as different from his own as Berg's *Wozzeck*, if he regarded them as exemplifying his own commitment to 'truth', something he could not discern in Ernst Křenek's 'boring' *Jonny spielt auf*, however much its runaway success might have seemed to have eclipsed the achievement of Berg in those years.[19] Nevertheless, his idea, expressed in the first of

[17] These two sources are quoted from Procházka, 'Z mrtvého domu', pp. 475–6.

[18] The interview was printed in *Literární svět*, 1 (1927–8), no. 12, of 8 March 1928, with this quotation reprinted in Procházka, 'Z mrtvého domu', p. 482. It is somewhat ironic that Ernst Křenek, the composer of *Jonny spielt auf*, should have written a glowing programme note for the first performance of Janáček's *From the House of the Dead* at Munich in 1961, at which a first attempt was made to eliminate the modifications of the opera by Bakala and Chlubna.

[19] Berg's *Wozzeck* was premiered in 1925 at the Staatsoper in Berlin, and first performed in Prague in 1926; Křenek's *Jonny spielt auf* was premiered in 1927 at the Neues Theater in Leipzig, and performed in its first season in more than forty opera houses (with more than 400 performances in Germany that year). It remains unclear, of course, how well Janáček knew *Jonny spielt auf*.

the two quotations above, that truth depends on the progressive stripping away of romantic bombast, has much in common with the attitudes of other composers of the time, including Křenek himself, even those working in other countries and in rather different styles – though Janáček's isolation from German-speaking and western culture, and his preference for models and ideas drawn from the eastern and Slavic sphere, mean that a direct influence is hardly to be expected from any of his western contemporaries.

Yet, however 'modern' Janáček's music may sound, he seems not to have wished to respond to contemporary ideas in Russia either; the influences in terms of thought come not from the composers, writers and thinkers of the first Soviet decade, but from the great nineteenth-century figures such as Tolstoy and Dostoyevsky. And even here, he seems to have preferred to ignore the generic differences between Tolstoy and Dostoyevsky: all the texts he selected from them (as from others, such as Ostrovsky) were such that could easily, and uniformly, be read as social criticism – even though Tolstoy's critique of marriage in *The Kreutzer Sonata* (supplying a narrative basis for Janáček's First String Quartet), for instance, is distinctly different from Dostoyevsky's of prison life in *The House of the Dead*. Yet the final choice of Dostoyevsky for what is arguably his greatest opera seems hardly coincidental: the epiphanic mode of Dostoyevsky had by 1928 become Janáček's preferred vein. He feigns an absence of formal artifice, and a naked directness of expression, in order to create empathy for his moral stance in the listener. It is, very precisely, the musical equivalent of the confessional dimension of Dostoyevsky – and thus one finds in this work a distinctly nineteenth-century style of thought, paradoxically wedded to a distinctly modernist style of musical expression.[20]

In this respect, Janáček is also not far removed from that other Russian, Musorgsky, who, like him, often seems at odds with the mainstream development of nineteenth- and twentieth-century music. Indeed, the obvious similarities have given rise to a whole literature of support –

[20] Perhaps one may suggest that the same concern on Janáček's part for directness of expression, most effectively constructed when springing from personal experience, lay behind Janáček's continual recourse to Kamila Stösslová as his inspiration, rather than a purely erotic concern, as emphasised, for example, in Tyrrell's 'Janáček, Leoš', *The New Grove Dictionary of Music and Musicians*, ed. Stanley Sadie (London: Macmillan, 1980), vol. IX, pp. 474–90 (p. 479).

and opposition – for the possibility that Janáček was able to become sufficiently familiar with the music of the Russian master to have been influenced directly by him.[21] (But in making comparisons between the two composers here, no assumption is made about any direct connection in terms of such traditionally conceived 'influences'.)

Carl Dahlhaus has written on the similarities between Janáček and Musorgsky, and it may be useful to examine his line of argument. He writes:

> The aesthetics that [Janáček] espoused: the proposition that music must above all be 'true' and ought not to flinch at the reality of ordinary life, agrees in almost every respect with the convictions formulated in letters by Musorgsky. And Janáček's practice of composing prose and developing melody from the rise and fall of speech is reminiscent of the 'realistic' dialogues in the inn scene from *Boris Godunov*.[22]

Dahlhaus argues that Musorgsky's particular search for 'truth' was one that led him down the path of realism in music. This path, he maintains, was one that predominated in literature, but hardly in music, in the late nineteenth century (despite the presence of realistic traits in many operas from several different national traditions), and not only for coincidental reasons. Since nineteenth-century idealist aesthetics gave a special place to music 'as "by nature" a romantic, non-realistic art, whose realm is the "strange" – E. T. A. Hoffmann's *Dschinnistan* or *Atlantis* – not the "prose of common life" (Hegel)',[23] it may be seen that realism in music is precarious, and that the unusual qualities in Musorgsky, often branded 'amateurish', arise as a natural consequence of the attempt to impose realism on music. They are in the nature of the case, so to speak, a price the composer has to pay. (We shall argue below that Dostoyevsky's and Janáček's brands of realism themselves require some refinement of this argument.) And Dahlhaus then proceeds, on the basis of a few examples, to suggest that Musorgsky's realism depends on an undermining of traditionally accepted conventions of hearing – and that this process, giving rise to Musorgsky's realism, is best understood in

---

[21] See, in particular, Abram Gozenpud, 'Janáček a Musorgskij', *Opus musicum*, 12, no. 4 (1980), pp. 101–9; 'Musorgskij a Janáček', *Opus musicum*, 12, no. 5, pp. i–iv, vii–viii.

[22] Dahlhaus, *Vom Musikdrama zur Literaturoper*, p. 39. Note that this chapter was omitted from the later revised edition of this book (Munich and Mainz: Piper/Schott, 1989).   [23] Ibid., p. 41.

terms of the 'defamiliarisation' (*ostranenie*) principle of the Russian Formalist school. Paradoxically, realism and Formalism are thus seen to depend, believes Dahlhaus, on the same principles, rather than being opposed to one another as Marxist critics have usually maintained.

For example, the central section of the monastery scene of *Boris Godunov* (Act I scene 1) comprises a monologue by Pimen in which he refers to the frequent custom of the tsars of renouncing the crown in favour of a monk's habit; this is illustrated, says Dahlhaus, by a harmonic caesura at this point in the monologue (the abrupt though not entirely unmotivated juxtaposition, at rehearsal number 25 in the score, of two primarily diatonic sections in E♭ and G, whose surprising effect is reinforced by the sudden drop to *pianissimo* coinciding with the harmonic change). Dahlhaus claims this represents *ostranenie* at work, and gives us a clue that Musorgsky was adhering to the aesthetic principles represented by the Russian Formalists. And he adds that one should not be misled by the opposition of realism (espoused by Marxist aestheticians) and Formalism (attacked by them), since 'the formalism of Viktor Shklovsky in his *Theory of Prose* was grounded and developed as an aesthetics of the realistic narrative technique of Gogol and Tolstoy'.[24]

So for Dahlhaus the technique of Musorgsky, and by extension that of Janáček, is grounded fundamentally in the aesthetics of Russian realism – but a kind of realism that is articulated through the techniques of 'defamiliarisation' (*ostranenie*) described by Shklovsky and other Russian Formalists. This places the weight of the characterisation of both the libretto and the music on those techniques, already mentioned, of abrupt juxtapositions of style and matter, rather than in homogeneous unfolding or *unendliche Melodie*, in the manner of Wagner. Such an account of Janáček's music of course immediately identifies, even though in relatively crude terms, one of its principal 'modernist' features, which he shares also with such other composers as Debussy, Stravinsky and Messiaen.

The possibility of interpreting these features in terms of theory worked out in the Slav world in the early years of the twentieth century is naturally tempting, but it should immediately be recognised that the theoretical agenda of the Russian Formalists was only in a very general sense aes-

[24] Ibid., p. 43.

thetic, and was not even specifically modernist. *Ostranenie* is the process of defamiliarisation by which the literary is made literary, and by which it is sharply divided from the rest of existence (as happens also when an author deliberately draws the reader's attention to the techniques by which fiction has been constructed, as for example in Sterne's *Tristram Shandy*). This occurs, in principle, in art works of every period, for it is what makes them art works, even though twentieth-century techniques of defamiliarisation (like those of the eighteenth century) are often particularly striking. Thus for the Formalists, Musorgsky and Janáček would no doubt have exemplified *ostranenie*, but could not have claimed kinship with them on this basis any more than Bach, Beethoven, Mozart or Wagner could have done. More seriously, Formalism implied a radical rejection of referentialism in art; in his critique of Formalism, Bakhtin points out its roots in the aesthetic writings of Eduard Hanslick.[25] And the aesthetic of both Musorgsky and Janáček, with their toleration of programmatic traits of every kind, is clearly very remote from Hanslick's in a number of respects – and equally remote, we would suggest, from the more specific aesthetic preferences of the Russian Formalists of the second and third decades of the twentieth century.

Dostoyevsky's own brand of realism in *The House of the Dead* is, however, not completely straightforward. It may seem to depend most obviously on the characteristics of the 'Siberian Notebook', which at least ostensibly represents records of sayings and events taken from life, and which – interspersed with songs, proverbs, etc. – contributes very markedly to the 'lyrical', allusive and oblique way in which the narrative is set up. But against this, apparently anti-naturalistic forces are at work in the book. Like the Abbé Prévost's *Manon Lescaut*, Umberto Eco's *The Name of the Rose*, or for that matter the series of poems by Ozef Kalda, published in the Brno newspaper *Lidové noviny*, that served as a literary source for Janáček's

---

[25] Pavel Nikolayevich Medvedev and Mikhail Mikhailovich Bakhtin, *The Formal Method in Literary Scholarship: A Critical Introduction to Sociological Poetics*, trans. Albert Wehrle (Baltimore and London: The Johns Hopkins University Press, 1978), pp. 41–2: 'Our formalism was formed in the same atmosphere and appeared as an expression of the same changes in art and the ideological horizon that caused West European formalism to develop ... The formal movement in Western art scholarship arose on the basis of the visual arts, and partly of music (Hanslick).'

own *The Diary of One who Disappeared*,[26] to cite three examples almost at random, Dostoyevsky's *The House of the Dead* makes use of the time-honoured fictional device of the recently discovered document to set up a first-person narrator who is suitably distanced from the person of the author. After the death of Aleksandr Petrovich Goryanchikov, a mysterious and unsociable ex-convict who had settled in a remote Siberian town after his release from prison, a bundle of papers is found in his lodgings:

> There was one fairly flat, voluminous exercise book, filled with microscopic handwriting and unfinished, perhaps abandoned and forgotten by the author himself. This was a description, albeit an incoherent one, of the ten years of penal servitude which Aleksandr Petrovich had undergone. In places this description was interrupted by another narrative, some strange, terrible reminiscences scribbled down in irregular, convulsive handwriting, as if following some compulsion. I read these fragments through several times and was almost persuaded they had been written in a state of madness.[27]

The 'terrible reminiscences' are not presented to the reader, but the text of *The House of the Dead* purports to be the other strand of notes in the exercise book, the description of ten years' penal servitude. The narrative 'I' who makes this discovery, and who is responsible for editing the notes, is there-

---

26 It is probable that the text of *The Diary of One Who Disappeared*, first published anonymously as 'From the Pen of a Self-taught Man' in *Lidové noviny* on 14 and 21 May 1916, was written by Ozef Kalda (born Nové Město na Moravě, 4 August 1871; died Prague 1 January 1921), a transport official in Prague who was well known as the author of childhood reminiscences and stories with a regional flavour. In a letter of 8 June 1916 to the author Antonín Matula, Kalda adds a postscript, 'Did you see the feature "From the Pen of a Self-taught Man" in the Brno *Lidové noviny* on 14 and 21 May? I allowed myself a little jiggery-pokery [*eskamotage*] there' (see Jan Mikeska, 'Jak jsem přispěl k odhalení?' [How did I Contribute to a Discovery?], *Opus musicum*, 29 (1997), pp. 97–100). In another article on this subject Jiří Demel adds some circumstantial evidence in favour of Kalda's authorship, mainly from the author's vocabulary and choice of theme, besides reviewing earlier alternative attempts at identifying the author (Jiří Demel, 'Kdo je autorem Zápisníku zmizelého?' [Who is the Author of *The Diary of One who Disappeared*?] *Opus musicum*, 29 (1997), pp. 93–6). See also Jan Vičar, 'Autor veršů Janáčkova Zápisníku zmizelého objeven' [The Author of the Verses of Janáček's *The Diary of One who Disappeared* Revealed], *Hudební věda*, 34 (1997), pp. 418–22.

27 Quotations are from the translation by David McDuff (Harmondsworth: Penguin, 1985), pp. 25–6.

fore not the 'I' of the book proper, nor can he be identified unproblematically with Dostoyevsky himself. He vanishes after the introduction, reappearing only once in Part II, chapter 7 to correct a misapprehension, and we are left to understand that the original experiment – which was to excerpt two or three chapters to see how the public reacted – has been allowed to proceed into the full text, propelled by its own momentum and without the need for further editorial intervention. At its most straightforward, the traditional device of the fictional discoverer of a lost manuscript is a means of enabling the story to stand on its own, of distinguishing the fictional memoir from the real thing – and the narrations of Prévost, Eco and Ozef Kalda are in no sense autobiographical. In Dostoyevsky's case, however, this feint is a double-bluff – indeed more than a double-bluff. An appeal to a well-known *fictional* strategy has enabled him to present a version of a *true* memoir; at the same time, it disguises the truth as fiction, with the advantage that it becomes more malleable and open to the full range of the other mechanisms with which fiction operates to communicate truth; and, further still, this disguise is itself a transparent device for emphasising that the 'incoherence' and 'madness' of the narrative themselves guarantee its authenticity as reported truth.

All this represents the means by which Dostoyevsky can intensify the *privateness* of the memoir – and paradoxically therefore project it successfully *publicly*, as self-revelation – and achieve the reverse of what is the case in his *Notes from the Underground*. There, the retired civil servant who is the narrator subscribes to Heine's view that true (that is, accurate) autobiography is not possible, quoting Heine's opinion that Rousseau's *Confessions* are riddled with lies, even self-accusing lies:

> But Heine was passing judgment on a person making a public confession. I, however, am writing for myself alone and declare once and for all that if I'm writing as if I'm addressing readers then it's quite simply for show, because it makes it easier to write. This is mere form, empty form.[28]

It is true that, in spite of Dostoyevsky's pretence, described here, that the events conveyed in the Notebook – and hence in *The House of the Dead* –

---

[28] Quoted from the Oxford World's Classics translation by Jane Kentish (Oxford: Oxford University Press, 1991), p. 39.

are so urgent and convulsive as to be without order and without sense, there are some key threads which counter this and which give the book a clear logical structure on at least one level. The primary one is the slow progress that is outlined from 'death' to 'resurrection', as the prisoners' tales gradually unfold and reveal the reality of the humanity that is present even in this inhumane setting. In the course of this process, the play within the play, presented in Dostoyevsky's version as part of the Christmas festivities, fulfils a key role in showing how enthusiasm at a common task can present Goryanchikov with quite a new view of the prisoners. And it is placed precisely at the midpoint of the action (the end of the first part), making a secondary (anticipatory) denouement in which Goryanchikov perceives the possibility of the freedom which is realised in the primary denouement at the end; in the process, it supplies a secure even if rudimentary framework to the narrative.

But, fundamentally, within this 'false fictional' framework, Dostoyevsky's narrative adaptation of the 'real' events of his imprisonment has an unexpectedly unstable quality that firmly allies *The House of the Dead* with Dostoyevsky's 'genuine' fiction – *Crime and Punishment*, *Devils*, *The Idiot* and so on. Where Tolstoy's realism is constructive and monumental, 'monologic', to use Bakhtin's term, so that all characters' voices are under the authoritarian control of the author, Dostoyevsky's is fragmented, and his novels are what Bakhtin called 'polyphonic': 'Dostoyevsky, like Goethe's Prometheus, creates not voiceless slaves (as does Zeus), but rather free people, who are capable of standing beside their creator, of disagreeing with him, and even of rebelling against him.'[29] The characters of *The House of the Dead* are so numerous, so comparatively little defined, their appearance and disappearance so beyond the control of the main character, that the effect is of an untidy, provisional collage of voices, and the framework described above supplies the justification for presenting the novel thus: one narrator has died without having made the material more presentable, the other disclaims responsibility for doing so. Dostoyevsky is deliberately evasive about providing an ordering identity for the material, as he had been in his first novel *Poor People*, an exchange of letters between a clerk and a girl who lives near him, with some letters missing yet referred to in others

---

[29] Mikhail Bakhtin, *Problems of Dostoevsky's Poetics* (Ann Arbor, MI, 1973).

and no one to fill in the gaps between. *The House of the Dead* is narrated as fiction and not as straightforward autobiography or journalism because of Dostoyevsky's ambition to write 'the deeper realism'. His aim was showing the fluidity and fragmentation of reality, and his technique in fiction was not to create solid alternative worlds but to use it to subvert the apparent solidities of our own – in order that a more 'reliable' truth about humanity may be constructed. 'The need for evasion in *The House of the Dead* matches a desire to evade.'[30]

One aspect of this evasion is description. Dostoyevsky's accounts of events and surroundings are often apparently very full: at the beginning of the episode in the hospital, for example, details are given of the striped quilt on the bed, the rest of the bedclothes, the little table with a jug and a cup, underneath which is the shelf on which patients could keep teapots, and so on.[31] Patients were officially not allowed to smoke, and in consequence they had to hide their pipes and tobacco under their beds. But the thrust is not to illustrate the external world so as to make it more precisely perceptible to the reader's imagination as it would be in the traditional nineteenth-century realist novel. Like Kafka, Dostoyevsky uses the objects in the hospital to furnish a consciousness, Goryanchikov's overwhelming awareness of decay, banality and restriction. Cumulatively, detail in the various episodes that constitute *The House of the Dead* makes up the atmosphere of oppression that defines Goryanchikov's experience, and from which the few moments of joy and exaltation detach themselves. And narratively, too, Dostoyevsky evades, as John Jones has indicated in his account of the flexibility of the first-person tale telling.[32] Jones analyses the sequence in which the convicts release the eagle they have captured and tried to tame, and shows how the narrator both distances himself from the group and includes himself within it.

Evasions are in evidence in Janáček's version also, serving a very similar aim of a 'deeper realism'. There are differences: the apparatus of the 'recently discovered document' falls away as it had in his setting of *The Diary of One who Disappeared*, and the complexities of Dostoyevsky's first-person narration are absent. But again there is no central character.

---

[30] Jones, *Dostoevsky*, p. 154.   [31] Dostoyevsky, *The House of the Dead*, p. 209.
[32] Jones, *Dostoevsky*, pp. 129–30.

Gorjančikov has no particular status, even though it is he with whom the narration begins and ends, and it is he who is closest to Aljeja, the purest symbol of humanity within the prison. And, even though the number of characters is drastically reduced, the impression of a 'polyphony' of uncoordinated voices remains, particularly outside the context of the long sustained narratives such as the stories of Akulka and Lujza.

In some respects, the process of evasion goes further in Janáček than it had in Dostoyevsky: the appearance of strict logic is often absent even in individual interchanges. Dostoyevsky's episodes usually have recognisable beginnings and endings, but Janáček's often seem incoherent. This is, of course, the almost inevitable result of Janáček's work of condensation, particularly when he conflates different incidents and different characters; as Melnikova points out, all the characters with the exception of Čerevin and one or two others are the products of conflations.[33] Most of what Janáček takes into the libretto is from the first part of Dostoyevsky's text; he preserves several of the incidents in Dostoyevsky's narrative, often in the same order, conflates others, but cuts out the bulk of it altogether. The combining of two of Dostoyevsky's prostitutes, Chekunda and Dvugroshovaya, in Part I, chapter 2, into a single anonymous prostitute at the end of Janáček's Act II, for instance, produces dialogue of particularly surreal inconsequentiality, since Janáček retains the precise wording of some of the original dialogue, but out of context; the comic tone of Dostoyevsky's anecdote (where, for example, the extreme ugliness of the girls forms part of the narration, rather than being relegated to stage directions) could only be projected through stage business in a production of the opera.

The apparent absence of logical consequence is heightened by the process, often described in the Janáček literature as resembling the 'cinematic' or filmic,[34] by which Janáček's setting is apt to 'cut' abruptly and rapidly between different dialogues and different registers of discourse; a good example of this is the sudden switch from the miscellaneous, disconnected dialogues in Act II, after the amateur theatricals, to the 'folk-song' 'Oj, pláče, pláče, mladý kozáče'[35] (Ah, how he weeps, the young Cossack),

33 Melnikova, 'Interpretace Dostojevského textu', p. 49.
34 See, for example, Procházka, 'Z mrtvého domu', p. 230.
35 Rehearsal number 39, p. 114 in the Universal Edition vocal score (Vienna, 1930; plate no. U. E. 8221).

and back again. One may wish to discount any dependence of Janáček on Eisenstein's (or any other) theories of cinematic montage, the placing of images in sharp juxtaposition for affective or rhetorical purposes; but the technique serves the same purpose as it does in film, of 'constructing realism' – creating the fiction that reality is unmediated, by evading the logical consequence of the discourse. The techniques that are used for the purpose might easily be described in terms of *ostranenie,* for they are thoroughly artificial in construction.

All these aspects of the opera might be described as examples of evasion, of the avoidance of clear exposition in the interests of constructing a fictional autonomy for the characters. Yet a clear understanding of them, and of the opera, requires that they be set against their converse, the constructions (in both libretto and music) that Janáček uses as affirmations, or as means of creating dramatic goals that act against the centrifugal tendency of much of this work – and that such central points of reference exist is already suggested by the tendency of some of the literature to speak of Janáček's music using Aristotelian terms such as catharsis (for example, in a remark by Melnikova concerning the 'Orel car' (The eagle is tsar) episode in the final scene).[36] First, Janáček sets up the action within the same two-part framework as was employed by Dostoyevsky (even though he distributes Dostoyevsky's material over three acts). The end of Janáček's Act II corresponds to the end of Dostoyevsky's Part I: the play within the play (no longer set in winter, though not necessarily 'in summer' as in the German stage directions in the score), somewhat abbreviated as compared with Dostoyevsky's version, occurs not long before the end of the act, which marks a clear turning-point in the action of the opera.

But Janáček's realisation of the drama, if one is to judge it with the help of the autograph synopses (scenarios) that survive (described above), has rather different nuances from that of Dostoyevsky. One of the synopses, that for Act II printed by Procházka,[37] represents the play within the play as a set of 'conflicts' (with the knight, the priest and the cobbler) – and this may supply a key to a conception of the whole narrative, not merely the Don

---

36 Melnikova, 'Interpretace Dostojevského textu', p. 47: 'The placing of Dostoyevsky's chapter ... before the end of the whole libretto of the opera functions as an expressive catharsis.'

37 Procházka, 'Z mrtvého domu', p. 229.

Juan/Kedril/Elvira and Fair Miller's Wife scenes in the amateur theatricals, as a succession of episodes, which, though apparently unrelated, unite in presenting a series of conflicts, some comical, some inconsequential, and some deeply serious. Like Dostoyevsky's episodes, they do not hang together in a coherent succession. Yet as an ensemble they too present a picture of the great, undeserved suffering of the human beings who happen, through a single, unexpected 'stab of Fate', to use Janáček's phrase,[38] to find themselves locked without any possibility of escape into this charnel house. Like Dostoyevsky, Janáček expects his audience to do some of the interpretative work themselves; if they do, they will follow Gorjančikov in recognising this view of humanity.

In accordance with his conception of the drama as a series of conflicts, Janáček does not end the Act as Dostoyevsky ends the Part, with Goryanchikov musing half-optimistically as night falls. Instead, he introduces, after the play within the play, several unrelated vignettes of interaction between characters at odds with one another, culminating in an episode where the Short Prisoner becomes very hostile and aggressive, finally hurling a samovar at Gorjančikov on account of his possession of money and his apparent violation of the prison code of equality. Instead of Gorjančikov, Aljeja is struck, and seems to have been mortally wounded. This, the most serious of the conflicts, besides motivating another highly theatrical end to the act, sets the scene for the beginning of Act III, set in the prison hospital, which was characterised by Janáček in one of his synopses as the 'climax of the suffering'.[39] (Elsewhere it is clear that Janáček had an idea of staging with Aljeja dressed in a white hospital robe at this point in the opera, as a visible emblem of the purity of humanity in its hour of direst suffering, and indeed as a kind of incarnation of Kamila Stösslová.)

However, there is a division between incidental, unimportant conflations such as these, whose tone (comic or serious) is not always easy to discern, and those conflations chosen by Janáček to give sharper definition to the direction of the drama. One such is the conflation of Goryanchikov and the 'Polish nobleman Ż—ski', which has the important consequence that Gorjančikov in the opera has admitted to being a political

---

[38] See ibid., p. 477.   [39] The synopsis of Act III printed in ibid., p. 232.

prisoner, and therefore that the lashing administered to him at the end of Act I is far more strongly motivated than in the book. The combination of the offstage beating with Luka's narration of his own beating further sharpens one's sense of the oppression endured within the prison, and heightens the importance of Gorjančikov as a character within the action (here signifying one who represents suffering humanity). Yet Janáček retains the comic response, 'And did you die?', to the account of Luka's beating (made in Dostoyevsky's narration by a slow-witted prisoner), and times it to coincide with the horrifying return of Gorjančikov after his ordeal; this shockingly abrupt juxtaposition of moods produces a highly theatrical effect, heightened by the fact that the curtain falls almost immediately.

Moreover, these techniques are complemented by the musical techniques, which run partly in parallel with the construction of the libretto (Janáček is never averse to writing 'realistic' descriptive music) but which also expand well beyond them, and sometimes appear to be at odds with them. Two brief examples from the closing scenes of Acts I and II may serve to illustrate this, for these are moments in which Janáček chooses to maximise his dramatic effects. In the final scene of Act I, Luka's narrative draws to an end; both text and music have been extraordinarily fragmented, with brief, curt interjections, often of no more than two or three notes or words, between pauses that were so long that Bakala and Chlubna added extra text to Janáček's original. While the narrative remains fragmentary (after rehearsal number 27), the music begins to change character, the fragmentary falling motif with slurred quaver pairs giving way to a more coherent, continuous rising motif in quadruplet crotchets, and this signals a process of increasing importance for the music as against the text; a climax (in textural and dynamic terms) ensues, *fortissimo*, in D♭ minor ('Vbodl jsem mu nuž do života' (I stuck the knife into his stomach)), although the dialogue is still fragmentary and abrupt. And then ('Tempo primo', *piano*, just before 'Aljeja, niti!' (Aljeja, more thread!)), with a tonal drop to B (C♭) minor, although the mood changes, there is clearly tonal continuity – with a reminiscence of the music of the overture, even to the use of two solo violins, through to the next section of the narration. This covers, and to an extent contradicts, Luka's breaking off the story (perhaps in an excess of emotion) in order to deliver his asides about the thread to Aljeja. At rehearsal number

30, the 'height of suffering' in this story and therefore perhaps in Janáček's mind its climax, the tonal centre returns to D♭ minor with another *fortissimo*; the dialogue ceases, after the comic interjection, and then the music continues through to the unforgettable final twenty-two bars of the act, where the D♭ minor turns out to have been a preparation for a shattering final affirmation of A♭ minor, with prominent percussion, as the ultimate tonal goal of the scene and indeed the act. This well illustrates the manner in which Janáček uses the fragmentary evasions of his original in this work to suggest a shattered universe – from which dramatic moments of great human significance are nevertheless built.

A comparable construction occurs at the end of the second act, after the amateur theatricals. The dialogue between the Young Prisoner and the Prostitute (after rehearsal number 37) is accompanied once again with fragmented lines (though of a very different character from those used for Luka in Act I). The progression towards coherence begins with the offstage interjections from the chorus of prisoners (before rehearsal number 39), and Luka's folk-song, with which the music settles firmly, at rehearsal number 39, on a modal A♭ minor tonal centre. The tonal voice-leading continues in a far from fragmented way through the next exchange between Gorjančikov and the Short Prisoner, settling once again at the offstage folk-song (rehearsal number 40, this time in E (F♭) minor). The movement from this point onwards towards another 'height of suffering', the point of maximum violence in the narration and thus the point at which the conflict is most starkly articulated, is once more a continuous preparation for another overwhelming tonal affirmation, this time of D♭ major, accompanied by the snare drum (and alternating, before the curtain falls, with a choral outburst, 'Ubijstvo!' (Murder), in E (F♭)); although the musical foreground is highly diversified, the sense of the progression, once it gets under way, is perfectly straightforward and clear.

Although these two passages are highly idiosyncratic (even in Janáček's work generally), they may serve to suggest general points about the ways in which literary models are transformed into musical settings within the twentieth-century *Literaturoper* repertory. If a literary model has any worth, it will have complexities that will never translate into opera, where, as Auden remarked,

> The quality common to all the great operatic roles, e.g., Don Giovanni, Norma, Lucia, Tristan, Isolde, Brünnhilde, is that each of them is a passionate and willful state of being. In real life they would all be bores, even Don Giovanni. In recompense for this lack of psychological complexity, however, music can do what words cannot, present the immediate and simultaneous relation of these states to each other . . .[40]

In *From the House of the Dead*, there are no great operatic roles of this sort, and clearly Janáček is attempting to follow Dostoyevsky in his epiphanic style of writing. Yet the great moments in the opera bear out Auden's point precisely, for at these points the music contradicts the evasive, ambiguous style of the model, even though it persists in the libretto. The characters, even Skuratov, Luka, Šiškov, cease being 'human' in the real literary sense that was of such importance to Janáček, and instead become 'human' in the antithetical operatic sense – which was his more essential concern. In order for the opera to be successful, at these moments a misreading, comparable to that of Tolstoy quoted at the beginning of this article, has to occur: the characters must cease being psychologically complex and interesting; they must become bores, and must for their great moments become Toscas and Carmens, adopting the 'passionate and willful' mode proper to opera of every period and style.

---

[40] W. H. Auden, 'Notes on Music and Opera', in *The Dyer's Hand and Other Essays* (London: Faber, 1963), pp. 465–74 (p. 470).

5 Direct discourse and speech melody in Janáček's operas

MILOŠ ŠTĚDROŇ

Introduction

One important aspect of Janáček's original approach to musical narratology has not hitherto been examined in detail.[1] This concerns what modern narrative theory terms 'direct discourse': i.e. 'a "quotation" of a monologue or a dialogue' (whether actual or conjectured), which 'creates the illusion of "pure" mimesis'.[2] Direct discourse occurs in Janáček's opera librettos from the very start. Moreover, this mode of speech presentation is one of the most important narrative principles in the libretto of his last opera, *Z mrtvého domu* (From the House of the Dead; 1927–8). The aim of my essay is to examine chronologically key moments containing direct discourse in Janáček's eight operas leading up to *From the House of the Dead*, and to demonstrate that the composer displays a progressive awareness of the considerable dramatic potential of this conventional narrative resource.

There is an obvious initial question: is there any relationship between direct discourse and Janáček's almost lifelong preoccupation with 'speech melodies' (*nápěvky mluvy*)? Speech melodies are essentially stylised snippets of everyday speech written in conventional musical notation. Janáček apparently began to collect them, from a wide variety of real-life situations, in around 1897, by which time he had already completed two operas: the mythological *Šárka* (1887; rev. 1888, 1918–19 and 1925), after an almost decadent libretto by Julius Zeyer; and *Počátek románu* (The

---

[1] I first raised briefly the topic of this essay in my study 'K některým konvencím u Janáčka' [On Some Conventions in Janáček], *Program* [Státního divadla v Brně], 3 (1968), pp. 8–9.

[2] Shlomith Rimmon-Kenan, *Narrative Fiction: Contemporary Poetics* (London: Methuen, 1983), p. 110.

Beginning of a Romance; 1891; rev. 1892), a comic opera in the *Singspiel* tradition.[3] Nevertheless, it seems that Janáček's systematic recording of speech melodies was a major influence on his operatic style and poetics in general. Furthermore, a careful examination of Janáček's speech melodies on the one hand and of vocal style in his operas on the other reveals that, in the operas, sung speech-melody stylisations are restricted almost exclusively to passages incorporating direct discourse and/or quotations from written texts. (The latter can be viewed as a subcategory of the former and will hereafter be treated as such.)

Although it is true that Janáček strongly resisted (instinctively and intellectually) the notions that he was a 'naturalist' and that he incorporated the speech melodies he collected into his actual compositions, it seems obvious that the everyday process of recording speech melodies must have had an impact on his vocal and operatic style. This argument is supported by the increasing significance of direct discourse set to music in the speech-melody style in Janáček's operas. In my essay I will attempt to record all the principal instances of this technique's use.

Before beginning the examination proper of the operas I should point out that many of the speech melodies Janáček collected still remain to be edited and published, even if this topic has attracted virtually every musicologist who has studied the composer. The early generations of Janáček scholars (i.e. Vladimír Helfert and his pupils Jan Racek, Bohumír Štědroň and Zdeněk Blažek), and even those writing in the 1950s and 1960s (Jaroslav Vogel, Hans Hollander etc.), did not distinguish between the artistic and the scientific value of the concept of speech melody, and (for all their differences of approach) they accepted without question Janáček's notion of speech melodies as objective, scientific records of the rhythms and inflections of real spoken language. Nowadays, speech melodies are more usually considered to be artistically stylised objects.[4] Clearly, only a critical edition of the whole surviving collection dating from 1897–1928 will help

---

[3] The genesis and content of this now incompletely preserved opera are examined in John Tyrrell, 'The Musical Prehistory of Janáček's *Počátek románu* and its Importance in Shaping the Composer's Dramatic Style', *Časopis Moravského muzea: vědy společenské*, 52 (1967), pp. 245–70.

[4] For further details see, for example, John Tyrrell, 'Janáček and the Speech-melody Myth', *Musical Times*, 111 (1970), pp. 793–6, and Paul Wingfield, 'Janáček's Speech-melody Theory in Concept and Practice', *Cambridge Opera Journal*, 4 (1992), pp. 281–301.

Example 5.1   Janáček, *Šárka*, Act I

Example 5.2   Janáček, *Šárka*, Act II

us determine the precise character of the stylisation process itself. However, a useful working definition of Janáček's speech-melody style would be vocal writing that creates the illusion of mimicking the rhythms, stress patterns and inflections of the spoken form of its text.[5] Bearing this in mind, we can now turn our attention to the operas.

Šárka and *The Beginning of a Romance*

In Zeyer's libretto for *Šárka* (which Janáček modified) there are only two passages of direct discourse, deployed at relatively unimportant points in the drama. Examples 5.1 and 5.2 show both, sung respectively by Ctirad in Act I ('To Vyšehrad I hastened, but my father bade me thus: "Go to Libice, the deserted castle"') and Šárka in Act II ('Here in the dark forest she hissed at me: "It was not Trut, who frightened you away from the vault"').[6] Although of limited significance in this opera, the obvious speech-melody mode of word-setting here foreshadows what was to become, especially after 1900, a favourite convention in Janáček's operatic works. The com-

---

[5]   A description of the stress patterns and rhythmic characteristics of spoken Czech can be found in John Tyrrell, *Czech Opera*, Cambridge National Traditions of Opera (Cambridge: Cambridge University Press, 1988), pp. 253–8. [ed.]

[6]   There is no widely available published score of this opera.

Example 5.3   Janáček, *The Beginning of a Romance*, No. 3a

poser's next opera, *The Beginning of a Romance*, also contains very little
material pertinent to our enquiry. The opera's one surviving (relatively
long) passage of direct discourse – sung by Poluška (who is quoting Baron
Adolf) at the start of the very first vocal number (no. 2) – is shown in
Example 5.3 (' "Here on this silken forest soil I shall see you tomorrow, as
the sunshine lures you out and the morning sky turns red" '). This is not
actually marked by any clear speech-melody characteristics and is more
reminiscent of a condensed conventional recitative–arioso structure.[7] But
elsewhere in this opera there are folk-song 'quotations', which have, in the
context of 1890s Czech opera, a quasi-realistic effect. There are four main
quotations of this kind: in nos. 3a, 7, 16 and 17 (the finale).[8] The folk-songs
occur in a form close to that in which they would have been taken down in
the field and thus, like speech melody, constitute 'natural' sonic objects that
are pitted against the 'artificial' nineteenth-century forms of recitative and
arioso.

Jenůfa

Janáček's third opera, *Její pastorkyňa* (Her Stepdaughter; Jenůfa; 1894–
1903; rev. 1906–7), was his most important in terms of international recognition. In this work, the composer exhibits for the first time an awareness of
the full potential of direct discourse, deliberately (if sparingly) deploying
this narrative device at the highpoints of the drama. (Janáček was his own
librettist for this opera.) The first example of a direct-discourse section
occurs as early as Act I scene 1 (Example 5.4), near the end of Laca's veristic
arioso 'Vy, stařenko' (Yes, old lady; Vocal Score – hereafter 'VS' – p. 17, b. 1, to

---

[7]   No score of this opera is currently available either.

[8]   For a fuller account see Tyrrell, 'The Musical Prehistory of Janáček's *Počátek
románu*', pp. 265–8.

Example 5.4   Janáček, *Jenůfa*, Act I scene 1

p. 21, b. 13).[9] In Example 5.4 Laca jealously recalls the favouritism that Grandmother Buryjovka used to show his half-brother, Števa, as a child, quoting some of her doting words: 'when you were fondling Števa on your lap, and stroking his hair that you said was "gold as the sun"!' Laca's jealousy of Števa is of course a linchpin of the drama. The actual direct-discourse bars of Example 5.4 (bb. 7–8 and 11–12) are barely differentiated from the preceding melodically and rhythmically homogeneous stream of arioso, although they do stand out a little owing to the emphatic varied repetition a tone higher of their initial two-bar motive.

There are two further instances of speech melody in Act I of *Jenůfa*. The first, in scene 5, is important because it occurs in conjunction with a subcategory of direct discourse frequently encountered in Janáček's operas from this point onwards: the immediate echo or quotation of an utterance of one character by another/others. In this case, the chorus of recruits echoes in an almost parodistic manner Grandmother Buryjovka's exhortation 'A vy muzikanti, jděte dom! Nesvádějte chlapců!' (And you musicians, go home! Don't lead the lads astray!; VS, p. 73, b. 6, to p. 74, b. 7). The last instance of speech melody in Act I is in scene 7, where Laca peevishly paraphrases Števa's boast to Jenůfa in the previous scene – 'mohly jste se dívat, jak o mne všechna děvčata stojí!' (you should have seen just now how much they thought of me, all the girls!; VS, p. 90, b. 22, to p. 91, b. 8) – as 'co prý se na něho všude smějú!' (those girls he says are smiling at him everywhere!; VS, p. 99, bb. 6–13). The mode of speech presentation here is, strictly speaking, 'indirect discourse, mimetic to some degree', which creates 'the illusion of "preserving" or "reproducing" aspects of the style of an utterance, above and beyond the mere report of its content';[10] this is of

---

9   4th edn, Hudební matice, plate no. H. M. 89 (Prague, 1943).

10   Rimmon-Kenan, *Narrative Fiction: Contemporary Poetics*, p. 109.

Example 5.5 Janáček, *Jenůfa*, Act II scene 3

Example 5.6 Janáček, *Jenůfa*, Act II scene 5

course a close relative of 'direct discourse', and Janáček seems to have viewed the two as variants of a single narrative device. Appropriately, Laca's utterance is a distortion of Števa's, recasting its rhythm profile if not its pitch content.

Very different in character are the three passages of speech melody in Act II sung by Kostelnička. In the first of these (scene 3), Kostelnička for the first time contemplates killing Jenůfa's illegitimate baby, formulating the words she will use when she confronts the father, Števa, with the consequences of his fecklessness: 'and throwing him [the dead baby] down at his feet: "There you are, on your conscience be it!"' (Example 5.5). Even if this utterance is once more firmly embedded within a larger section of arioso, both its rhythm and its stress patterns are reminiscent of speech melody. Kostelnička's next speech-melody interpolation – an echo – occurs at the start of scene 5 (Example 5.6). Her ' "In a moment ..." ' here alters the intonation and rhythm of Laca's simple promise at the end of the previous scene to return soon ('Co chvíla budu tady' (In a moment I'll be back)), reflecting her dawning realisation that in this short period of time she will alter irrevocably the course of her life by seizing the opportunity to murder the baby. Act II scene 5 is widely considered to be the key scene of the whole opera and has been much analysed and interpreted by Czech musicologists. At its climax, Kostelnička is, as in scene 3, predicting future events. Envisaging how she and Jenůfa will be persecuted, she utilises direct discourse in con-

Example 5.7   Janáček, *Jenůfa*, Act II scene 5

Example 5.8   Janáček, *Jenůfa*, Act II scene 7

junction with speech melody to imagine the village people shouting accusingly at her: 'They would all be down on me, and on Jenůfa! "Look at her, Kostelnička!"' (Example 5.7). The alterations of intonation when the phrase '"Look at her"' is twice repeated are typical of Janáček's compositional method; exact repetition is far less characteristic.

One last example from Act II (scene 7) – another echo – marks an equally important moment in the drama: 'And your little boy died', Kostelnička announces. Jenůfa, shocked and disbelieving, partly repeats the statement – 'So he's died' – feebly reversing the melodic direction of Kostelnička's utterance (Example 5.8). Act III has only a single snippet of direct discourse, but this could hardly be more prominently situated. After she has confessed to the murder, Kostelnička pleads for Jenůfa's forgiveness in a veristic arioso ('Odpusť mi jenom ty' (It is only your forgiveness I ask)), at the heart of which she sings: 'Včil už nemůžeš volat: "Mamičko, aj mamičko!"' (Now you won't be able to cry out any more: 'Mother, oh Mother!'). This passage stands out because of its cathartic effect.

The shift in the deployment of direct discourse in Janáček's third opera is obvious. The composer had by now discovered that this mode of speech presentation could be combined effectively with speech melody to highlight key moments, thereby underpinning the whole dramatic structure. He was to develop this important discovery in his later operas.

Živný

Example 5.9   Janáček, *Fate*, Act I scene 11

Example 5.10
(a)   Janáček, *Fate*, Act II scene 2
(b)   Janáček, *Fate*, Act II scene 2

Fate

Janáček's exploitation of direct discourse in his fourth opera, *Osud* (Fate) (1903–5; rev. 1906, 1907), obviously stems directly from *Jenůfa*. The convention occurs in six situations, on which I shall comment in some detail. The first is Živný's brief paraphrase, within his long monologue musing on the past in Act I scene 11, of the intonation of a statement about him and his lover (Míla – later his wife) by her mother: ' "Dreamers, romantics and parasites!" ' (Example 5.9).[11] Musically, the direct discourse is not greatly emphasised, although its realistic rhythm and wide vocal range are expressive in character. The next example, from Act II scene 2, is more concrete (we never hear the original utterance 'quoted' in the previous example): Živný's ' "Come, oh come to me! Fate!" ' is immediately echoed offstage by Míla's mother (see Examples 5.10a and 5.10b). This speech-melody echo constitutes the apex of a larger pattern of musical logic: it caps a lengthy veristic arioso for Živný, whose 3/8 metre imparts realistic syllabic stresses to its entire text. Also, the ramifications of this passage extend to the disastrous turning-point of the whole opera. In Act II scene 6, just before Míla's mother throws herself off the balcony dragging Míla with her, the mother

---

[11]   No printed edition of *Fate* is widely available.

Example 5.11   Janáček, *Fate*, Act II scene 6

Example 5.12   Janáček, *Fate*, Act III scene 1

repeats the word 'Fate!' on enharmonically equivalent pitches, the first of which is emphatically prolonged (see Example 5.11).

Act III scene 1 of *Fate* brings a large 'quotation' from a fictional musical work that forms the crux of the plot of this act: Živný's unfinished opera, the incomplete finale of which the music conservatory students preview here on stage. This 'opera-rehearsal-within-an-opera' is not unique, even in Czech opera. Several similar examples can be found in works from *Erat unus cantor bonus* by František Xaver Brixi (1732–71) to Dvořák's *Jakobin* (The Jacobin; 1887–8; rev. 1897) – the novel features of Janáček's scene are merely its conservatory setting and the specific character of the 'rehearsal'. Nor does this 'opera finale' contain any direct discourse. Nevertheless, the scene does exemplify an increasing predilection on Janáček's part for 'quotation'; and, more significantly, it is followed by a passage of 'indirect discourse, mimetic to some degree', apparently viewed by Janáček as a variant of direct discourse (see p. 83 above). Verva explains to the students in a patently realistic vocal style that Živný went to the theatre for the first official rehearsal of his opera 'saying he'd brought the whole of the opera except for the last act. That's still in God's hands and there it'll stay!' (see Example 5.12); this statement is made all the more prominent by its juxtaposition with an immediate echo: the students' *sotto voce* sequential repetition of its last clause.

A later passage of Act III scene 1 illustrates *par excellence* the dramatic power of Janáček's operatic direct-discourse/speech-melody technique.

Verva opines to the students that Živný's opera is autobiographical, remarking 'Povím vám ještě z opery pěknou scénu, dětskou scénu' (I'll perform for you another nice scene from the opera, a scene with a child). He sits at the piano and sings, imitating a child's voice, a short dialogue between child and mother:

> 'Mami! Mami! Víš co je láska?'
>   'Mé dítě, vím, ach vím!'
>   'Nevíš, nevíš!'
>   'Mé dítě, vím, ach vím!'
>   'Nevíš, nevíš! Když se mají Žán a Nána rádi!'
>   'Ale jdiž! Žán a Nána?'

> ['Mummy, Mummy! Do you know what love is?'
>   'My child, I do, oh I do!'
>   'No you don't, no you don't!'
>   'My child, I do, oh I do!'
>   'No you don't, no you don't! When John and Nanny love each other!'
>   'What do you mean, "John and Nanny"?']

On one level, this is an extended, minimally modified intratextual quotation. The reference is to Act II scene 4, where this very same dialogue takes place between Míla and her son, Doubek, to virtually the same music. Both times, the mother's closing question imitates the child's immediately preceding naive speech melody,[12] mimicking its rising seventh at pitch (Example 5.13a shows Verva's Act III version of this passage). This part of the text is thus marked out as a type of direct discourse. Moreover, after Verva's Act III narration of this scene, the students repeat key phrases from it; in other words, they quote from a quotation, enhancing the effect of the initial intratextual reference. On another level, the child's speech melody is actually intertextual: its characteristic seventh invokes Jenůfa at the moment of her deepest crisis, numbed by the shock of her baby's death into child-like passivity – 'Thank you, Laca, for all the kind things . . .' (Act II scene 8; see Example 5.13b). In summary, within a veristic, art nouveau context, Janáček's direct-discourse convention takes on a partly new,

[12] Strikingly, Janáček drew attention to this very passage as early as 1903 in an article in the periodical *Hlídka* – see John Tyrrell, *Janáček's Operas: A Documentary Account* (London: Faber, 1992), pp. 110–11. [ed.]

Example 5.13
(a) Janáček, *Fate*, Act III scene 1
(b) Janáček, *Jenůfa*, Act II scene 8

expanded role, often clinching larger sections of veristic arioso (especially in Act II).

The Excursions of Mr Brouček

The fantastic locations of Janáček's next opera, *Výlety páně Broučkovy* (The Excursions of Mr Brouček; 1908–17), give rise to several outbursts of direct discourse. There are three in the moon excursion. In the first (Act I) Lunobor reads Brouček 'three chapters' from a volume on 'aesthetics' (VS, p. 77, b. 7, to p. 78, b. 6).[13] Every one of the identical 'chapters' (the first of which is shown in Example 5.14) is sung prominently to a repeated single variant of a four-note motive, which is gradually expanded, and whose rhythm fits the trochaic tetrameters of the text: ' "Krá-sy lu-ní pro-jdi v ká-zni, / boj se v lá-sce, mi-luj v bá-zni, / v ká-zni, bá-zni ne-u-vá-zni!" ' ('Tread the beauty of the moon with discipline, / fear love-making, love with awe, / do not get bogged down in discipline or awe!'). In Act II of this excursion, Etherea's exclamation, 'I will shout it like the Muslim "Allah!" ' underlines the word 'Allah' by a quasi-oriental ascending tritone and a lengthened second syllable in imitation of the Muslim call to prayer (see Example 5.15). Near the end of Act II, as Brouček prepares to fly away on Pegasus the winged horse, Lunobor reiterates the end of his reading from his book on

---

[13] Universal Edition, plate no. U. E. 6185 (Vienna, 1919).

Example 5.14   Janáček, *Mr Brouček's Excursion to the Moon*, Act I

Example 5.15   Janáček, *Mr Brouček's Excursion to the Moon*, Act II

'aesthetics' to three further variants of the four-note motive (VS, p. 144, bb. 6–7, 12–13 and 18).

Act II of Brouček's second excursion – to the fifteenth century – occasions several structurally more significant examples of direct-discourse technique. At the start of the act Brouček conducts a 'dialogue' with an imaginary Hussite warrior in front of Domšík's house, a scene which presages his later cowardice during the battle – the focal point of the act. Brouček's cowardice is emphasised dramatically all the more by the fact that his 'dialogue' is feigned rather than real. As his defence of his non-combative stance becomes more animated, he questions his fictional interlocutor directly: 'Don't you think, Johnny, that I'll allow myself to be cut up like a beefsteak! To what end? Why?' (Example 5.16). The dramatic import of this statement is reinforced by the striking antiphonal 'dialogue' between Brouček's speech melody and the orchestra's punctuating blocks.

A much more substantial passage of speech melody occurs in Act II when Kunka, returning from church, quotes extensively from Rokycana's sermon. Kunka's narration is set to what amounts to a bipartite arioso (**AB**) in a modally inflected A♭ minor (VS, p. 221, b. 1, to p. 223, b. 6 – some thirty-five bars of music). Janáček's favourite 'Lydian' fourths (D), 'Mixolydian' sevenths (G♭), intervallic successions of a fifth followed by a second and pentatonic inflections abound. Example 5.17 quotes part of this 'number': 'He said: "Therefore stand firmly in the Truth, everything you do, do as though you were the sons of God." '

Example 5.16 Janáček, *Mr Brouček's Excursion to the Fifteenth Century*, Act II

Example 5.17 Janáček, *Mr Brouček's Excursion to the Fifteenth Century*, Act II

A little later on in the act, during a dry debate about church vestments, the Student quotes St Bede and St Augustine in defence of his view that those who wear the vestments are the Church's highest dignitaries: 'Or as Bede says in his chapter "Quicumque", and St Augustine in his chapter "Omnis catholicus": "Ita fit", "Sic enim" . . . um . . . um, "Et ponitur" . . .' (Example 5.18). These words, which need to be clearly audible, are appropriately delivered in the manner of an ecclesiastical recitation. Also, the actual quotation is differentiated from the text that prepares it by the transposition of the initial F♯–D♯ dyad to E♭–C followed by G–E. Such quotations are not invariably emphasised in this way. After the climactic battle of Act II, Brouček takes off his Hussite disguise and dons his own clothes. Plagued by the troublesome Kedruta, he drives her away with an old Czech proverb: 'Ha, nýčko ti to povím srozumitelně, po staročesku: "Čerta se uchovati muože, rač zlé baby uchovati, Bože, Bože!"' (Ha, now I am going to say to you bluntly in good old-fashioned Czech: 'I can deliver myself from the Devil, but I beseech thee, Lord, to deliver me from this evil old hag!'; VS, p. 256, bb. 1–17). The concluding quotation is not highlighted registrally, even if the entire passage in question displays speech-melody characteristics. Nevertheless, registral underlining in such instances is quite common.

91

Example 5.18   Janáček, *Mr Brouček's Excursion to the Fifteenth Century*, Act II

Example 5.19   Janáček, *Mr Brouček's Excursion to the Fifteenth Century*, Act II

When Brouček boasts untruthfully of his heroic deeds in the battle, the actual direct discourse is marked by a shift to a higher register within an overall speech-melody vocal style: 'Then I meet Žižka: "Things are bad, very bad there on that hill, very bad; you should hasten there to help!"' (Example 5.19). Similarly, when Petřík subsequently provides evidence of Brouček's cowardice, his speech melody moves to a higher register as he quotes Brouček's snivelling attempts to ingratiate himself: 'Tu, ajta, zřím, an kleká před rytířem a volá: "Majne hern, majne hern! Jsem váš! Ne Pražan, ne Hus! Knáde!"' (And there I see how he kneels before a knight and cries out: 'Meine Herren, meine Herren! I'm one of you! I'm not from Prague, nor am I a Hussite! Gnade!'; VS, p. 282, b. 11, to p. 283, b. 3).

Kát'a Kabanová

In Janáček's next opera, *Kát'a Kabanová* (1920–1), the two 'folk-songs' that frame Act II scene 2 (Kudrjáš's 'Po zahrádce děvucha' (Through the garden this young maid) and Kudrjáš's and Varvara's 'Všecko domů, domů' (Get back home, one and all)) strictly speaking do not constitute direct discourse

Example 5.20   Janáček, *Kát'a Kabanová*, Act III scene 1

Example 5.21   Janáček, *Kát'a Kabanová*, Act III scene 1

and have a function similar to that of the folk-song quotations in *The Beginning of a Romance*. Hence, passages relevant to our enquiry are confined to Act III. The first of these occurs near the start of the act, during the discussion between Dikoj and Kudrjáš about storms and lightning conductors. Kudrjáš quotes Dyerzhavin in support of his theory that storms are merely electricity as opposed to acts of God: 'Savël Prokofijevič! Your worship! Dyerzhavin writes: "Tho' Mankind's body turn to dust, his mind has quelled the thunder!"' (Example 5.20).[14] The entire speech-melody utterance is permeated melodically by pentatonic inflections arising from Janáček's favourite intervallic patterns (fourth followed by second, and third–fourth–second) and is mainly governed by a second-inversion A♭ minor chord; there is little differentiation between the quotation proper and its preparation. Shortly after this, there is an echo, Dikoj mockingly imitating Kudrjáš's realistically intonated 'Apparently' (see Example 5.21).

The final scene opens with a classic snippet of direct discourse, which, although short, has great dramatic import. Tichon and the servant, Glaša, are searching at twilight by the Volga for Kát'a, who has confessed her

---

[14]   Universal Edition, plate no. U. E. 7103 (Vienna, 1922).

Example 5.22   Janáček, *Kát'a Kabanová*, Act III scene 2

infidelity publicly and fled. Tichon makes a remark that draws together all the principal threads of the drama: 'Oh Glaša! Could anything be worse? A beating would be nothing! Mama says: "Let her [Kát'a] be buried alive to atone for her sins" ' (Example 5.22). Tichon adopts unequivocally a speech-melody mode of utterance throughout; once again the quotation is distinguished musically only minimally from its preceding text: the larger intervals of Tichon's initial exclamations to Glaša (beginning with a typical fourth–second pattern) are a little more expressive than his later bursts of recitation on single pitches ($e\flat^1$–$d\flat^1$–$e\flat^1$).

This episode is followed quickly by the opera's last piece of direct discourse, once again attesting to Kabanicha's cruelty. Varvara complains to Kudrjáš about her treatment by Kabanicha for her part in arranging Kát'a's trysts with Boris: 'She keeps locking me in my room and tormenting me. I said to her: "Don't lock me in, or there'll be trouble!" Will you teach me, how I now must live?' (Example 5.23). The quotation itself is differentiated from the surrounding text by rhythmic augmentation (quavers to crotchets) and by the two progressively higher repetitions of 'there'll be trouble', which retain the motivic shape of the original statement despite contracting the initial falling seventh to a major sixth. In addition, the realistic rising intonation at the end of Varvara's question is echoed in the very next bar by Kudrjáš ('Jak žít?' (How to live?)). Equally worthy of note are the repetitions of Varvara's six-note ascending and descending motive spanning the tetrachord $c\sharp^2$–$f\sharp^2$ ('x' in Example 5.23) by the violins (VS, p. 140, bb. 2, 4 and 5), which not only increases the tension but also demonstrates that speech melody can infiltrate the instrumental fabric.

Example 5.23   Janáček, *Kát'a Kabanová*, Act III scene 2

With *Kát'a Kabanová* Janáček's speech-melody/direct-discourse technique has acquired the status of a full-blown operatic convention: although it is honed rather than developed significantly in this opera, its pointed, sudden deployment imparts considerable dramatic force to key moments.

The Adventures of the Vixen Bystrouška

Quotation and direct discourse play a larger role in *Příhody Lišky Bystroušky* (The Adventures of the Vixen Bystrouška; 1922–3); as a result, there are some important developments in their musical treatment in this opera. Overall, there are five episodes to be examined, three of which incorporate several relevant utterances. The first episode forms part of the Inn scene near the start of Act II. The Priest twice quotes a Latin code of ethics, ' "Non des [sic] mulieri corpus tuum" ', each time singing on an 'ecclesiastical' recitation tone – VS, p. 62, bb. 8–11 and p. 66, bb. 12–14 (Example 5.24a).[15] The Gamekeeper makes the Priest translate this into Czech, which he does so by inflecting his speech-melody rhythms with whole-tone intonation: 'In the vernacular, then: "Give not thy body to a woman" ' (Example 5.24b). The next pertinent episode, which occurs a little later in the same scene, also involves a quotation, this time a biblical reference by the Gamekeeper: ' "V potu tváře jísti budeš chléb svůj!" ' ('In the sweat of thy brow shalt thou eat thy bread!'; VS, p. 69, bb. 19–20). This too is intoned on a single pitch.

A rich source of speech melody is the very next scene of Act II, where

---

[15]   Universal Edition, plate no. U. E. 7564 (Vienna, 1924).

(a)

Non des mu - li - e - ri cor - pus tu - um

(b)

Tož čes - ky: "Ne - dáš že - - ně tě - la své - ho".

"Ne - dáš že - ně tě - la své - ho".

Example 5.24
(a) Janáček, *The Adventures of the Vixen Bystrouška*, Act II scene 2
(b) Janáček, the *Vixen*, Act II scene 2

Ó, ó Te - ryn - ko!

Example 5.25 Janáček, the *Vixen*, Act II scene 3

byl bych dáv - no o - pu - stil ob -žer - ní - ky o - ba.

Example 5.26 Janáček, the *Vixen*, Act II scene 3

the inebriated Schoolmaster conducts a 'dialogue' with a sunflower, mistakingly believing it to be his distant beloved, Terynka (VS, p. 77, b. 14, to p. 80, b. 1). This passage is in effect a veristic arioso studded with speech melodies. In his initial invocation, 'Oh, oh, Terynka!' (Example 5.25), the Schoolmaster employs the familiar intervallic sequence of third–fourth–second. He goes on to lament that, had he known she were there, 'I would long since have deserted those two drunkards' (Example 5.26), his vocal line now taking on whole-tone inflections. The association of the whole-tone collection here with a form of direct discourse bears out Zdeněk Sádecký's observation that whole-tone elements in Janáček's operas (and in the *Vixen* in particular) tend to be associated with moments of plot complication.[16] The

---

[16] Zdeněk Sádecký, 'Celotónový charakter hudební řeči v Janáčkově "Lišce Bystroušce"' [The Whole-tone Character of the Musical Language of Janáček's *Vixen Bystrouška*], *Živá hudba*, 2 (1962), pp. 95–163.

Example 5.27   Janáček, the *Vixen*, Act II scene 3

Example 5.28   Janáček, the *Vixen*, Act II scene 3

Example 5.29   Janáček, the *Vixen*, Act II scene 3

Example 5.30   Janáček, the *Vixen*, Act II scene 3

Schoolmaster's next gambit, 'You love me, do you? Oh, speak!' (Example 5.27), introduces the interval of the sixth, which is frequently employed hereafter to highlight key words – see also Example 5.28 ('I have adored you for years and years; your fate is in my hands')[17] and Example 5.29, whose more conventionally melodic 'arioso' style marks out the climax of his declaration ('I shall follow you now. I shall clasp you in my arms!'), each sentence of which commences with a descending sixth.

At the end of this episode the Schoolmaster switches to talking to himself: 'Aha, she's already making room for me! What next . . .' (Example 5.30). To begin with, he abandons his previously heightened vocal style for a more prosaic speech-melody mode of utterance (bb. 1–2 of Example 5.30). The melodic pattern here of descending perfect fourth followed by ascend-

---

17   The second clause of text here is clearly supposed to be 'my fate is in your hands'; the Schoolmaster's erroneous transposition of 'my' and 'your' is clearly intended to emphasise his befuddled state. This comic effect is adopted by Janáček directly from the original novel by Rudolf Těsnohlídek, on which his libretto is based.

Example 5.31   Janáček, the *Vixen*, Act II scene 3

Example 5.32   Janáček, the *Vixen*, Act II scene 4

ing minor third – which is common in Janáček's music after 1900 – attests to the influence of Stravinsky, for example. In the final two bars of Example 5.30 the Schoolmaster returns to his earlier 'arioso' style (see Examples 5.28 and 5.29), also recalling the prominent g♭¹–b♭ descending sixth of his assertion that he has adored Terynka for years (see Example 5.28). The end of the Schoolmaster's soliloquy is then sharply delineated by a further recitation on a monotone by the Priest (suddenly 'approaching from below'): ' "Remember to be a man of virtue!" ' (Example 5.31). In his ensuing narration of an incident in his youth when he was wrongly accused of seducing a girl, the Priest adds a further quotation recited on a monotone, this time in Greek from 'Xenophon's Anabasis': ' "Memnestho, aner agathos einai" ' (VS, p. 84, bb. 7–10).

There is a further, yet more substantial and highly distinctive episode in Act II, this time utilising orthodox direct discourse. After the third change of scene, the Vixen relates to the Fox the events that led to her doing 'a bunk' from the Gamekeeper's lodge (VS, p. 95, b. 15, to p. 99, b. 14). She quotes the Gamekeeper's threats after she was caught stealing (Example 5.32), employing the melodious succession perfect fourth–minor third–major second for the textual cue introducing the quotation ('The gamekeeper bragged:') but delivering the gamekeeper's actual words mainly on a succession of repeated monotones (d♭²–e♭²–a♭¹): ' "Don't

Example 5.33   Janáček, the *Vixen*, Act II scene 4

Example 5.34   Janáček, the *Vixen*, Act II scene 4

Example 5.35   Janáček, the *Vixen*, Act II scene 4

worry, I'll finish her off. When she's dead I'll slit that greedy throat of hers and you, wife, will get a fur fit for a countess." '

The following speech-melody passage in which the Vixen quotes her own retorts to the Gamekeeper is more varied melodically, unfolding a deliberately structured succession of expressive interval sequences. As she mimics herself standing up to the Gamekeeper, the Vixen's tone is at first aggressive, musically giving rise not only to an emphatic sixth (this time ascending) but also to two sets of pitches (an A–F dyad and an A–B–D♯–F tetrachord) referable to the whole-tone collection: ' "Aren't you ashamed of yourself, gaffer, being cruel to animals?" I said. "If you hit me again I'll get my own back. Are you so mean that you begrudge me a bit of food?" ' (Example 5.33). Then she turns to wheedling, bringing diatonic intervallic successions (fourth–second and second–third) centred around the pitches of the accompanying second-inversion chord (D♭ with an added sixth): ' "You've got everything you want here, and I've got nothing at all" ' (Example 5.34). After that, the Vixen explains: ' "I'm not the sort to go

(a)

(b)

Example 5.36

(a) Janáček, the *Vixen*, Act II scene 4
(b) Janáček, the *Vixen*, Act II scene 4

Example 5.37   Janáček, the *Vixen*, Act II scene 4

begging, so I just took a bit"' (Example 5.35). Her first clause is set to a sinuous intervallic succession that mixes the chromatic and the diatonic (minor second, tritone and major second descending, then perfect fifth ascending). Her second clause sees this motive's sequential repetition a tone lower with a narrowing of the final interval also to a tritone. This hints at a return to the more strident mode of discourse allied to the whole-tone scale, which indeed erupts in the orchestra as she exclaims ' "Hit me if you want!"' (Example 5.36a), giving way to an arpeggiated half-diminished seventh concluding with a threatening three-bar trill as she defiantly cries: ' "Hit me if you want! But if you do –"' (Example 5.36b). Her literal quotation now breaks off momentarily with 'So he hit me', the setting of which contracts the intervals of the ' "Hit me if you want"' motive and is highlighted by the lack of orchestral accompaniment (last three bars of Example 5.36b). The episode concludes with the Vixen's parting words: ' "Tyrant! You can have what you wanted"' (Example 5.37), set to a repeated (triplet) monotone followed by a descending and ascending minor third.

The last example of direct discourse in the *Vixen* is a short section near the start of Act III. Harašta (a poacher) enters with an empty pannier on his back; the Gamekeeper, who is walking down the same path, notices

100

Chtĕl jsem ho vzít,   a- le   eš-če že mi,   že mi co- si řek- lo:

Example 5.38 Janáček, the *Vixen*, Act III scene 1

Ne - ber,_____   Ha - ra -što,   mo — hl bys být   v os- tu - dĕ!

Example 5.39 Janáček, the *Vixen*, Act III scene 1

Harašta from a distance. Harašta sees a dead hare and is about to pick it up when he espies the Gamekeeper; he rapidly desists. In the ensuing dialogue between the two men Harašta quotes an 'inner voice' that warned him not to pick up the hare: 'I was just going to pick it up when something, something said to me: "Harašta, leave it alone! Or you'll get into trouble!"' In this instance, the setting of the introduction to the quotation (Example 5.38) – which has a pentatonic cast (ascending minor third followed by ascending tone) so typical of Janáček's sound – is more varied than that of the quotation itself, which is declaimed on a single recitation tone (Example 5.39). The Gamekeeper then immediately assumes the role of the inner voice, repeating its words menacingly on a recitation tone a minor third higher (VS, p. 140, bb. 8–11).

In the *Vixen* Janáček consolidates his speech-melody principle, differentiating quotations in Latin, Greek and Czech, and beginning to employ single recitation tones for emphasis. The placing in this opera of direct discourse at dramatic peaks continues a convention that he invented in *Jenůfa* and never forgot, utilising it most extensively in his last opera, *From the House of the Dead*.

The Makropulos Affair: an opera of quotations

In Janáček's penultimate opera, *Věc Makropulos* (The Makropulos Affair; 1923–5) speech melody takes on a notably different hue owing to the very large number of quotations in the libretto. Indeed, the resolution of legal difficulties through quoting precedent is a major factor in the plot. Another

Example 5.40   Janáček, *The Makropulos Affair*, Act I

Example 5.41   Janáček, *Makropulos*, Act I

important element is the quotation of phrases in Greek and Spanish: Greek is of course the mother tongue of Elena Makropulos, alias Emilia Marty, and Spanish is a language she has spoken a great deal during her unnaturally long life of more than 300 years.

At the beginning of the opera the lawyer's clerk, Vítek, is standing on a stepladder replacing files relating to the all-important case *Gregor* v. *Prus*. He quotes and excerpt from a speech by Danton, retaining only one word of the original French: 'Soudí se to sto let! Špinavec! "Citoyens! Občané! Strpíte nadále, aby tento stav, jenž děkuje za výsady jen tyranii…"' (Fighting the case for a hundred years! The swine! 'Citoyens! Citizens! Will you continue to tolerate this class who owe their privilege to tyranny alone…'; VS, p. 14, b. 14, to p. 15, b. 3).[18] The entire passage is set to naturalistic rhythms, Janáček's favourite euphonious melodic fourth–second pattern, used initially to highlight the switch to French then back to Czech (see Example 5.40), permeating throughout. The next quotation in the opera occurs after Marty's first entrance. Acknowledging that she has a specific reason for coming, and sitting down and opening a newspaper she remarks: 'Indeed. I read here: "Final day of court case *Gregor* v. *Prus*"' (Example 5.41). Again, the quotation is set to a favourite melodic intervallic succession – descending fourth then rising minor third, often employed in close conjunction with the fourth–second pattern to produce pentatonically oriented melodies.

---

18   Universal Edition, plate no. 8656 (Vienna, 1926).

Example 5.42   Janáček, *Makropulos*, Act I

Example 5.43   Janáček, *Makropulos*, Act I

The lawyer Dr Kolenatý is the main purveyor of quotations in the opera. On his first appearance, he cites extensively from an alleged witnessed declaration by the late Joseph Ferdinand Prus (who died childless and intestate in 1827) that he was bequeathing the Loukov estate to a certain Ferdinand Karel Gregor (VS, p. 29, b. 9, to p. 31, b. 2). His monologue is a mixture of paraphrase and exact quotation (mainly in German). The text of the first section is as follows: 'His [Gregor's] claim to the Loukov estate rested on the following facts: first, the deceased had personally approached the director of the Theresianum, *höch[st]persönlich* [in person]' (Example 5.42). Its setting acts as a blueprint for the whole monologue: each clause is narrated in natural speech rhythm on a monotone without any note-values being specified for individual syllables until particularly important phrases occur, most usually in the form of precise quotations. These key phrases are set to more varied intervallic patterns, often involving a simple upward leap of a fourth, or two rising fourths a minor third apart – see Example 5.43: '(And declared that) he was bequeathing the estate in question *dem genannten Minderjährigen* [to the said minor], the said Gregor'.

After a brief discussion with Marty about Baron Emerich Prus's objections to the claim of Ferdinand Karel Gregor on the estate, Kolenatý

MILOŠ ŠTĚDROŇ

Example 5.44 Janáček, *Makropulos*, Act I

Example 5.45 Janáček, *Makropulos*, Act II

quotes from a file the alleged 'verbal disposition' made by the deceased on his deathbed in favour of another person, one Gregor Mach: '"As he lay dying in a high fever he declared several times that the Loukov estate *Herrn Mach Gregor zukommen soll*" [should go to Herr Mach, Gregor] . . . Or in Czech "Řehoř Mach"' (Example 5.44 – NB here 'Gregor' is claimed to be the first name, not the surname, of the supposedly intended inheritor). As a rule, Janáček does not set any Czech translations of the German with the same intonation (the two languages are after all very different), but in this case Kolenatý highlights in his Czech translation of the German the name 'Mach, Gregor' through exact correspondence of pitch.

Quotations play a crucial role in Act II as well. In the scene involving Hauk, the highpoint is his and Marty's recalling their affair of over fifty years before. They do so mainly in Spanish, the language in which they used to communicate (VS, p. 101, b. 1, to p. 103, b. 7).[19] In my first example from this scene (Example 5.45), Janáček subtly differentiates between 'kiss me' as enunciated in the two languages: although the two phrases have the same rhythm, the initial falling minor third of the Czech form represents the harshness of the Czech first-syllable stress in comparison with the less stri-

[19] This scene is examined at length by Michael Beckerman in his essay on pp. 109–26 of this volume. [ed.]

Example 5.46   Janáček, *Makropulos*, Act II

Example 5.47   Janáček, *Makropulos*, Act II

Example 5.48   Janáček, *Makropulos*, Act II

dent accentuation of the Spanish form, which is sung on a monotone. Nevertheless, the Spanish text does not cause any major alterations of Janáček's characteristic melodic style: Hauk's sharply rhythmicised exclamation, 'Eugenia, darling, beloved, black lass!', incorporates all the usual intervals (Example 5.46).

Later on in Act II Prus's probing brings him close to discovering Marty's true identity. He has established that Ferdinand Karel Gregor's real surname was 'Makropulos': 'in the birth register is the following: "*Nomen infantis*: Ferdinand Makropulos; status: illegitimate; father – omitted; mother – Elina Makropulos" ' (Example 5.47). Here the introduction to the quotation is, after an initial recitation tone, marked by a strong descending perfect fourth. In contrast, the quotation proper has little melodic variation. Certainly, the father's details are downplayed: his name is declaimed on a single b♭, the qualifying information a minor third lower. It is only the name of the mother – identical to Marty's own – that is highlighted, by Janáček's favourite intervallic pattern of second followed by fourth; this clearly reveals Prus's suspicions.

Prus

Můj   je - di - ný syn!   "Tá - - to,   buď

šťa - sten,   a - le   já".

Example 5.49 Janáček *Makropulos*, Act III

Kolenatý

E - u - ge - ni - a Mon - tez,   El - sa Mül - ler, de - va - de - sát de - vět,

Vítek

Sa - mé E. M.

Kolenatý

E - li - an Mac - gre - gor,   E - ka - te - ri - na Myš - kin

Example 5.50 Janáček, *Makropulos*, Act III

The next passage including a quotation in Act II – the point where Marty tells Janek what is written on the envelope she wants him to steal – has a similar structure; once again the introduction to the quotation is more varied melodically than the quotation itself: 'it says on it: "To be handed to my son Ferdinand"' (Example 5.48). Even Prus's quotation from his son's suicide note at the start of Act III – 'My only son! "Father, be happy – but as for me"' (Example 5.49) – adopts the same basic format: the exclamation that precedes the quotation is expressive, with its rising second followed by a descending fifth (an intervallic succession which was a particular favourite of Janáček's), whereas the quotation itself is mainly on a monotone, varied only by an understated closing pattern of falling tone then rising minor third. Just before Marty's true identity is revealed, Dr Kolenatý lists four of the names that have come up during this convoluted legal case ('Eugenia Montez, Elsa Müller, ninety-nine, Ellian MacGregor, Ekaterina Myshkin'), his clerk, Vítek, immediately pointing out that they all have the initials 'E. M.' (Example 5.50). Noteworthy here are the domination of the melodic line by seconds and fourths and the highlighting of the moment

106

Example 5.51   Janáček, *Makropulos*, Act III

Example 5.52   Janáček, *Makropulos*, Act III

Example 5.53   Janáček, *Makropulos*, Act III

where the initials 'E. M.' are spelled out by Vítek by two overlapping pentatonic subsets (last two bars of Example 5.50).

As is often the case, in the closing stages of Act III the textual cues for
the quotations are not differentiated from the quotations themselves. As
Marty relates how she came to take the longevity potion in the first place,
she explains: 'But Emperor Rudolf was scared, and he said: "Try it on your
daughter, first try it on your daughter!"' (Example 5.51). The setting of all
this text is wide-ranging in terms of pitch, recalling together with the
orchestra over the dominant of A♭ minor the work's opening fanfares (used
throughout the work in conjunction with references to Marty's distant
youth). Marty's subsequent quotation of the beginning of the Lord's Prayer
in Greek, 'Pater hemon, hos eis en uranois', is similarly expressive melodically, outlining an ascending second and falling fifth (Example 5.52).
Marty's last quotation – in the finale before the catharsis – is the most

heightened melodically of all. As she at last holds the formula devised by her father that will give her eternal life, she reads her father's opening words of the document: 'It is written here: "*Ego Hieronymos Makropulos, iatros kajsaro Rudolfu*" [I, Hieronymos Makropulos, physician to the emperor Rudolph]' (Example 5.53). Her speech-like rhythms are accompanied by some extravagant leaps, including one of a ninth.

My overview of Janáček's direct-discourse technique ends here, as the composer's last opera, *From the House of the Dead* (1927–8), would require a separate study. That work constitutes the apex of the technique's application: direct discourse not only forms the basis of the three central narratives but also provides the backbone of the entire opera. The highly individual narrative structure of the original Dostoyevsky text on which the opera is based afforded Janáček a unique opportunity to exploit one of his strongest operatic conventions. In this essay, I have tried to show how Janáček rapidly realised the potential for combining direct discourse with speech melody. My detailed catalogue of all such passages from his first eight operas demonstrates eloquently the maturation process of this powerfully expressive convention.

Translated by Paul Wingfield

6   Kundera's eternal present and Janáček's ancient Gypsy

MICHAEL BECKERMAN

It is well known and will doubtless become part of operatic lore that there was a real live death at the 1996 Metropolitan Opera premiere of Janáček's *Věc Makropulos* (The Makropulos Affair; 1923–5). The tenor playing the lawyer's clerk Vítek, Richard Versalle, fell off the ten-foot ladder on to the Met stage after singing the words 'One should not live so long'. Actually the Czech 'Nic netrvá věcně' is better translated as 'Nothing lasts for ever'. The response of the audience, of course, was a kind of hushed disbelief and shock. I received many telephone calls in the following days from people who had been completely traumatised by the event. Some blamed the Met for having the actor up so high, others simply shuddered.

Nothing could more easily illustrate the line between illusion and harsh enactment, or between realism and reality, making it abundantly clear that it is the *former* audiences wish to see, never the latter. The reasons for this are not necessarily self-evident. After all, Janáček's *Makropulos* deals quite specifically with issues of life and death. Could it not be argued that such an unpredictable event allows the spectator to have an even deeper experience, to reflect more profoundly on the transitory nature of existence? Would it be heartless for even a Janáček lover to say: 'The death of the tenor moved me even more deeply than any performance of the opera'? No one has come forward and suggested either in this case.

There was another striking phenomenon. All the callers (and to be honest, E-mailers) tried, Rashomon-like, to reconstruct the event in all its complexity. Most of them admitted that they were unable to remember or really put together what actually happened at the time: even the exact moment the tenor fell was a matter of controversy. They had impressions, it is true, and strong ones; but the intense present, that moment in which we live, that which makes possible past and future, they did not find easy to grasp. Yet it is the relationship between such a living present and the spectre of death which is the core of Janáček's opera.

This aspect of literature and music is explored in a book by the Czech writer Milan Kundera, entitled *Testaments Betrayed*. Kundera devotes a chapter to a story by Ernest Hemingway called 'The Hills Like White Elephants'. Seeking to rehabilitate both the story and the writer, Kundera turns to what he terms Hemingway's 'artistic obsession' with creating illusions of real-life conversation. Kundera challenges the reader:

> Try to reconstruct a dialogue from your own life, the dialogue of a quarrel or a dialogue of love. The most precious, the most important situations are utterly gone. Their abstract sense remains ... perhaps a detail or two, but the acousticovisual concreteness of the situation in all its continuity is lost.[1]

Eventually Kundera turns to the sonic quality of these lived moments: 'But how is this sentence spoken in a real situation? What is the *melodic truth* of this sentence? What is the melodic truth of a vanished moment?' To answer this question Kundera takes us, not to Hemingway, but to Janáček, a fellow Moravian and the teacher of his father, Ludvík Kundera. He writes:

> The search for the vanished present; the search for the melodic truth of a moment; the wish to surprise and capture this fleeting turn; the wish to plumb by that means the mystery of immediate reality constantly deserting our lives, which thereby becomes the thing we know least about. This, I think, is the ontological import of Janáček's studies of spoken language and, perhaps, the ontological import of all his music.[2]

Kundera gives a few short examples of Janáček's sense of stage reality, citing moments from *Její pastorkyňa* (Her Stepdaughter; Jenůfa; 1894–1903; rev. 1906–7) and *Příhody Lišky Bystroušky* (The Adventures of the Vixen Bystrouška; 1922–3), but of course does not go into much detail. Feeling the pressure both of Kundera's provocation and the death of Versalle, I would like to explore in some greater depth the way Janáček constructs a scene in his attempt to create the illusion of a kind of living present truth on stage. Yet I would like to show that this present is rarely something which simply refers to a particular moment happening on stage, but in reality comprises

[1] Milan Kundera, *Testaments Betrayed*, trans. Linda Asher (London: Faber, 1995), p. 128.   [2] Ibid., p. 138.

110

multiple psychological time zones combining real and imagined pasts with real and imaginary presents.

For my example I would like to turn to the very middle of the middle act of *Makropulos*, where we find one of the most peculiar and, I believe, one of the most extraordinary scenes in twentieth-century opera (Act II, Figs. 40–63; see the vocal score (hereafter VS), p. 94, b. 13, to p. 103, b. 20.)[3] The great singer Emilia Marty has been entertaining her many admirers backstage after a performance. (We might quickly note the illusion of reality created by turning the theatre on its end and emanating the action from behind the curtain.) Marty is mysterious, distant, imperious. Since she is so disdainful, someone asks her if there is anything in the world which really moves her. 'Nothing, nothing at all', she replies. Slowly, a strange old man carrying a bouquet wanders in and walks in her direction: 'Allow me, please allow me . . . You're so, so like her!' He is Hauk-Šendorf, and the assembled admirers look on with some embarrassment as he describes his devastating love affair with an Andalusian Gypsy named Eugenia Montez, 'la chula negra' – 'the black wench'. Marty watches with interest as he tells his story of love and describes his complete mental destruction as a result of his affair. Finally he comes to his senses: 'But what do you care about a woman long since dead?' Suddenly the icy Marty rises crying out 'Dead? That's silly! Maxi!' and begins to make love to him – many productions have them rolling on the floor together. We, the audience, are stunned, but not nearly so much as Marty's admirers, for we know from hearing about the opera or actually reading our programme notes, that Marty is over 300 years old, that her original name was Elena Makropulos, and she actually *was* Eugenia Montez in a former life, in which she did indeed seduce and abandon Hauk.[4]

The opera is based on a 1922 play by Karel Čapek, who among other things gave the word 'robot' to world languages from his play *R. U. R. – Rossum's Universal Robots* (1920). The pre-plot of *Makropulos* takes us back to the sixteenth-century Bohemia of Rudolf II – incidentally, the same place where Hindemith's opera *Die Harmonie der Welt* (The Harmony of the World; 1950–7) is set. While Johannes Kepler, Tycho Brahe and their col-

---

[3] Universal Edition, plate no. U. E. 8656 (Vienna, 1926).

[4] There are certain works which, I believe, are never encountered without a hefty knowledge of the pre-plot. I would be surprised if anyone has seen *Makropulos* and not known the story behind the story.

leagues were merging the scientific method and various occult practices on the famous 'Zlatá ulička' (Golden Lane) in the area of Prague Kafka was later to immortalise as the 'Castle', the fictional father of Elena Makropulos was mixing a longevity potion for Rudolf. The Emperor, suspicious of any plot against his life, made him try it on his daughter first; she collapsed in a coma and her father was imprisoned. She woke up, weeks later, feeling her normal self, but over the years gradually realised that she was no longer ageing at the same rate. Wandering through the world, changing her name and identity every few decades – yet always retaining the initials 'E. M.' – she became a singer. (It turns out that hundreds of years of vocal lessons actually do help.) Shortly after the curtain rises in both play and opera she majestically breezes into a Prague law office just as an important court case is about to be settled. Although she is unknown to the litigants in this case, she has a vested interest in the outcome. A century earlier she had lent her only copy of the longevity potion to one of her previous lovers and he had not returned it. Now it's beginning to wear off, and she is terrified of dying.

Incidentally, when Čapek first heard that Janáček was interested in making an opera from his play he is reported to have said: 'That old crank! Soon he'll even be setting the local column in the newspaper.'[5] But Janáček knew what he wanted. This science-fiction plot, like many of Čapek's writings, is not a simple thriller in any sense, but rather is a pretext for dealing with larger issues, in this case a meditation on the theme of life cycles.[6] The potion that has kept Marty alive has destroyed her soul, and she has undergone that archetypal passage (as does Dvořák's Rusalka) from an innocent young girl to femme fatale. Although men no longer have any attraction for her, she exerts the most profound erotic hold on them, which ultimately results in their destruction. In the previous scenes in Act I we saw how a range of men found her strangely irresistible. Yet we have never seen her seduce someone, and we have never seen the effects of her seduction. This is one of the purposes of the scene I am about to discuss.

Before looking at the music I would like to mention two things. First,

5   John Tyrrell, *Janáček's Operas: A Documentary Account* (London: Faber, 1992), p. 307.

6   Although most critics consider the play as a kind of response to George Bernard Shaw's *Back to Methuselah* (1922), Čapek maintained that the model was H. G. Wells's *The Food of the Gods*.

by this time in his career, Janáček was writing his own librettos. This usually consisted of a combination of paring and reorganising. In making his version of this scene Janáček cut roughly two-thirds of the original dialogue. In Table 6.1, the left-hand column shows the text Janáček extracted from Čapek's play in its original chronological sequence; groups of three dots show cuts, italics denote text in Spanish, and round brackets identify words within clauses omitted by Janáček. The right-hand column shows the order in which the same text appears in Janáček's libretto; Janáček's textual additions are in square brackets, small textual changes are underlined, Spanish text is again in italics, and stage directions are in bracketed italics. An English translation of Janáček's text is also provided. Janáček essentially divides Čapek's text into thirteen chunks (which I have numbered) and re-orders them completely: the chaotic numeration sequence in the right-hand column of Table 6.1 shows just how extensively Janáček ripped up the material. The major changes are as follows. First, Janáček wants Hauk to introduce himself as an idiot before we find out what made him that way. Further, Janáček wants to give Hauk a much longer speech in the middle, to allow him to tell his story in a concentrated manner. Finally, in Čapek's original there is no real motivation for Marty to kiss Hauk. Janáček sees the seduction as the natural response to the presumption that Montez is dead.

En passant, also, we might note that Janáček had a peculiar horror of death and rejected the notion that because he was an old man he had to reconcile himself to it. After the premiere of the *Glagolitic Mass* (1926; rev. 1927; first performed on 5 December 1927), which Janáček began a year after he finished *Makropulos*, Kundera's father wrote: 'Janáček, an old man, now a firm believer, feels with increasing urgency that his life's work should not lack an element expressing his relationship to God.' Janáček sent back a postcard saying: 'No old man, no believer! You youngster!'[7] The composer is also reported to have said to his niece, Věra: 'A church is concentrated death. Tombs under the floor, bones on the altar, pictures full of torture and dying. Rituals, prayers, chants – death and nothing but death. I don't want to have anything to do with it.'[8]

---

7 Paul Wingfield, *Leoš Janáček: Glagolitic Mass* (Cambridge University Press, 1992), p. 17.

8 Jaroslav Vogel, *Leoš Janáček: A Biography*, trans. Geraldine Thomsen-Muchová, rev. 2nd edn (London: Orbis, 1981), p. 336.

MICHAEL BECKERMAN

Table 6.1 *Comparison of Čapek's and Janáček's texts for the 'Madman' scene from* Makropulos, *Act II*

Čapek's text	Janáček's text
(1) **Hauk**	(1) **Hauk** (*vejde s kyticí*)
Dovolte, dovolte prosím…	Dovolte, dovolte prosím.
dovolte, abych…	(*padá na kolena, vzlyká*)
kdybyste věděla…	[Ó, ó, ó, ó, ó, ó, ó –]
Vy jste jí tak, tak podobná!…	Dovolte, abych –
	(*kleká před trůnem*)
(2) **Marty**	[Ó] kdybyste věděla – (*vzlyká*)
Kdo je ten dědeček?…	[Ó, ó, ó, ó, ó, ó, ó –]
	Vy jste jí tak, tak podobná!
(3) **Hauk**	
I ten hlas, oči… čelo…	(3) I ten hlas, oči, čelo -
Vy jste celá ona!…	[Ó] vy jste celá ona! [Celá ona!
	Ó, ó, ó, ó, ó, ó, ó,
(4) Co vám je po (nějaké) dávno mrtvé	ó, ó, ó.]
ženě?	
Marty	(2) **Marty**
(Copak je) mrtvá?…	Kdo je ten <u>stařeček</u>?
To je hloupé…	
	(10) **Hauk**
(5) **Hauk**	Já jsem totiž idiot.
Já jsem ji totiž miloval…	**Prus**
	Slabomyslný.
(6) ona byla cikánka.	**Hauk**
Říkali jí *la chula negra*.	[Tak, tak,]
Totiž tam dole, v Andalusii…	Hauk idiot.
	Marty
(7) Před padesáti lety.	Ó, [ó –]
Osmnáctset – sedmdesát.	
Marty	(5) **Hauk**
Ano…	Já jsem ji totiž miloval
(8) **Hauk**	(7) před padesáti lety,
(Bože) jak (po ní) bláznil celý svět!	osmnáctset sedmdesát.
Vaya, Gitána!…	**Marty**
	Ano.
(9) Já (jsem,) pak zůstal pro celý život	
jako pitomý.	

114

Table 6.1 (*cont.*)

Čapek's text	Janáček's text
(10) **Marty** Oh! **Hauk** Já jsem totiž idiot, (slečno.) Hauk idiot … **Prus** Slabomyslný.	(6) **Hauk** Ona byla cigánka, říkali jí *chula negra*. Totiž tam dole, v Andalusii. (8) Jak <u>se</u> bláznil celý svět! *Vaya Gitana!* [Jak se bláznil celý svět! *Vaya Gitana!*]
(11) **Hauk** Všecko jsem nechal tam, u ní	(11) Já všecko tam zanechal, [všecko] u ní! (9) Ja pak zůstal <u>po</u> celý život pitomý,
(12) račte rozumět? Já už (jsem) pak nežil, to byla jen dřímota …	(12) račte rozumět? Já už pak nežil, to byla jen dřímota. (4) [Ale] co je <u>vám</u> po dávno mrtvé ženě? **Marty** Mrtvé? To je hloupé. [Maxi! (*nakloní se*) Polib mne! **Hauk** Eugénie!] (*rozpláče se*)
(13) **Marty** Polibte mne! **Hauk** Jak, prosím? **Marty** *Besa me, bobo, bobazo!* **Hauk** *Jesús mil veces, (Eugénia -)* **Marty** *Animal, un besito!* **Hauk** *Eugénia, moza negra –* *(niňa –) quérida –* *carísima –*	(13) **Marty** <u>Polib</u> mne! **Hauk** Jak, prosím? **Marty** *Besa me, bobo, bobazo!* **Hauk** *Jesús mil veces!* **Marty** *Animal, un besito!* **Hauk** (*políbí ji*) *Eugénia, moza negra* *querida* *carísima!*

Table 6.1 (*cont.*)

Čapek's text	Janáček's text
Marty	**Marty**
Chito, tonto! Quita! Fuera!	*Chito, tonto! Quita Fuera!*
Hauk	**Hauk**
Es ella, es ella! Gitana endiablada . . .	*Es Ella, es ella! Gitana endiablada!*
Marty	*[Ella es ella, Gitana endiablada!]*
Další.	(*ukloní se Prusovi a ostatním, odchází*)
	[Já zase přijdu!
	Ó, ó, ó, ó, ó, ó, ó -]
	Marty
	Další.

English translation of Janáček's text

(1) **Hauk** (*enters with a bouquet*)
Allow me, please allow me.
(*falling to his knees, sobbing*)
[Oh, oh, oh, oh, oh, oh, oh -]
Allow me to -
(*kneeling in front of the throne*)
[Oh] if you only knew - (*sobs*)
[Oh, oh, oh, oh, oh, oh, oh -]
You're so, so like her!

(3) Even your voice, eyes, brow -
Oh, you're the very image of her!
[The very image!]
[Oh, oh, oh, oh, oh, oh, oh
oh, oh, oh.]

(2) **Marty**
Who's this grandpa?

(10) **Hauk**
Well, you see, I'm the madman.
Prus
Feeble-minded
Hauk
That's it, that's it,
Hauk the madman.

Marty
Oh, [oh -]

(5) **Hauk**
You see, I was in love

(7) fifty years ago,
in eighteen seventy.
Marty
Yes.

(6) **Hauk**
She was a Gypsy,
they used to call her *the black
wench.*
Down south, that is, in Andalusia.

(8) The whole world was crazy about
her.
Hey Gypsy!
[The whole world was crazy about
her.
Hey Gypsy!]

(11) I left everything behind,
everything] with her!

116

Table 6.1 (*cont.*)

(9) Ever since then I've been half-witted,	**Hauk** *Jesus, Jesus!* **Marty** *One little kiss, you ass!*
(12) You know what I mean, I hope? I haven't really been alive since then, just dozing.	**Hauk** (*kisses her*) *Eugenia,* *Darling, beloved, black sweetheart!*
(4) [But] what do you care about a woman long since dead? **Marty** Dead? That's silly! [Maxi! (*she bends down*) Kiss me! **Hauk** Eugenia!] (*he bursts into tears*)	**Marty** *Hush, fool! Go away! Be off with you!* **Hauk** *It's her, [it's her,] that devil of a Gypsy girl!* [*Her, it's her, that devil of a Gypsy girl!*] (*bows to Prus and the rest, exits*) I'll be back again!
(13) **Marty** Kiss me! **Hauk** What are you saying? **Marty** *Kiss me, you fool, you great big fool!*	Oh, oh, oh, oh, oh, oh, oh - **Marty** Next.

This critical scene proceeds through the alternation of three different musical worlds, which I shall refer to as the 'cafe waltz reminiscence', the 'idiot motive' and the 'Gypsy dance'. (Examples 6.1 to 6.3 show all three types of music; Example 6.1 is what may be regarded as the 'definitive' statement of the cafe waltz reminiscence, first introduced at VS, p. 95, bb. 3–14.) The primary material, the cafe waltz, is arrived at in a deceptive manner, through a kind of musical stutter (see Example 6.4) followed by a lament (VS, p. 94, b. 13, to p. 95, b. 8), in a way reminiscent of the fool in Musorgsky's *Boris*. (We may note that, especially these days, madwomen in opera have been treated at some length, but the strange and sometimes prophetic role of madmen, such as the fool in *Boris*, Hauk and Wozzeck has not yet been tackled.)

(più mosso)

Example 6.1   Janáček, *Makropulos*, Act II, 'Madman' scene: VS, p. 101, bb. 8–15

Allegro (♩ = 56)

Example 6.2   Janáček, *Makropulos*, Act II, 'Madman' scene: VS, p. 97, bb. 9–10

In Dashiell Hammet's *Maltese Falcon* the character Joel Cairo is forever imprinted on the reader's imagination by references to the wafting cloud of vaguely levantine perfume which always surrounds him. 'The fragrance of *chypre* came with him', Hammet writes. One of the limitations of film is its lack of anything related to the sense of smell. For this reason, in the famous film version of the book, a caricature exotic 'feminised' oboe riff is used to conjure up Cairo's exoticism and his homosexuality, assisted of course by the acting talents of Peter Lorre. Long before Bogie set up his dame for the fall, Janáček employed a similar device; for we cannot help but believe

118

Example 6.3   Janáček, *Makropulos*, Act II, 'Madman' scene: VS, p. 98, bb. 9–20

Example 6.4   Janáček, *Makropulos*, Act II, 'Madman' scene: VS, p. 94, b. 13

that this sentimental, unfinished and unfinishable cafe waltz is something which Hauk brings with him everywhere, a symbol of his loss, his existence in a kind of perpetual past. Obviously meant to suggest a popular tune of an earlier day, it hovers constantly throughout this scene, its core progression remaining perpetually suspended on the dominant. Carolyn Abbate some years ago coined an attractive one-liner asserting that 'music seems not to "have past tense".[9] But, in another, less narrative way, the ability of music to evoke the past is as real as that of language. Even before we find out what kind of past is being recollected, there is a suggestion of memory in this tune.

[9]   Carolyn Abbate, *Unsung Voices: Opera and Musical Narrative in the Nineteenth Century* (Princeton: Princeton University Press, 1991), p. 52.

(Janáček also uses this kind of material at the end of the Act II inn scene in the *Vixen*, when the old men are reminiscing about their good old days.)

We should bear in mind, though, that the identity of the first section of the scene (VS, p. 94, b. 13, to p. 97, b. 8) is created not only by the waltz itself, but by its juxtaposition with the upward stutter, and a kind of buzzing repeated tone, perhaps suggesting Hauk's inability to concentrate on anything real. We only gradually realise that Hauk's wordless lament (VS, p. 95, bb. 3–5 etc.) is actually the tag of the cafe waltz. Up to this point Marty does not know yet who Hauk is, and she interrupts his tag with 'Who is this grandpa?' His answer, 'Já jsem totiž idiot' (literally 'Well, you see, I'm the idiot') introduces a second motive (Example 6.2 – VS, p. 97, bb. 9–10), a descending chain of major triads a major third part (E–C–G♯). This is obviously intended as a musical portrait of Hauk's dissociation, a kind of vacuous downward spiral over which Marty reveals that she knows just who he is, and is somehow rather shocked. Several bars later, after Marty's crucial 'Ano' (meaning 'Yes, I remember'), the third musical event of the scene is introduced (Example 6.3 – VS, p. 98, bb. 9–20). Although its castanets immediately suggest Spain, the dance does not derive from any proto-Iberian style but is a musical dialect that Janáček has used many times before. The dance passage has four variants, the second (VS, p. 98, b. 21, to p. 99, b. 11) and third (VS, p. 99, bb. 15–20) separated by a re-articulation of the 'Hauk Idiot' motive (VS, p. 99, bb. 12–14), and the final one occurring towards the end of the scene (VS, p. 102, b. 14, to p. 103, b. 7). Each version becomes progressively more exotic and disjointed. The first features a kind of scale found occasionally in Moravian folk music, which Czech scholars have given the unlikely name of 'Lydian minor', since it features a minor third and a raised fourth. In the second variant the dance theme is altered to include a Phrygian tetrachord at the top of the scale.

One part of Čapek's script that certainly caught Janáček's eye was the reference to Eugenia as a 'Gypsy', a 'black wench'. For centuries the Gypsies, hated and reviled, nonetheless furnished material for myriad erotic fantasies, becoming the dark *tabula rasa* on to which all the base and sensual fantasies of white society were projected. While there are severe problems today concerning the Gypsies in the Czech Republic and Slovakia (poverty, over-population, crime, racism), the situation in the Czech Lands at the beginning of the twentieth century was quite different.[10] In 1918 the new country of Czechoslovakia was formed, guaranteeing equal rights to all citizens. While today there may be as many as half a million Gypsies in the Czech Republic and Slovakia, in those days there were perhaps 20,000, and more than 95 per cent of those were in what is now Slovakia.[11] Far from being a harsh, disturbing or sinister presence, the Gypsies at this time functioned as what we might call 'orientalism from within', an exotic symbol of freedom, passion and improvisation. We may keep in mind that it was those countries with the greatest colonial interests and holdings in the Far East – such as France and Russia – which most notably explored exotic oriental paradigms. For the Central Europeans, the Gypsies were exotic enough.

Janáček had explored this phenomenon explicitly in one of the great song cycles of the twentieth century, *Zápisník zmizelého* (The Diary of One Who Disappeared; 1917–19; rev. 1920), finished two years after the emancipation of Czechoslovakia. In the cycle a Czech boy 'from a good family' is eroticised by 'Zefka', a 'dark Gypsy', and is gradually lured into the 'free' life of the traveller. (A more comic example of this theme occurs in a story by Bohumír Hrábal called 'Romance'. A boy in love with a Gypsy confesses all to an old watchman, who says: 'So you've got yourself a Gypsy girl. But what will they say at home? Supposing your mam says "A Gypsy? Over my dead body." What will you say then?' The boy replies, 'I'll say, "Stretch out, Ma, I'm crossing over."')[12] In his song cycle, just as in the central scene from *Makropulos*, Janáček pulls out all the stops, deploying a wide variety of different musical scales in an attempt to capture this alien, exotic quality he associated with the Gypsies.[13] In sum, the idea of Eugenia Montez (aka Marty) as a force which could easily have destroyed someone like Hauk fits

---

[10] This situation has recently received much attention as a large group of Czech Gypsies have emigrated to Canada.

[11] See David Crowe, *A History of the Gypsies of Eastern Europe and Russia* (London: I. B. Tauris, 1995).

[12] Bohumír Hrábal, *The Death of Mr. Baltisberger* (New York: Doubleday, 1975), p. 21.

[13] See Jaroslav Volek, 'The "Old" and "New" Modality in Janáček's *The Diary of One Who Vanished* and *Nursery Rhymes*', in Michael Beckerman and Glen Bauer, eds., *Janáček and Czech Music* (Stuyvesant, NY: Pendragon Press, 1995), pp. 57–81.

in perfectly with the super-erotic image of the Gypsy in Janáček's mind and European thought in general.[14]

We also know that at the time he wrote *Makropulos* he was deeply infatuated with Kamila Stösslová, nearly forty years his junior. Almost all his great female roles, with the exception of Jenůfa, were written with her in mind, as hundreds of letters demonstrate. Since she was Jewish and dark-skinned, he often referred to her as his 'Gypsy', both the source for Zefka in the song cycle, and a model for Emilia Marty. Here are passages from some of the letters he wrote to her:

> Will you believe that I've not yet got out of the house? In the morning I potter around in the garden; regularly in the afternoon a few motifs occur to me for those beautiful little poems about that Gypsy love [i.e. *The Diary of One Who Disappeared*]. Perhaps a nice little musical romance will come out of it – and a tiny bit of the Luhačovice mood would be in it.　　(Brno, 10 August 1917)

> It's too bad my Gypsy girl can't be called something like Kamilka. That's why I also don't want to go on with the piece.
> 　I can't explain why you don't write to me ...
> 　I have nothing more than memories – well then, so I live in them.
> 　　　　　　　　　　　　　　　　　(Brno, 2 September 1918)

> And Kát'a, you know, that was you beside me. And that black Gypsy girl in my *Diary of One Who Disappeared* – that was especially you even more. That's why there's such emotional heat in these works. So much heat that if it caught both of us, there'd be just ashes left of us. Luckily it's just I who burn – and you who are saved.　　(Hukvaldy, 24 July 1924)

> Because you're in me, because you've dominated me completely, I don't long for anything else. I don't have the words to express my longing for you, to be close to you. Wherever I am, I think to myself: you can't want anything else in life if you've got this dear, cheerful, black little 'Gypsy girl' of yours.
> 　　　　　　　　　　　　　　　　　　(Brno, 30 April 1927)

---

[14] There have been a large number of books dealing with this and related questions in recent years. Perhaps the most conspicuous are the books by Crowe (see note 11) and Isabel Fonseca (*Bury Me Standing: The Gypsies and Their Journey* (New York: Knopf, 1995)). The most thorough treatment of the subject in the musicological literature is Jonathan Bellman, *The 'Style Hongroise' in the Music of Western Europe* (Boston: Northeastern University Press, 1993), especially Chapter 4, 'Stereotypes: The Gypsies in Literature and Popular Culture'.

> I told [Zdenka] how in my compositions where pure feeling, sincerity, truth, and burning love exude warmth, you're the one through whom the touching melodies come, you're the Gypsy with the child in *The Diary of One Who Disappeared.* (Hukvaldy, 8 June 1927)

> You noticed a nice passage in my *Diary of One Who Disappeared*!
> You know, it would be like under that fir tree of mine in my forest.
> And there's another nice one! At the end – Žofka [Zefka] with the child in her arms – and he follows her.
> And I always thought about you in that work. You were that Žofka for me!
> (Brno, 24 December 1927)[15]

Though there is no doubt about the fact that Kamila was an important model for Emilia Marty, he revealed his ambivalence towards both Kamila and Emilia. Both are hot and cold at the same time. Black Gypsy and White Ice:

> I think that for me you'll turn into that 'icy one'. Well now, she's liked in spite of it all, and universally. Those outfits of hers! In Act 1 a sort of greenish fur as a lining. Those pearls and long gold earrings [!] In Act 2 a white fur, a long train, in Act 3 a dress made out of gold, as if out of scales. What a sight! And everyone falls in love with her . . . So you'll come and see that 'icy one' in Prague; perhaps you'll see your photograph. (Brno, 28 January 1928)[16]

In his conflation of Kamila and Emilia he had created a powerful symbol both super-erotic and exotic. The freedom and supposed sexiness of the Gypsy were for Janáček, in effect, what made life worth living, but Emilia Marty/Elena Makropulos was a kind of lethal overdose of this ethos, capable, like Carmen, of driving men mad. This process is revealed in a passage which illustrates Hauk's madness. Another 'elongated' version of the Gypsy dance (VS, p. 99, bb. 15–20), now above an A♭ pedal, combines with three things to reflect Hauk's past desperation: the text ('I left everything behind, everything with her'); the inclusion of the 'idiot motive' in the bass; and the utter collapse of the tune into dribbling semitones.

The next few bars demonstrate Janáček at his declamatory best. The line 'I left everything behind, everything with her' descends chromatically from f^1 to leave Hauk hanging on $e♭^1$ (VS, p. 99, b. 20). Over a general pause

[15] John Tyrrell, ed. and trans., *Intimate Letters: Leoš Janáček to Kamila Stösslová* (London: Faber, 1994), pp. 10, 23, 53, 105, 121 and 171. [16] Ibid., p. 98.

Table 6.2 *Design in the 'Madman' scene from* Makropulos, *Act II*

VS references	Bar totals	Sections	Units
94(13) to 97(8)	40 (3+6+6+7+8+10)	A	$a+a^1+a^1+a^2+a^1+a^3$
97(8) to 98(8)	12 (5+7)	B	$b+b^1$
98(9–20)	12 (6+6)	C	$c+c$
98(21) to 99(11)	12 (6+6)	C^1	c^1+c^1
99(12–14)	3	B^1	
99(15–23)	9 (3+3+3)	C^2	$c^2+c^2+VA(c)$
99(24) to 100(16)	17 (14+3)	A^1	$a^4+VA(a)$
101(1–15)	15 (7+8)	A^2	a^5+a^6
101(15) to 102(13)	13 (5+5+3)	A^3	$a^1+a^1+a^7$
102(14) to 103(7)	10 (5+5)	C^3	c^1+c^1
103(8–20)	13 (12+1)	A^4	a^1+VA

Note:

In column 1, page numbers appear first, bar numbers following in brackets; in column 4, 'a' units are based on the 'cafe' waltz' and/or the 'stutter' motive, 'b' units on the 'idiot' motive, and 'c' units on the 'Gypsy dance' – see Examples 6.1 to 6.3; 'VA' in column 4 denotes 'voice alone' and any clear motivic derivation is indicated in brackets; VS, p. 101, b. 15 functions as both the end of one section and the beginning of the next.

(p. 99, b. 21) Hauk intones 'Ever since then I've been half-witted.' The descent continues from d^1 to b♭ on the words 'You know what I mean, I hope?', accompanied by the madman rhythm (p. 99, bb. 22–3). The waltz theme returns and the repeated note continues its obsessive buzz (p. 99, b. 23, to p. 100, b. 13). Though Hauk can remember Marty's erotic charge, it is the endlessly whirring cafe memory which has destroyed him, it is what's left of the fire after the flame has gone.

Hauk's return to some sense of reality is couched in one of Janáček's most wonderful bits of intonation, a series of rising semitones imitating the stutter theme at the beginning, hitherto heard only as an instrumental sound (see Example 6.5: VS, p. 100, bb. 13–15). It is this question, 'But what do you care about a woman long since dead?', which finally rouses Marty out of the spiritual torpor that has afflicted her since the opening of the opera. Not only is she afraid of death, but she cannot even stand being thought of as dead. She replies indignantly: 'Dead? That's absurd!' (p. 100, bb. 15–16). To the sound of the waltz theme she practically brings him to climax (p. 101, b. 1, to p. 102, b. 13), and this section moves directly into a

Example 6.5 Janáček, *Makropulos*, Act II, 'Madman' scene: VS, p. 100, bb. 13–15

completely exoticised version of the Gypsy dance (p. 102, b. 14, to p. 103, b. 7), which uses the scale also employed by Janáček for the actual 'Gypsy song' in the *Diary*.

A final statement of the waltz theme hauntingly refers not only to Hauk's past, but to the immediate past which has become our past too (p. 103, bb. 8–17). It does not resolve, though, and Hauk resumes his strange wordless wail (p. 103, bb. 18–20[1]) and also leaves without resolving the motive. Marty's 'Další' (Next) ghoulishly comes out of the silence. (By the way, it is a difficult moment for the singer playing Marty. It is easy to play it for laughs, as she immediately loses her apparent passion and becomes cold again: 'Next. Who wants what?' (p. 103, b. 20, to p. 104, b. 1). It can be played with frustration, or perhaps most effectively, with desperation, since Marty is keeping the barest hold on her sanity at this point in the opera.)

Our scene with Hauk the Madman reveals, among other things, some of the critical differences which exist between musical and dramatic form. Musical time tends to be innately circular, or rather spiral, since it can only have meaning by referring back to itself. Perhaps the same is ultimately true for dramatic time on the deepest level, but the patterns are vastly different, and the structure of the narrative gives a much greater illusion of continuous progress or, what we might call in music, 'through composition'. As Table 6.2 shows, Janáček achieves his effect through repetition which, if not literal, is often quite close to it. Thus maximum power is derived from rather small changes. In addition, he has emended the original drama of Čapek in such a way as to musicalise it and maximise the musico-dramatic effect (see Table 6.1).

Janáček's previous opera, the *Vixen*, is a parable which illustrates what kind of spiritual rebirth is possible when human beings overcome their resistance to nature and allow themselves to participate in the round of natural cycles. *Makropulos* is in a way the dark side of this formula, a searching attempt to present the dangers of violating the cycles of life. The juxtaposition at this one moment of the gorgeous Marty and the decrepit Hauk-Šendorf perfectly dramatises her fears (and perhaps ours) about ageing, senility, madness and death. At the same time, the way she throws herself at Hauk reveals that after centuries of life she is so jaded and bored that even a fleeting memory stirred by old Hauk is more exciting than anything else the assembled characters can offer her.

In a well-known article in the field of philosophy Bernard Williams meditates on the problem of Emilia Marty, particularly in regard to the question of when to die:

> Necessarily it tends to be either too early or too late. EM reminds us that it
> can be too late ... If that is any sort of dilemma, it can ... if one is
> exceptionally lucky, be resolved, not by doing anything, but just by dying
> shortly before the horrors of not doing so become evident.[17]

Our scene might, from Williams's perspective, be seen as a drama between two people: one who has lived too long, and another who, though still breathing, has died too soon. Their lives only have meaning in relation to what Kundera refers to as an 'eternal present'. By seeking to capture, through both motive and intonation, a 'real' present, and linking that with other hallmarks of realism such as the backstage locale and a series of interruptions, Janáček has illustrated some of Kundera's vanished moments which, not surprisingly, shed light on the past and future as well.

Finally, let us remember that the immediate present Kundera seeks to recapture, and the one in which Janáček works so well, is an *imaginary* present. When the tenor falls from a ladder and dies of a heart attack, we are talking about a very different kind of spectacle, one which yields even less to our methods of analysis than the traditional machinations of the stage.

---

[17] Bernard Williams, 'The Makropulos Case: Reflections on the Tedium of Immortality', in *Problems of the Self* (Cambridge: Cambridge University Press, 1972), pp. 82–100 (p. 100).

7   Janáček's folk settings and the *Vixen*

ZDENĚK SKOUMAL

Introduction

Janáček writes in the preface to a collection of Moravian folk-song arrangements:

> Dance songs are characteristic; which is why their accompaniments must not
> lack those typical rhythmic figures (*sčasovky*)[1] that are tied to the beautiful
> movements of dance. In slow songs the musicians even pause on longer tones
> and fill them with the little tones of the tune ... What a rich source of
> accompanimental motives! Song accompaniments are even more beautiful if
> at the same time they are truthful.[2]

This statement reveals two important elements that shaped Janáček's own
musical language: his profound admiration of the folk musicians' art on
the one hand, and his nineteenth-century heritage on the other. His
genuine love of folk-songs went back to his youth and influenced his entire
philosophy of existence: 'Folk-song! I've lived and breathed it since I was
small. In folk-songs we find the whole person, body, soul, environment,
everything, everything. Whoever grows up with folk-song, grows up into a
whole person.'[3] Folk-songs touched Janáček's emotions for nostalgic
reasons – as well as for the beauty of the music. To him, they encapsulated
the genuine emotions and concerns of ordinary people, and they were

---

[1] See pp. 221–5 below of my chapter in this volume for a full explanation of
   'sčasování' and this term's derivative, 'sčasovka'. [ed.]
[2] Leoš Janáček (with František Bartoš), *Moravská lidová poesie v písních*
   [Moravian Folk Poetry in Songs] (Telč: Emil Šolc, 1892–1901; 2nd edn 1908);
   the quotation here is taken from the 4th edn, ed. Bohumír Štědroň (Prague:
   Hudební matice, 1947), pp. i–iii (p. i).
[3] Quoted in Theodora Straková, 'V životě a práci' [In Life and Work], *Opus
   musicum*, 6, nos. 5–6 (1974), pp. 194–202 (p. 197).

creations equivalent in stature to those from the art-music repertory. Their apparent simplicity was necessitated only by the lack of notation, which did not affect their quality. Folk-songs also echoed Janáček's fervent nationalistic concerns. The Austro-Hungarian domination of the Czech lands fuelled his desire to help preserve Czech language and culture as much as possible, in as pure a state as possible. Authentic Czech (especially Moravian) folk-songs were an ideal medium to accomplish that goal. He studied, collected and arranged folk-songs throughout his life.[4]

Janáček reveals his nineteenth-century heritage through his interest in 'unity' and motivic relationships. Composers of the time seem to have striven to achieve unity in their works; indeed, the artistic merits of nine-teenth-century compositions were often judged on the basis of whether or not they were deemed to display unity. For nineteenth-century composers, the quest for unity became paramount. The gradual dissolution of estab-lished structural paradigms (and ultimately the dissolution of tonality itself), as well as the changing make-up of audiences, made unity a more pressing problem. Composers could no longer rely on established forms and harmonic practices, and they could no longer expect their listeners to possess the required technical knowledge. Comprehensibility had to come more from internal cues than familiar patterns.[5]

While coherence may arise from various musical parameters – style, affect, key schemes, instrumentation, rhythmic organisation etc. – one source of unity cultivated increasingly and valued more and more as the nineteenth century progressed was that derived from motivic relationships. Throughout that century, the composers that relied most on intricate motivic relationships either were predominantly Germanic (e.g. Beethoven, Schubert, Wagner and Brahms) or had a strong affinity with Germanic music (e.g. Chopin, Smetana and Dvořák). Janáček was, of course, well acquainted with the works of many of these composers. Indeed, since he grew up and studied in Central Europe, his musical education

---

[4] At the time of his death Janáček was in the midst of publishing (with Pavel Váša) the collection *Moravské písně milostné* [Moravian Love-songs], which was eventually issued posthumously (Prague: Státní ústav pro lidovou píseň, 1930–6).

[5] See Leonard Meyer, 'A Pride of Prejudices; Or, Delight in Diversity', *Music Theory Spectrum*, 13 (1991), pp. 241–51.

would have revolved around this very repertory.[6] It is not surprising, then, that practically all of his works show a highly developed motivic technique. Even the early works, such as the *Idylla* (Idyll) for string orchestra (1878), display remarkable motivic organisation.

Having a deep respect for folk music, as well as a solid grounding in art music, Janáček was thrilled to find relationships between the two. In his fieldwork he discovered similarities in rhythmic and melodic gestures, and similar philosophical and structural principles – particularly concerning form and motivic technique. He thus came to believe that Czech folk music and art music were really one and the same. While of course he did admit that art music is more complex, he felt that this is mainly due to the availability of notation: 'Do not allow a musical genius manuscript paper, notes, or a pen – and he will compose nothing more than a folk-song.'[7]

Janáček's awareness of the folk musicians' creative technique and his own adaptation of it betrays his nineteenth-century outlook. The quotation cited at the beginning of this essay describes the way folk musicians generate their accompaniments from the tunes themselves; in other words, he points to the inherent 'unity' of the songs. In calling such accompaniments 'truthful' Janáček suggests that they do not add extraneous or foreign elements; they take what is given and expand on it. With regard to his own folk accompaniments, Janáček notes: 'I search out a song's characteristic motive and then by means of this I harmonise – I accompany'.[8] Such an awareness of – and interest in – organic relationships is highly characteristic of nineteenth-century thought. But in Janáček's case it goes beyond interest: it forms an essential part of his own compositional technique.

In this study I will examine three of Janáček's folk settings to show his incorporation of the folk musician's technique into his own artistic idiom. I will look primarily at motivic technique, but I will also consider musico-

---

6   See Jaroslav Šeda, *Leoš Janáček* (Prague: Státní hudební nakladatelství, 1961), p. 115. In addition to studying in Brno (1869–72) and Prague (1874–5), Janáček also studied briefly in Leipzig (1879–80) and Vienna (1880).

7   Leoš Janáček, 'O lidové písni' [On Folk-song] (notes for a 1922 lecture), in *Leoš Janáček: O lidové písni a lidové hudbě: dokumenty a studie* [Leoš Janáček: On Folk-song and Folk Music: Documents and Studies], Janáčkův archív, Second Series/Vol. 1, ed. Jiří Vysloužil and Jan Racek (Prague: Státní nakladatelství krásné literatury, hudby a umění, 1955), pp. 434–41 (p. 440).

8   Quoted in Šeda, *Leoš Janáček*, p. 111.

textual relationships and larger structural issues. I will conclude with an analysis of a section of *Příhody Lišky Bystroušky* (The Adventures of the Vixen Bystrouška; 1922–3) to demonstrate the use of similar techniques at a higher structural level. The texts of all four of these songs are translated in an appendix (pp. 146–7 below).

'Pérečko'

'Pérečko' (Little Feather) is no. 19 of the collection *Moravian Folk Poetry in Songs*, arrangements that Janáček made between 1892 and 1901,[9] around the time he was composing *Její pastorkyňa* ((Her Stepdaughter; Jenůfa) (1894–1903; rev. 1906–7). In general, the accompaniments to the songs in this volume are texturally simple, intended to add colour to the tunes without disturbing their inherent beauty. Some merely double the melodic line and add a few tremolos or arpeggios in imitation of the cimbalom, a folk instrument (see, for example, nos. 7 and 9 of the collection). Others, like 'Pérečko', are motivically oriented. On the most fundamental level 'Pérečko' itself (see Example 7.1a) exemplifies the folk musicians' technique that Janáček describes in the introduction to this volume ('In slow songs the musicians even pause on longer tones and fill them with the little tones of the tune'). But, as we shall see, the accompaniment also reflects the tune in a more structural way that is obviously related to the art-music repertory. Furthermore, the content of the text is vital to the design of the accompaniment.

The song consists of four three-bar phrases; the final tone of each phrase is lengthened by a fermata. Three of the fermatas (bb. 3, 6 and 12) are embellished in the piano part by a rapid turn figure. This figure, marked as 't' in Example 7.1a, derives from the tune itself: in fact, the piano turn in b. 12 delineates almost exactly the same sequence of pitches as the voice does in bb. 8–9, the only difference being the substitution in the piano variant of A♯ for A. The parallel is even closer because both turns are preceded by a D. Janáček most likely focussed on this particular motive for a textual reason. In the first stanza, the third phrase (bb. 7–9) corresponds to the girl's plea to her mother 'Let me out, my good mother', of which motive 't' sets the words 'my good mother'. Thus, by pre-echoing and recalling this melodic motive in the piano, Janáček effectively reiterates its accompanying text several times. The

[9] See note 2.

Example 7.1

(a) Janáček's arrangement of 'Little Feather'

(b) Reduction of 'Little Feather'

131

melodic line in b. 9 implies a shift to the relative major, an implication that Janáček realises in his setting. The third phrase is the only one that ends in the major, possibly illustrating the daughter's affection for the mother.

Apart from motive 't', Janáček also fills three other places with 'little tones of the tune'. First, the piano's ascending pentad (E–F#–G–A–B) from the end of b. 3 to the first beat of b. 4 imitates the opening of the vocal line (bb.1–2^1). Then the parallel gesture in bb. 6–7^1, which now outlines the tetrachord B–C#–D–E, imitates the opening of the voice's second phrase (bb. 4–5^2). And finally, in b. 10 the piano's descending fifths in three octaves echo the voice part of the same bar ('I will go to him').

In the great Lieder of Schubert, Wolf and other song composers, the accompaniment and the overall structure often relate directly to the text itself. In 'Pérečko', these two elements are almost inseparable, both in matters of detail and on the broadest scale. Bar 4 contains simple but effective reference to the text: 'He is tapping at me' occasions three repeated Bs, which Janáček leaves unharmonised, the piano's b–b^1 octave merely doubling the voice and illustrating the hollow sound of tapping. When the same figure recurs in b. 10 it is more urgent (triplet quavers replacing regular quavers), and Janáček once again leaves it unharmonised.

As regards its broader design, the melody of 'Pérečko' projects a rather simple shape: the focal points outline a rising e^1–b^1–e^2 pattern to the mid-point (b. 7), then the mirror image in the second half (see Example 7.1b, a straightforward reduction of the song). Up to b. 8 the bass follows the melody in parallel octaves, as if illustrating the close bond between mother and daughter. However, in the third phrase the melody and bass begin to move independently, and as this phrase ends the two parts come to rest on different notes (B and G respectively). Although they are still consonant and part of the same harmony, the bass no longer doubles the melody. We might observe that the daughter is becoming more independent. The last phrase begins with the girl's assertion of her intention: 'I will go to him' (b. 10). This brings the loudest dynamic ('*ff*'), a new bass tone (A), and a new harmony (a bare A–E fifth, expanded to an A minor triad in the next bar). Although bb. 11–12 are the same melodically as bb. 2–3, they are harmon-ised differently. The bass A clashes with the B of the melody, as if A repre-sents the boy who creates a true conflict between mother and daughter. In b. 11 the bass A turns the B into an appoggiatura and pulls it down to A. Both parts then proceed to E, ending as they began, in perfect harmony. However, this harmony now seems to be between the two young people, not between mother and daughter. The evidence lies in the last line of the song's second stanza: 'Like my cheek with his right cheek'. It is significant that the first chord of the final cadence (b. 12^1) does not include the expected B in the bass that would establish it as a dominant. Although each of the first three phrases does conclude with a standard V–I cadence, at the end a diminished seventh is substituted for the dominant chord. The substitution allows the bass to remain on A; B does not return. In terms of the story, the boy replaces the mother in the girl's life.

'Pérečko' exemplifies the folk-song/art-song mixture that characterises Janáček's own development as a composer. While it is a genuine folk tune, and while Janáček does in many respects employ the folk musicians' technique, it also contains elements that point to a musician familiar with the masterworks of the art-song repertory. Musico-textual relationships such as those described here are ever-present in the songs of Schubert, Schumann, Brahms and Wolf. 'Pérečko' evidences a musician well acquainted with the past.

'Na horách, na dolách'

'Na horách, na dolách' (In the Hills, In the Valleys) is an arrangement dating from 1916 (Example 7.2a). It is no. 7 of the eight *Detvan Songs (Brigand Ballads)*.[10] The text is initially somewhat puzzling, and it turns out to be tragic. For the first part of the song the listener does not know what is being described, or even whether the song is happy or sad. The initial images are positive: mountains, something white. It is only in the last line of the song's third stanza that the dire truth is revealed: a young man is lying dead with his head battered in. Janáček responded to the initial ambiguity and created a setting where that uncertainty and ultimate tragedy infiltrates the musical structure.

The tune illustrates the text in ways that point to the unhappy outcome. Although the melody begins conventionally with an implication

[10] Leoš Janáček, *Písně detvanské (Zbojnické balady)* [Detvan Songs (Brigand Ballads)], arranged 1916, published as part of *26 Balad lidových* [26 Folk Ballads] (Prague: Hudební matice, 1950).

Example 7.2

(a) Janáček's arrangement of 'In the Hills, In the Valleys'

(b) Reduction of 'In the Hills, In the Valleys'

of a tonic G major harmony, it ends inconclusively on the supertonic scale degree. The open ending suggests the asking of a question. The rising contour of the first section (bb. 1–5) gives way to a falling contour in the second (bb. 6–13). The positive images of the song's opening give way to the negative aspect of the ending. Finally, the Lydian C♯ of b. 6 becomes C♮ in bb. 9 and 12, the same images seen from a different point of view.

Janáček's accompaniment reflects the melodic material as well as the mysterious text. His harmonisation moves from an implied tonic G at the beginning to the dominant D at the end. Ending on a dominant fittingly portrays the uncertainty of the text. The harmony also changes mode: the initial Lydian-inflected major mode gradually gives way to the minor: B♭ replaces B in b. 5, C cancels C♯ in b. 8, and E♭ effaces E in b. 9. Example 7.2b summarises the entire harmonic progression. It includes harmonies that Janáček omits but which are implied by the melody.

The song is rhythmically free, offering many opportunities to fill in the longer tones with motivic material. As he does in many of his folk arrangements, Janáček doubles the melody with the left hand, while the right hand fills the longer notes with the primary motive. The motive is an evenly spaced neighbour-note motion D–D–E–D, taken from b. 4 of the tune (motive 'n'). It recurs much more frequently than did the 'characteristic' motive of the earlier 'Pérečko'. The piano anticipates motive 'n' on the same pitches in b. 3, repeating it in bb. 9, 11 and 14, and on two occasions (bb. 5 and 13) stating an important variant outlining a minor rather than a major second. In addition, bb. 7, 8 and 12 contain only the motive's second half, a type of motivic fragmentation typical of art music. Though Janáček could have chosen other melodic figures as the main motive (for example D–C–A, which ends the tune and appears rotated in bb. 7–9), this one stands out. One reason for this is its sighing quality. Particularly when the neighbour-note motion involves a minor second it forms the traditional sighing figure, so familiar from Baroque rhetorical theory and countless classical works. The continual repetition of the figure imparts to the entire song a sense of foreboding or even a tragic mood. The second reason that the neighbour-note motive stands out is that it also serves as the larger structure of the tune (see the beamed melodic notes of the reduction in Example 7.2b). Analysis of Janáček's other music shows that he had an awareness of larger motivic structures, and it is unlikely he would have missed it here.

The last three bars of Janáček's arrangement show a deeper-level version of the same motive, this time in the piano part. The motive appears simultaneously in the right hand and inverted in the left. Each of the motive's first two pitches also begins a higher-level motivic statement, in effect embedding two further statements of motive 'n' within one larger statement. Motivic enlargement of this sort is an important technique throughout much of his original music, including the *Vixen* excerpt to be examined later in this study. Although it is not inconceivable that a folk musician would create a structure of this type, it is really a technique from the more learned repertory. While arranging a simple folk-song, in these bars Janáček speaks to us in a more sophisticated musical language. It is a tribute to his genius that he is able to incorporate techniques derived from art music while maintaining the sound and apparent simplicity of the genuine folk-song.

'A chot' sem děvucha'

The third folk-song, 'A chot' sem děvucha' (Even Though I am a Daughter), comes from the collection *Slezské Písně* (Silesian Songs; 1918). The collection consists of ten songs, six of which have highly motivic piano parts. The accompaniments once again originate within the melodies themselves. Not all of these songs are slow like the two discussed above, and they do not contain suitable long tones which may be motivically filled. Nevertheless, from the melodic motives Janáček weaves complete accompaniments. The most pertinent details of the tunes become ever-present backgrounds.

The story of 'A chot' sem děvucha' is an old favourite: unrequited love. The heroine loves to dance, but she does not get to dance enough; her beloved ignores her because she is poor. In the first stanza her acknowledgement, 'I am poor', corresponds to the melodic climax (Example 7.3a, bb. 5–6). The climactic tone (b. 5^3) occurs on 'I', slightly past the middle of the melodic phrase.[11] These bars also bring the loudest dynamic ($\boldsymbol{f}$).

---

[11] In fact, here the climax occurs at the primary golden section (after 14.832 crotchets to three decimal places). Although Janáček seems to have been familiar with this ratio, unlike Bartók he does not appear to have attached any particular musical importance to it. [See my comments on this subject on pp. 236–7 below of this volume. (ed.)]

Example 7.3
(a) Janáček's arrangement of 'Even Though I am a Daughter'
(b) The motives of 'Even Though I am a Daughter'

Moreover, bb. 5^1–6^2 generate three motives: 'x' – the step-down/leap-up approach to the high d^2; 'y' – the descending tetrachord from D to A; and 'z' – the rhythmic pattern of quaver followed by two semiquavers. Janáček combines these three motives to form the right-hand ostinato pattern of the accompaniment (motives 'x' and 'z' stems up, motive 'y' stems down in Example 7.3b). The pattern persists throughout the entire song. A syncopated 'mirror' rhythm adds energy in the left hand.

Motive 'y' – the descending tetrachord – undergoes two transformations. The first involves the changing modal inflections characteristic of Moravian folk music.[12] Within the melody itself D moves to A through C♯ and B♮ (bb. 5–6). Three further variants exhaust all the possible combinations involving chromatic alteration of the middle two pitches: D–C♯–B♭–A, D–C♮–B♭–A, and D–C♮–B♮–A. Janáček's accompaniment uses all three. The first two alternate in bb. 1–4, while the third appears in the lower part of the right hand in b. $5^{1–2}$. The climactic vocal descent in bb. 5–6 thus presents the fourth and last possible version of this figure.

The second transformation of motive 'y' concerns its length. The basic form of this motive (right hand, lower part, bb. 1–4) spans four notes, covering a perfect fourth (d^1–a). In b. 5 (also right hand, lower part) it acquires two new opening notes (F and E), expanding to a minor sixth (f^1–a). The sixth (now major) immediately returns in bb. 6–7^1, descending from $c♯^2$ to e^1. (This descent – heard again in the right hand – is not beamed as it is in b. 5, probably because of the necessary alterations to the direction of the stems.) The motive's expansion culminates in the melodic descent of the vocal part in the last two bars: the motive is now stretched to seven notes and spans a diminished seventh ($b♭^1$–$c♯^1$), a dissonance resolved upwards by step in the last bar. This final descent appropriately evokes the singer's sinking heart, particularly in the second and third stanzas: 'you . . . rarely want to dance with me' and 'he dances with another'. Perhaps to underscore the emptiness of the disappointment, in bb. 7–8 Janáček's accompaniment omits the accentuating low bass notes on the downbeats.

The expansion of motive 'y' also relates directly to the song's rhythmic structure. Janáček initially sets the four-note motive as even quavers, creat-

---

[12] For a lengthy examination of modal fluctuations in folk-songs see Jan Trojan, *Moravská lidová píseň* [Moravian folk-song] (Prague: Supraphon, 1980), pp. 17–29 and 83–202.

ing a 2/4 metrical pattern which cuts across the 3/4 maintained by the syn-copated left hand, producing hemiolas in bb. 1–2 and 3–4. Like the right hand of the piano, the melodic line contains even quavers, but in bb. 1–4 its contour and the textual accents create the impression of the metre alternat-ing between 6/8 and 3/4 (6/8 in bb. 1 and 3; 3/4 in bb. 2 and 4). Hence bb. 1 and 3 feature three metres simultaneously: 3/4, 2/4 and 6/8 (bb. 2 and 4 omit the 6/8). This metrical conflict is resolved by an overall 3/4 in b. 5, coincid-ing once again with the climactic point of the melody. The metrical change in the right hand emanates from the expansion of motive 'y'.

In 'A chot' sem děvucha' we see motivic play that sounds very simple and natural, and yet it is doubtful that it would arise out of the improvised performance of folk musicians. Although the mixed rhythms could easily arise in a folk group, the treatment of melodic motives suggests a more intense thought process. It shows the value of notation, a resource not avail-able to the folk musician.

Harašta's song

My last example is from the beginning of Act III of *The Adventures of the Vixen Bystrouška*; specifically, the instrumental prelude to the act (Vocal Score – hereafter 'VS' – p. 131, b. 1, to p. 133, b. 8),[13] and Harašta's first song, which has an instrumental introduction and an instrumental postlude (VS, p. 133, b. 9, to p. 135, b. 18). Harašta is a poacher, a rather carefree character, who later in the act has the dubious distinction of killing the Vixen. At the beginning of the act he is walking up a hill, singing a song about his beloved. The song is distinctly folk-like in character – see Example 7.4, which repro-duces the first of Harašta's three musically identical stanzas along with its surrounding purely instrumental sections (VS, p. 133, b. 9, to p. 134, b. 7). It begins essentially in a Dorian C♯, but also stresses the lowered fifth, G (bb. 8 and 10 of Example 7.4). It ends tonally in C♯ minor.

The melody's most 'characteristic' motive is the rising minor third, 'h', which appears at the beginning (b. 8) and recurs three times (bb. 10, 16 and 18). The last two statements involve the inflected tone G (marked with an arrow). The minor third also appears once as a descending interval, landing

---

[13] Universal Edition, plate no. U. E. 7564 (Vienna, 1924).

Example 7.4   Harašta's song from Act III of the *Vixen*: VS, p. 133, b. 9, to
p. 134, b. 7

Example 7.4 (*cont.*)

rather prominently on the Dorian scale degree, the raised sixth – A♯ (also marked with an arrow). Janáček uses the third to form the oscillating bass accompaniment for the entire song. The oscillation well illustrates walking: Harašta is singing about walking and wandering, and he is of course walking himself.[14] At times the accompaniment simply doubles the voice, but it mostly acts as an independent part. As in the folk-song arrangements, the accompaniment grows out of the tune. Nevertheless, here the motivic influence goes beyond the song itself; it shapes the entire instrumental prelude to Act III, both in its details and in its large-scale structure. The minor third first appears in the bass in bb. 7 and 8 of the act (C♯–E in VS, p. 131, bb. 7–8), growing out of the contraction of the interval of a minor seventh first to a perfect fifth and then to a minor third (bb. 5–7) and appearing several times subsequently (p. 131, b. 13, p. 132, bb. 5–6 etc.). The act begins on the same tonic (spelled as D♭ rather than C♯), and the initial one-bar ostinato immediately features both of the song's characteristic tones, the G and the A♯ (spelled B♭).

For the large-scale structure, Janáček provides an overriding motivic coherence through melodic expansion: i.e. he uses figures that originate as melodic details and expands them to cover larger passages of the music. We have already seen evidence of this in the song 'Na horách, na dolách', where the closing bars feature the main motive on two levels simultaneously. In the prelude to Act III of the *Vixen* Janáček foreshadows in an expanded version the melodic core of Harašta's ensuing song. The song's melodic

---

14 The Czech word 'chodit' means 'to walk' as well as 'to go' or 'to visit'. Harašta begins his song by recalling the time when he used to 'visit' his beloved.

Example 7.5

(a) The beginning of Harašta's song, simplified

(b) Summary of the Prelude to Act III of the *Vixen*: VS, p. 131, b. 1, to
     p. 133, b. 8

tones are also the primary bass tones that shape the introduction's harmonic structure. To demonstrate this, Example 7.5a shows a rhythmically
simplified summary of the beginning of Harašta's song, and Example 7.5b
offers a reduction of the Act III prelude. The structural bass tones of
Example 7.5b replicate the first five bars of Harašta's melody.

It is fascinating that this motivic expansion underpins such a varied
musical surface. The prelude consists of two contrasting motives that are
juxtaposed throughout: the opening ostinato of the act (see the first six
notes in the upper part of the left hand of Example 7.5b); and the descend-

142

ing scale figure that first appears in bb. 5–7 (the first group of beamed quavers in the right hand of Example 7.5b). The two motives alternate – or interrupt each other – continually, in a Stravinskian fashion. Like the great Russian composer, Janáček generates momentum in his music through interlocking passages, which on their own may be relatively static, but which in combination create a sense of urgency and unrest. As the prelude comes to a close, the two motives are united. At the beginning of the song proper (p. 133, b. 16; b. 8 of Example 7.4) the violin counterpoint to the tune contains elements of both: it descends a fifth stepwise from $g\#^2$ to $c\#^2$, passing through $g\natural^2$, the inflected fifth (Example 7.4, bb. 8–9). This is of course accompanied in the bass by the oscillating minor third motive. The motivic expansion thus gives the prelude an overall coherence despite the varied character of its musical surface. It prepares the subsequent song in a very subtle – practically subconscious – manner.

Conclusion

The influence of folk music on Janáček's compositional process can hardly be overestimated. But there is a danger in thinking that he was primarily a folk composer and forgetting about other aspects of his musical education. He received a mainstream, Central European grounding in all the major musical disciplines (in Brno, Prague, Leipzig and Vienna), he knew the music of the masters (he conducted Beethoven's *Missa Solemnis*, for example), and he was well read in music theory ('during the past year I have got to work and read all the harmony manuals, beginning with Reicha-Paris up to Schoenberg').[15] Thus, when he describes the ingenious motivic treatment of the folk musician and feels that he is adapting it, we must remember that he is viewing all this through the filter of his past. In other words, is his perception of the ingenious motivic treatment of the folk musician perhaps coloured by his knowledge of classical masterpieces? Did he attach a much greater importance to this technique than the folk musicians themselves? Ultimately, we have to acknowledge that although – as is well known – Janáček adopted many folk idioms in his musical language,

---

[15] Quoted in Alena Němcová, 'Janáčkovy vztahy k české a světové hudbě' [Janáček's Relationship to Czech and World Music], *Opus Musicum*, 6, nos. 5–6 (1974), pp. 209–18 (p. 213).

these idioms were combined with techniques from the classical repertoire. While the type and frequency of his motives are similar to those of the folk musicians, their use – especially in larger structures – exhibits the more complex thought processes of a classically trained musician. This is particularly true of the early works, written before his intense involvement with folk music.

Of course, the instance of motivic expansion we discovered in the *Vixen* is hardly unique. We could find many similar examples in other parts of the opera, in Janáček's other works and indeed in the music of other composers from Mozart to Berg. What is unique to Janáček, however, is the degree to which he employed this technique and the manner in which it interacts with his characteristic musical language. The folk-derived pedals and ostinatos that permeate his music are ideal for exactly this type of compositional logic. The static nature of the blocks in his music allows the motives to stand out clearly, whether they are in the foreground or deeper in the structure. It allows them to function more readily as structural determinants. As far as the evolution of this technique is concerned, we might observe that the technique itself did not develop, but rather that the musical language around it did. As Janáček moved from the world of nineteenth-century harmony into that of folk-influenced twentieth-century extended tonality, the motives became more prominent and took on a greater structural role, directing the musical flow.

It is pertinent to speculate how Janáček's motivic technique relates to his preoccupation with 'speech melodies'. Both appear to be part of the same way of looking at the world. We know that Janáček was influenced by Herbartian philosophy, a philosophy that relates the whole to its smallest constituent components.[16] Motives are the simplest of musical constructs; speech melodies likewise reduce the human utterance to its characteristic bare minimum. Janáček's profound involvement with speech melodies may have made him much more sensitive to the presence of motives in the music he heard, although the reverse is also possible: that his acute awareness of the motivic dimension of music reinforced his belief that motives were important in daily life. What seems certain is that he tried to view

[16] See Michael Beckerman, *Janáček as Theorist* (New York: Pendragon Press, 1995), pp. 15–24.

music like a folk musician, associating it with everyday experiences, feelings and concerns. To him, music was life itself, with all its beauty as well as hardships:

> For the folk composer the tone is more than a refined sound from an instrument; it is ruffled with murmurs, it is wet as if from the Danube's swift water, green as if from a meadow, white as if from a handkerchief, trustworthy as if from a swain. It does not spout from note-heads, nor does it run from the furrows of the five lines, nor expand with five fingers on the violin, nor intertwine with the holes of the bagpipes (*gajdy*), nor crawl under the strings of the cimbalom (*cimbál*).
>
> The composer crumbles with delight, stretches with longing and hope, takes lustre and strength from white cheeks; he catches sweetness from eyes like forget-me-nots. He reaches out to the stars. He is connected with everything of which he thinks. His thoughts in general and thoughts in tones are one and the same.[17]

This quotation encapsulates an ideal for which Janáček strove throughout his life, whether in simple folk arrangements or his most complex operas. But that is not the only aspect of composition; there is the basic matter of putting pitches together in a coherent manner. And Janáček's fundamental technique of composition is just as much rooted in the nineteenth-century art-music style as it is in the water of the Danube, probably more. His works are thoroughly unified on all structural levels. No matter how much of the folk idiom Janáček adopted, his music testifies that he was above all a highly sophisticated, 'classical' composer.

---

[17] Leoš Janáček, 'Nota (Na pamět' Frant. Bartoše)', [The Note (František Bartoš in memoriam)], *Lidové noviny* (28 July 1926); reprinted in *O lidové písni a lidové hudbě* (see note 7), pp. 457–61 (p. 458).

Appendix: English translations of the texts

Pérečko (Little Feather)

A swain stands under our window,
he's tapping at me with his gold ring:
let me out, my good mother,
I will go to him for two, for three words.

My dear mother, I beg you for God,
I have already even made him a little feather;
how it suits him on his hat,
like my cheek with his right cheek.

Na horách na dolách (In the Hills, in the Valleys)

In the hills, in the valleys, something white appears:
are they geese, or is it snow?

If they were geese, they would have already flown away,
if it were snow, it would have already melted.

The white is a ready-made bed,
there lies a young swain, his head battered.

On one side lies a steel cutlass,
on the other side sits his lass.

In one hand he holds a white handkerchief,
in the other hand he holds a green sprig.

A chot' sem děvucha (Even Though I am a Daughter)

Even though I am a daughter of a poor father,
and no-one wants to take me dancing;
and even though I am poor,
still I am ready to dance.

A poor mother had me,
she did not make me expensive clothes;
you, poor boy,
rarely want to dance with me.

I come to the dance, I do not join the circle,
my beloved is dancing, he does not fear God,
he brushes against me,
then he dances with another.

Harašta's Song

When I went a-wandering
the band played,
my own darling,
gazed from the window.

Do not stay a-gazing,
come instead with me,
and I will buy thee
a skirt all green.

A skirt all green,
made of muslin,
so that thou canst
come a-wandering with me.

8   Janáček's operas in Australia and New Zealand: a performance history

ADRIENNE SIMPSON

Adelaide, with its well-proportioned buildings and wide expanses of parkland, is one of the most tranquil and elegant cities in Australia. By comparison with the bigger, busier centres of Sydney and Melbourne it is often considered something of a backwater, yet it has an enviable reputation for enterprise in the arts. The showpiece of the city's musical life is the Adelaide Festival. Held biennially since 1960, it has become noted for its adventurous programming and, in particular, for the presentation of important twentieth-century operas not previously seen in Australia.

The festival's major opera productions were initially given by visiting ensembles because the city had no resident professional company of its own. This situation changed when the Australian Opera, which had been a regular visitor, decided to bypass the 1974 festival in order to concentrate its resources on building up a strong summer season at the recently opened Sydney Opera House. The festival's general manager, Anthony Steel, who was a great believer in using local talent wherever possible, promptly approached the New Opera of South Australia – a small and penniless ensemble which had begun its professional existence just a few months earlier – and suggested that it should fill the gap by mounting a production of *Idomeneo*. The company's young administrator, Justin Macdonnell, had studied in Prague and was an enthusiastic admirer of Janáček's music. He countered by proposing *The Makropulos Affair* as an alternative. Steel's response was that *Makropulos* had been performed often enough in other countries and 'if it had to be Janáček, then it should rather be *The Excursions of Mr Brouček*'.[1]

---

[1] Justin Macdonnell, 'Extraordinary List of Firsts', *Opera Australia*, 121 (January 1988), pp. 3–4 (p. 4).

It was an extraordinary decision. At the time, Janáček's name was barely known in Australia. None of his operas had ever been staged there. A few performances of the *Sinfonietta* and the *Glagolitic Mass*, conducted by Charles Mackerras, had been favourably reviewed but had not created any lasting interest in the composer's music. Nor had the contributions made by Mackerras and other Australian performers to Janáček productions in the United Kingdom attracted much attention at home. Macdonnell later ascribed his company's readiness to tackle a Janáček opera to 'the brashness that only the newly-born can muster'.[2] Steel championed *Brouček* because he had enjoyed a performance of the work given by musicians of the Prague National Theatre at the 1970 Edinburgh Festival. He 'knew it was not often done but that audiences would find it entertaining and accessible if they could be persuaded to buy tickets'.[3] Planning was well under way before the two men realised that theirs would be the first fully staged production of the work in English.

The logistics of mounting such a large-scale opera were daunting, given the company's tiny resources. The problems were compounded when the chosen producer, Stefan Haag, was diagnosed as having cancer and had to withdraw. John Tasker, a well-known drama producer with an instinctive flair for catching the mood of an audience, stepped in at short notice. His experience in opera was limited, but he was intensely musical and very keen to be involved. The set designer, Stanislaus Ostoja-Kotkowski, had achieved fame with a series of spectacular 'sound and image' productions in the 1960s. His innovative designs made use of flashing laser beams, back projections and hanging perspex shapes, grouped to suggest everything from a massive cathedral to the transparent facades of medieval houses. They looked superb on paper but proved extremely difficult to realise in practice. There were headaches, too, with Ross Anderson's fanciful costumes, which had to be modified and redesigned.[4]

Many local commentators felt that the project was far too ambitious to succeed with untried forces. Doubts were also expressed about the box-office potential of an unknown opera by an obscure composer. William

2 Ibid., p. 4.
3 Personal communication of 29 October 1996 from Anthony Steel to the author.
4 Difficulties outlined in a letter of 2 October 1996 from Justin Macdonnell to the author.

Mann's programme notes seemed almost to apologise for the work in advance by concluding with the comment that 'Anybody who finds the whole thing too stupid for words should quickly be reassured that Janáček did write other operas of a more romantically appealing nature – *Jenůfa* and *Katya Kabanová*, to name but two.'[5] Tasker's attitude was more positive. Interviewed by an Adelaide newspaper a month before the premiere, he emphasised *Brouček*'s visual appeal, tunefulness and abundance of action: 'Opera-haters' he predicted 'would love the rarely performed work' (*News*, 14 February 1974).

The New Opera of South Australia's production of Janáček's *The Excursions of Mr Brouček* opened on 11 March 1974. To the relief of all those involved, the public and critical response was overwhelmingly favourable. 'A small theatrical miracle is taking place at the Festival Theatre' declared one reviewer. 'Adelaide's recently formed and impecunious local opera company has attempted the almost impossible – and brought it off' (*South Australian Sunday Mail*, 14 March 1974). Within a short time, the remaining performances were sold out and *Brouček* became an unlikely triumph. Many factors contributed to its success. One was the quality of the venue. An overseas visitor, Andrew Porter, memorably described the city's new Festival Theatre, with its fine technical facilities and capacious pit, as 'a building which, roughly speaking, cost a tenth of what the Sydney Opera House did, was put up in a tenth the time, and is ten times as successful' (*Financial Times*, 2 April 1974). Everyone, from performers to audience, relished the ample space and luxurious surroundings. Another bonus was the sympathetic playing of the South Australian Symphony Orchestra under Patrick Thomas. A noted interpreter of twentieth-century music, Thomas greatly admired Janáček and although he found that it took the musicians time 'to become conversant with the quicksilver Janáček idiom' he felt they 'played the difficult music brilliantly'.[6]

Gregory Dempsey's fine performance as Matěj Brouček was a vital component in the opera's success. He had been offered the role at the urging of the original producer, Stefan Haag, and Macdonnell later described the casting as 'almost psychic. He captured the at times larrikin, at times craven,

[5] William Mann, 'Leoš Janáček and Mathias Brouček', 1974 Adelaide Festival Programme Book, p. 48.

[6] Letter of 1 September 1996 from Patrick Thomas to the author.

character of Brouček exactly.'[7] Frances Kelly, in the *National Times* (18–23 March 1974), noted his 'great understanding and empathy for Janáček's idiosyncrasies'; Kenneth Hince in the *Australian* (21 March 1974) felt that 'He might have been more mobile on stage, but he made a good fist of this rapscallion character, in whom there is at least a strand of Mozart's Masetto, or the Háry János of Kodály, and of the average Ocker digger.' Others invariably singled out for favourable mention were Marilyn Richardson (Málinka/Etherea/Kunka) and Thomas Edmonds (Mazal/'Mazulan' [Blankytný]/Petřík), but all the soloists were generally felt to be of a high calibre and many critics were surprised that an Adelaide-based company could achieve such an excellent standard.

Ostoja-Kotkowski's designs had been difficult to implement, but they made a tremendous impact in performance. The influential Maria Prerauer wrote excitedly in the *Sunday Telegraph* (17 March 1974) of 'the most imaginative, effective and colorful scenery ever sighted in this country'. Tasker's production, however, did not find favour with everyone. 'A plot so exotic needs astute production to avoid a hollow collision with Disneyland' commented Kelly. She thought the producer had not entirely avoided the potential pitfalls, particularly in the excursion to the Moon, where he 'had the burly male chorus and soloists camping around as ethereally as a Les Girls production of "Iolanthe" . . . Janáček in his wildest dreams could not have envisaged such fairy floss, which, in contrast to the darker dramatic trip back in time, was destructive. The Hussite wars became a cardboard spear-carrying farce.' Hince also deplored 'the ubiquitous Australian tendency to make every comedy a farce' and felt that Tasker had done Janáček 'less than complete justice'.

There was considerable puzzlement over the composer's intended message. 'Some say it is Janáček's attack on snug, sleepy bourgeois indifference to matters of artistic taste or philosophical commitment' wrote the critic of the *Sydney Sun Herald* (17 March 1974). 'Actually, in emphasis Janáček's motive seems here to be the opposite – to defend the values of honest common sense against any sort of obsessively intolerant extremism.' Prerauer considered the biggest joke of a delightful evening was 'the way the composer himself has now been caught in a time-

---

[7] Justin Macdonnell, letter of 2 October 1996.

machine. He wanted us to despise Mr Brouček for his cowardice and philistine ways. But it's our anti-hero's pacifism in the 15th century and his common sense on the ivory-towered moon . . . that win, instead of alienating, our sympathies.'

It was the musical qualities of the work that most impressed commentators. It 'is of unfaltering inspiration, buoyant, yeasty and swift and airily open-textured' enthused the *Sydney Sun-Herald* reviewer. Andrew Porter, the only overseas critic to notice the event, provided a more detailed evaluation in his *Financial Times* piece:

> The moon music is flighty, delicate, strange, beautiful, sometimes delightfully satirical. The Hussite music is in Janáček's most fervent national vein and includes an affecting elegy on a fallen hero. There is also music on earth: brief lovers' exchanges that bring Fenton and sweet Ann Page to mind, small sharp character sketches (the lunar and medieval characters are dream-variants of these), and Mr. Brouček's grumbles about taxes and peccant tenants – surely life on the moon must be easier? The 'time-travelling' interludes are magical. All in all, it is an enchanting opera, and the brilliantly imaginative Adelaide presentation . . . swiftly dispelled any doubts about the 'viability' of the work in the theatre.

In hindsight, the Australian premiere of *The Excursions of Mr Brouček* can be seen as an extraordinary gamble that succeeded against overwhelming odds. It marked a significant step forward in the fortunes of the New Opera of South Australia, which was transformed almost overnight from a local ensemble to an organisation worthy of national recognition. The reception the work itself received was remarkable. Yet the handful of performances had little effect in popularising the opera elsewhere. *Brouček* did not reach London until 28 December 1978, when it was presented by English National Opera at the London Coliseum with Charles Mackerras as conductor and Gregory Dempsey reprising the title role he had undertaken in Adelaide four years earlier. The United States stage premiere did not take place until the 1996 Spoleto Festival. It remains one of the most under-appreciated and under-performed of Janáček's major stage works.

Less than six months after the Adelaide *Brouček*, another of the composer's operas received its first antipodean performance. This time, it took place in the context of a regular subscription season rather than a festival. The Australian Opera's production of *Jenůfa* opened at the Sydney Opera

House on 25 July 1974. It was conducted by the company's artistic director, Edward Downes, who also supplied the English version of the libretto in association with Otakar Kraus. The director was Covent Garden's John Copley, a frequent and popular guest with the Australian Opera since 1970. A young New Zealander, Allan Lees, provided the designs. The trio held extensive discussions on the best way of presenting the work to an audience unfamiliar with Janáček. They wanted to depict the life of the village and its inhabitants graphically enough to make the audience 'understand why the birth of Jenůfa's child brings such a terrible shame on the family'.[8] However, because the company planned to take the opera to several other cities, the designs had to be suitable for theatres with different stage areas and widths of proscenium opening. The final decision was to adopt a realistic rather than an abstract approach, with brown timbered peasant dwellings evocative of rural decay, autumn-toned costumes, and a massive water wheel in the background that was both a symbol of the repetitive drudgery of peasant life and a constant reminder of the stream in which Kostelnička would drown Jenůfa's illegitimate baby.

The work was soundly cast. Robert Gard's blond, feckless Števa made an excellent foil for Ron Stevens's dark, tense Laca. Jenůfa was played by an experienced Danish soprano, Lone Koppel. The wife of the company's general manager, John Winther, she confounded those who had raised the cry of favouritism over her casting. Her voice, with its distinct beat, was not altogether ingratiating but the touching simplicity of her acting disarmed criticism. Nevertheless her performance, like those of the other singers, appeared almost colourless when set against the commanding Kostelnička of the then little-known Elizabeth Connell. She was 'nothing less than sensational both vocally and dramatically . . . Overnight she leapt the barrier between great promise and near stardom' reported one commentator.[9] 'She combined immense feeling, awesome power, heart-rending agony [and] impeccable tonal quality into a thoroughly gripping and moving performance' observed David Gyger, who added: 'Her second act was electrifying, her last act spellbinding even when she merely sat immersed in thoughts of

8 Allan Lees, 'Designing *Jenůfa* for the Australian Opera', *Opera Australia*, 3 (July 1974), pp. 12–14 (p. 13).
9 Maria Prerauer, 'Janáček Debut Down-under', *Opera*, 25/12 (December 1974), pp. 1072, 1089–90 (p. 1072).

her own, only intermittently aware of the stage reality around her'
(*Australian*, 29 July 1974).

Connell's dominating performance threatened, at times, to take over
the production. The audience at the premiere was so overwhelmed by it that
– seeking, perhaps, to release their pent-up tension – they exploded into an
ovation at her last exit, reducing Jenůfa's and Števa's final scene from apotheosis to anticlimax. Although many critics conceded that this was a flaw,
they were moved by the powerful impact of the theatrical experience. Some
considered it the company's finest achievement to date. Downes 'gave the
unique score Slav fire, warmth and beauty and a quite shattering intensity'.[10] Copley's stage movement was 'consistently economical, meaningful
and visually interesting' and the crowd scenes 'filled with fascinatingly
evocative characters and props, establishing a vivid atmosphere of middle
European peasant life' (David Gyger in the *Australian*, 29 July 1974).

The effect of the work on an unprepared public was electric. 'People
were wondering why they had never encountered this marvellous dramatic
composer, when this opera had been around since 1904, as long as *Madama
Butterfly*' recalled a member of the audience later.[11] Reviewers struggled
to find analogies. Lindsay Browne invoked Thomas Hardy and the
Lear–Cordelia reconciliation as parallels 'for the kind of aching swell of
generosity which shines forth from Janáček's resolution of many sorrows'
(*Sun-Herald*, 28 July 1974). Brian Hoad stressed the contemporary relevance of the drama and the compelling force of Janáček's music, 'which
semaphores strange insights along the arteries and up and down the spine
with sparse and urgent repetitive phrases' (*Bulletin*, 3 August 1974). The
first night audience found clapping inadequate and vented their enthusiasm by stamping and shouting. The work's reception exceeded the
company's most optimistic expectations and tickets became so eagerly
sought after that they fetched more than their face value on the black
market.

Jenůfa proved to be one of the Australian Opera's most enduring productions, remaining part of the company's repertory for nearly two
decades. In 1975 it was seen not only in Sydney, but in Canberra, Melbourne

[10] Ibid., p. 1072.
[11] David Garrett, 'Leoš Janáček's First Masterpiece', *Opera Australasia*, 168
(December 1991), pp. 10–11 (p. 10).

and Adelaide. The most significant change from the original cast was the introduction of Elizabeth Fretwell, who took over the role of the Kostelnička from Connell in time for the Melbourne season and displayed rather less high-voltage intensity than her predecessor. Her interpretation was probably more convincing overall because of its restraint. A 1979 revival was notable for the masterly conducting of Charles Mackerras. The production was eventually restudied and made its final appearance in 1992 with Mackerras again at the helm, Eilene Hannan singing the title role and the original Jenůfa, Lone Koppel, as the Kostelnička. However the most remarkable event in its long history occurred in October 1976, when the production was taken across the Tasman to give New Zealand its first experience of a Janáček opera.

The tour was the Australian Opera's first overseas venture. Made possible by support from the governments of both countries, it took place at a time when opera in the dominion was in a state of recession following the collapse of the New Zealand Opera Company five years earlier. Just two cities – Wellington and Auckland – were visited and the touring repertory consisted only of *Jenůfa* and another Copley production, *Rigoletto*. These had been chosen as the most logistically feasible of the works in the Australian Opera's current programme. Even so, to save money, only the principals and a nucleus of chorus and technical staff were brought across the Tasman. Further chorus members were recruited locally and the New Zealand Symphony Orchestra was used. The five performances of *Jenůfa* – two in Wellington and three in Auckland – were conducted by the experienced Georg Tintner, who was a familiar figure in both countries.

In a newspaper article before the Wellington premiere on 16 October 1976, David McGill, a journalist who had seen the work in Sydney, tried to give prospective patrons an inkling of the excitement the work had created there. 'Get as close as you can!' he adjured. 'This is theatre like Brecht, music like Stravinsky, the kind of experience rock groups dream of generating' (*Evening Post*, 16 October 1976). The opening night reaction was certainly enthusiastic, with thunderous applause and the same foot-stamping and shouts of 'bravo' that had greeted the first performance in Sydney. The critics of the city's main dailies were clearly moved by the work. They were quick to notice the extent to which the drama was expressed in the orchestra and the quality of the New Zealand Symphony Orchestra's contribution

ADRIENNE SIMPSON

won their approval. Fretwell's dignified Kostelnička was much admired; Lone Koppel began slowly but wrung hearts with her singing of the heroine's lament for her dead child in Act II and Ron Stevens's forthright Laca also made a good impression.

The major disappointment of the premiere was the number of unsold tickets. Russell Bond, noting reports that it had been almost impossible to get seats for the opera in Sydney, suggested that it would almost have paid people to fly across the Tasman to fill the vacant places – 'But perhaps after word of "Jenůfa's" resounding success gets around it may be a different story' (*Dominion*, 18 October 1976). Attendances subsequently improved and there was no denying the tremendous effect the work had on those who saw it – not only in Wellington but in Auckland, where it was premiered on 23 October 1976. For the first time, New Zealanders were made aware of Janáček's stature as an opera composer. However, because the country had no permanent professional company at the time, there was no chance of building on the interest created.

Jenůfa was more successful than *Brouček* in fuelling antipodean enthusiasm for Janáček. Encouraged by its popularity, the Australian Opera quickly decided to add another of his operas to its repertory. *The Cunning Little Vixen*, first performed in Melbourne on 17 March 1976, was seen in a Jonathan Miller production borrowed from the previous year's Glyndebourne Festival. In those intimate surroundings it had been a great success and Miller's decision to avoid Czech tradition and have the animals appear as almost human had been generally approved. Transferred to the larger venues of Melbourne and then Sydney, it was much less convincing. Although Brian Hoad praised 'its exquisitely sensitive control of character, colour and mood' (*Bulletin*, 26 June 1976), most felt the production so ponderous and excessively stylised that it weakened the musical impact of the opera. It 'turned too much of this innately agile and precise work into a species of fuzzy slow motion' wrote Roger Covell in the *Sydney Morning Herald* (18 June 1976). He also pointed out that the actions Miller had assigned to the various characters did not seem to match their specific qualities as delineated by Janáček in his score.

There were compensations. Patrick Robertson's back projected settings, which altered in size and perspective depending on whether the animals or the humans held the stage, worked just as well as they had at

156

Glyndebourne. Eilene Hannan won praise for her fresh-voiced, delightfully feminine vixen. Ron Stevens as the fox, and Ronald Dowd as the schoolmaster and the dog, acquitted themselves with credit and Robert Allman's Forester was considered a masterly portrayal. The orchestra, despite some intonation problems, played eloquently under Carlo Felice Cillario. On the debit side, the school children appearing as insects and small animals seemed ill at ease and the decision to telescope the three acts and play the work without a break did not make it easy for audiences to come to grips with an unconventional opera written in an unfamiliar idiom. Despite these deficiencies, Covell felt the work possessed a special kind of magic. He urged people to see it because it would 'get under their guard, live with them like a benign virus, and eventually turn into a memory they will yearn to renew'. So far as the public was concerned, however, the extent to which the magic worked depended on the quality of the production and performance. On both grounds, *Vixen* failed to emulate the impact made by *Jenůfa*.

There was a four-year hiatus before the Australian Opera attempted another Janáček work. This time, the choice was *Kát'a Kabanová*, which was premiered at the Sydney Opera House on 28 July 1980. Its staging was entrusted to the team of David Pountney (producer) and Maria Bjørnson (costume designer), who had first worked on the opera at the 1972 Wexford Festival and been reunited for the joint Scottish/Welsh Opera production in 1979. There were predictions beforehand that *Kát'a* would generate the same kind of furore as *Jenůfa*. In the event, the most striking aspect of the opening night was the quality of the orchestral contribution. Mark Elder's conducting proved inspirational. He 'transformed the Elizabethan Trust Sydney Orchestra, making it play with both passion and precision, switching from the most delicate of transparent sounds to the brutally barbaric with apparent ease'.[12] Pountney's direction was generally praised for its sensitivity and avoidance of melodrama. Helped by Roger Butlin's stark sets 'its visual frugality exactly suited the concentrated economy of the music' (Fred Blanks in the *Sydney Morning Herald*, 30 July 1980). To ensure the transitional orchestral passages were listened to, the curtain remained raised throughout and scene changes took place in the full view of the audience.

---

[12] Maria Prerauer, 'Saved by the Slavs', *Opera*, 32/2 (February 1981), pp. 168–9 (p. 168).

The staging was not free of inconsistencies. During most of the opera, for example, the Volga was imagined as out beyond the audience. Yet, when Kát'a made her fatal leap into the river she did so from the back of the stage – an error which critics noted with relish. There were also miscalculations. The most debated scene was the pivotal one between Kabanicha and Dikoj at the end of Act II scene 1, during which Rosina Raisbeck's poisonously malevolent Kabanicha stuffed herself with sweets as Neil Warren-Smith's bear-like Dikoj groped beneath her skirts. The divergence of opinion on this episode ranged from Brian Hoad – who noted that it tended to provoke giggles from the audience rather than reflections upon the town's hypocritical moral standards (*Bulletin*, 12 August 1980) – to David Gyger, who found the grotesqueness of the scene 'particularly effective' in underscoring the dramatic points made in the orchestra.[13]

The singing was generally good, although Gyger felt that Robert Gard, as Tichon, and Gregory Dempsey, as Boris, might have been better suited had they exchanged roles. Ron Stevens was considered perfectly cast, if a little dry of voice, as Kudrjáš and Warren-Smith's initially low-key Dikoj expanded as the season progressed. Raisbeck sang splendidly as Kabanicha. If her unrelieved nastiness verged on caricature, the fault was felt to be the composer's for 'the character itself is vouchsafed no human warmth of the sort, for instance, that enriches the Kostelnička in *Jenůfa*'.[14] The most crucial casting was that of Marilyn Richardson as Kát'a. One critic felt that she 'revealed hitherto unsuspected emotional depths, dominating the action with her radiant presence'.[15] Another suggested it was 'surely one of the greatest performances of her . . . career. While one could picture a more girlish figure in the role, or wish for enunciation less likely to cloud under vocal pressure, it is impossible to imagine more committed acting or a more heartfelt radiance of tone' (Fred Blanks in the *Sydney Morning Herald*, 30 July 1980).

Overall, *Kát'a* provided satisfying rather than incandescent theatre. It was summed up by Gyger as 'an impressive team effort full of promise and free from major flaws, a worthy stab toward the epicentre of Janáček's creative soul'. The presence of artists such as Richardson, Stevens, Dempsey,

---

[13] David Gyger, 'Piha was Memorable as Katya', *Opera Australia*, 32 (September 1980), pp. 16, 15 (p. 15).   [14] Ibid., p. 16.
[15] Prerauer, 'Saved by the Slavs', p. 169.

Raisbeck and Gard, who had all taken part in previous Australian productions of Janáček, indicated that a core of local performers versed in the composer's idiom was being established. Perhaps the most noticeable aspect of the critical reaction to *Kát'a* was the change in attitude that it demonstrated. The opera's stature was readily acknowledged and it was clear that, just six years on from the first staging of a Janáček work in the antipodes, the composer's music was no longer regarded as a curiosity.

Since the premiere of *Brouček* in 1974, the Adelaide Festival had continued its policy of presenting operas new to Australia. Keen to surpass the exceptional success they had achieved with Britten's *Death in Venice* in 1980, the festival management and the former New Opera (which had been renamed the State Opera of South Australia in 1976) again turned their attention to Janáček. Their plans crystallised when they found that Elisabeth Söderström was available. Attracted, according to newspaper reports, by the opportunity of working with the acclaimed Melbourne-born director Elijah Moshinsky, she agreed to make her Australian operatic debut playing Emilia Marty in an English-language presentation of *The Makropulos Affair*.

The premiere took place at Adelaide's Festival Theatre on 4 March 1982. The keynote of the production was elegant austerity. With little money available, the design team of Brian Thomson and Luciana Arrighi decided to lavish much of it on superb costumes for the main character. Marty's opening outfit, topped by a black coat, richly trimmed with fur and featuring a striking red satin lining, set a tone of hard-edged glamour that was maintained throughout. Against the predominantly dark-hued sets, her sumptuous gowns and glittering jewellery emphasised her icy demeanour while hinting at the sad emptiness of her life.

Financial constraints did not preclude imaginative staging. In a novel opening, workers were seen pasting a poster on a billboard. As the music began, the lights – which had initially hung at stage level – rose to reveal it as a gigantic portrait of Marty. Glimpsed through the slatted blinds of Kolenatý's office, it became the backdrop of the first act and continued to dominate the stage until the climactic moment of Marty's death, when it ripped jaggedly apart in a startling *coup de théâtre*. The huge expanse of the Festival Theatre's stage was deliberately kept free of clutter. To Elizabeth Silsbury, this mirrored 'the vast and apparently unlimited emptiness of

Emilia's bizarre and heartless life'.[16] David Gyger took a contrary view, feeling that 'the title character's solitude and despair at her external life ought to be contrasted at every turn with the busyness, and sometimes the claustrophobia, of daily life in the real world'.[17] Most critics, however, thought that the muted, severely linear sets, allied to Moshinsky's unassertive production, kept the audience's attention focussed where it belonged – on the characters.

The production was unashamedly built around Söderström. She commanded the stage from the moment she walked onto it, magnetising those around her and displaying 'a whole spectrum of vocal colours, unified by flawless technique and crystal-clear articulation of both music and words'.[18] She was 'unbearably right' for the role, wrote Ralph Middenway: 'It would be worth going to see her or to hear her: to be able to do both is a privilege beyond words' (*South Australian Register*, 8 March 1982). Many commentators remarked on what a coup her presence was for the company and all agreed that she had amply fulfilled expectations. The response to Gregory Dempsey's performance as Albert Gregor was more equivocal. There was no doubting his affinity with Janáček's music but Ken Healey in the May 1982 issue of *Theatre Australia* summed him up as 'insufficiently beautiful of voice, feature and figure' to succeed in the role. Apart from Söderström and Dempsey, who was then a member of the Australian Opera, the rest of the cast comprised singers who performed regularly with the State Opera of South Australia. Several reviewers commented on the quality of the performances Moshinsky drew from them. James Christiansen excelled as a dignified Prus and Roger Howell was a convincing Kolenatý, 'fierce and relentless in pursuit of rational truth in the face of increasingly irrational events'.[19] There were also scene-stealing character studies from Thomas Edmonds as a fussily eccentric Vítek and Geoffrey Harris as a supremely dotty Hauk-Šendorf.

The Makroupulos Affair created a great deal of critical interest, but selling the work to the public was not easy. Söderström, despite her interna-

---

[16] Elizabeth Silsbury, 'Janáček and Britten', *Opera*, 33/11 (November 1982), pp. 1171–2 (p. 1171).

[17] David Gyger, 'Söderström Triumphs in Masterwork of Janáček', *Opera Australia*, 51 (April 1982), p. 16.   [18] Silsbury, 'Janáček and Britten', p. 1172.

[19] Gyger, 'Söderström Triumphs in Masterwork of Janáček', p. 16.

tional reputation, was not well known in Australia. The performances were also undermined by a consistently overloud orchestral contribution. Throughout the rehearsal period the State Opera of South Australia's General Manager, Ian Campbell, tried to convince conductor, Denis Vaughan, that the balance between pit and stage was not right, 'but he could not master the problem and, frankly, did not try very hard since I think he found the score difficult enough'.[20] Because the orchestra was too loud, the singers were not able to get their words across clearly. Audiences found it hard to follow the story and, perhaps as a consequence, attendances failed to match those of previous festival productions.

There was, moreover, considerable debate over the quality of the work itself. Several critics were unimpressed. Kenneth Hince felt that no amount of special pleading could make it into either good theatre or good opera. 'What is painful', he wrote, 'is to see a man of Janáček's talent engaged, perhaps through absurd passion for a young woman, with a *grand guignol* libretto like this' (*Melbourne Age*, 8 March 1982). Ken Healey was equally scornful of the libretto, which he thought 'better suited to the talents of, let us say, Menotti, than to the man who wrote *Jenůfa* and *Katya Kabanová*' (*Theatre Australia*, May 1982). Despite the work's perceived faults, however, Roger Covell felt encouraged that the battle to make the composer's works an accepted part of the repertory was being won. 'I believe Janáček to be greater in several ways as a composer for the theatre than Richard Strauss' he wrote. '[He is] certainly more reliably trenchant and concise – but I fully understand why Strauss is likely to retain the bigger audience' (*Sydney Morning Herald*, 6 March 1982).

No other Janáček operas have been premiered in Australia since *The Makropulos Affair*. In New Zealand, where an operatic resurgence has taken place over the past decade, there has been only one further premiere since the 1976 *Jenůfa*. The New Zealand International Festival of the Arts, held biennially in Wellington since 1986, has made a feature of mounting works too large or demanding to be contemplated by the country's regional professional companies. When its artistic director, Joseph Seelig, decided to make Janáček's music the focus of the 1996 festival, he chose *Kát'a*

---

[20] Letter of 4 October 1996 from Ian Campbell (now General Director of San Diego Opera) to the author.

Kabanová to represent the composer's operas. This was not just for its dramatic and musical strengths and because it would be new to local audiences, but because it was 'a work which the festival could cast and produce to the highest international standard, within a workable budget'.[21]

The opera was premiered on 2 March 1996 at the Michael Fowler Centre. A concert hall rather than a proper theatre, it posed several problems. There was no proscenium arch or fly tower, so dealing with load-bearing machinery and the water-sprinkling equipment used to simulate a realistic rainstorm at the beginning of Act III caused some technical headaches. The greater distances between performers and audience contributed to a loss of intimacy. Above all, the lack of a pit meant that the orchestra had to be strung out in a long line across the front of the stage. Most critics deplored the fact that the conductor and players were distractingly visible throughout. There was, however, consistent praise for the skill with which David Parry marshalled his widespread forces and the full-blooded and idiomatic playing he drew from the New Zealand Symphony Orchestra.

Unlike all previous antipodean productions of Janáček, which had been given in English translation, Wellington's *Kát'a* was performed in the original Czech. The standard of singing was high. After the scheduled Kát'a, American soprano Ashley Putnam, withdrew before rehearsals started, Charles Mackerras recommended a young Slovak, Eva Jenis, as a replacement. Her interpretation, 'rich with dramatic insight', impressed everyone.[22] 'I have seldom seen a performance on any operatic stage that marries such musical splendour with such absolute dramatic conviction' noted Tim Bridgewater (*Dominion*, 4 March 1996). 'Her singing was firmly in focus and truly memorable in its radiance and beauty' wrote the critic of *Opera* magazine. 'Moreover, she portrayed every step in Katya's progress from optimism to despair with moving dignity and total conviction.'[23]

If no other member of the cast could quite match Jenis, all were highly

[21] Personal communication of 27 September 1996 from Joseph Seelig to the author.
[22] Rod Biss and others, 'The Sixth International Festival of the Arts, 1–24 March 1996', *Music in New Zealand*, 32 (Autumn 1996), pp. 44–52 (p. 44).
[23] Adrienne Simpson, 'New Zealand *Festival Fare*', *Opera*, 47/8 (August 1996), pp. 965–6 (p. 965).

effective. The experienced Czech mezzo-soprano Antonie Denygrová made 'a dauntingly ferocious Kabanicha' according to a visiting Australian critic, David Gyger.[24] The wide vibrato evident in her upper register and the moments of stress in her singing were felt to be no handicap in context and she resisted all temptation to overplay the part. The cosmopolitan cast also included an English tenor, Mark Luther, as a personable Kudrjáš and an American specialist in twentieth-century opera, Peter Kazaras, as Boris. Both sang strongly, although Gyger felt that Luther 'could have used a little more fire in his dramatic belly'. He found Kazaras 'a suitably ardent illicit lover for Katya in the early stages, and horrifyingly credible when it came time to abandon her without hope and run away from the nasty situation he has been instrumental in creating'.[25]

The other roles were played by New Zealanders. Richard Greager's finely realised Tichon succeeded in eliciting sympathy for the man he might have been, in happier circumstances. His physical similarity to the Boris of Kazaras did not pass unremarked – one commentator feeling that it 'lent a new and fascinating pyschological dimension to the plot'. Conal Coad's resonantly sung and robustly acted Dikoj made a considerable impact, but Margaret Medlyn's Varvara 'failed to invoke the necessary ingenuousness of the character' (William Dart in the New Zealand Listener, 23 March 1996).

The work was staged with stylised simplicity. Indoor scenes were differentiated from outdoor only by the addition of a solitary chair and a flown wall of pollarded saplings. Guy Cadle's costume designs, in subtle variants of grey and black, underlined the drabness of the environment and Gale Edwards's direction emphasised the lack of communication between the characters by keeping them well spaced from each other. A deep blue cyclorama, suffused by ominous storm clouds, allowed her to create some striking silhouette effects. In tandem with designer Peter Davison, she provided two startling theatrical moments. The first occurred when the monolithic slab of granite, which had been suspended above the stage throughout, abruptly split apart to admit the driving rain in Act III scene 1; the second was Kát'a's death leap from the raised front of the stage –

---

[24] David Gyger, 'Rewarding NZ Don Giovanni, Gripping Katya – in Czech', Opera Australasia, 221 (May 1996), pp. 20, 18 (p. 20).   [25] Ibid., p. 18.

directly, as it seemed, into the bowels of the orchestra. Critics found both heart-stoppingly realistic. Most also approved the dramatic momentum generated by the director's decision to observe the composer's wishes and play the opera without a break.

Seelig had wondered whether *Kát'a* would catch the public's imagination, given that Janáček's music was relatively unfamiliar to New Zealanders. The excellent attendances and overwhelmingly positive reaction reassured him. In retrospect, he thought that 'perhaps some came with as much apprehension as curiosity, but they were gripped and convinced... it felt as though a huge number of people were very proud of what had been achieved'.[26] One reviewer went so far as to call the production 'a quantum leap for opera in New Zealand' (Lindis Taylor in the *Evening Post*, 4 March 1996). Despite the enthusiasm, however, most commentators recognised that the exigencies of operatic life in the country meant that there were unlikely to be any further Janáček premieres in the foreseeable future.

Across the Tasman, the composer's acceptance into the operatic mainstream is much more advanced. Rather than expand the repertory, however, the country's leading company, the Australian Opera (renamed Opera Australia in December 1996) has embarked on a second generation of Janáček productions with a projected cycle of four operas. This comprises *Kát'a Kabanová* (introduced in 1995), '*The Makropulos Secret*' (1996), *The Cunning Little Vixen* (opening on 3 October 1997) and *Jenůfa* (to open on 2 July 1998). All four have been entrusted to Neil Armfield, one of the finest representatives of the younger generation of Australian directors.

Interviewed before the premiere of *Kát'a* at the Sydney Opera House on 12 January 1995, Armfield spoke of his desire to avoid all superfluous clutter (*Bulletin*, 17 January 1995). A minimum of props would be used to suggest location and instead of three-dimensional scenery, he planned to create 'a rich visual environment' by using cinematic projections behind, above and around the stage. The audience would be forced to concentrate on the drama rather than diverted by externals. His minimalist concept found general favour. Its starkness, according to Maria Prerauer of the *Australian* (16 January 1995), 'uncovered the core of the work, letting the

---

[26] Joseph Seelig, communication of 27 September 1996.

164

music speak for itself and opening the way to Janáček's exploration of the uncharted chasms of the human mind'. Naturalistically acted and excellently sung, *Káťa* was felt to be an ensemble triumph for the company and a marked dramatic improvement on the 1980 production.

'*The Makropulos Secret*' (Sydney Opera House, 20 January 1996) was a company premiere. A talking-point was provided by the use of the word 'secret' in the title, rather than the more commonly used 'affair'. It was adopted when Charles Mackerras suggested it as a more accurate contextual translation of the Czech word 'věc'.[27] The production sparked considerable debate. Much of it was occasioned by Armfield's Hollywood-style ending, which had Marilyn Richardson, in the role of Emilia Marty, borne upwards, as if to heaven, while a double writhed in death agony below. The result was not only distracting but, to some critics, risible. It deprived 'Richardson's marvellous performance of what ought to have been its crowning glory, and the entire opera of much of the punch that ought to have been there at the final curtain'.[28] As had happened after the first Australian performance at the 1982 Adelaide Festival, doubts were also expressed about the work's intrinsic merits. There was a feeling that the opera had not worn very well and Fred Blanks concluded that it was destined to be 'relegated to the intellectual fringes of our own time' (*Sydney Morning Herald*, 22 January 1996).

Nearly a quarter of a century has now elapsed since the pioneering Adelaide Festival presentation of *The Excursions of Mr Brouček* in 1974. During that time, a great change has taken place in attitudes to Janáček's music. Almost total ignorance has given way to admiration and his operas have come to be accepted as an important part of the repertory. As yet, they do not appear regularly in antipodean programme schedules. The only Janáček production to have toured widely, or stayed in the repertory for a

---

[27] 'Věc' translates as 'thing' literally, but it is a word whose meaning can vary considerably according to context. Paul Selver was the first to render the word as 'secret', in his English translation of the play by Karel Čapek on which Janáček's opera is based. Other suggested renditions have included 'case', 'document' and 'affair' (employed in this volume). Unfortunately, no single English word conveys the wealth of nuances that Čapek's title evokes. For further details see John Tyrrell, disc notes to *Věc Makropulos*, conducted by Charles Mackerras, Decca 430374–2 (1979; CD 1991), p. 9. [ed.]

[28] David Gyger, 'Questionable Ending Mars Triumph', *Opera Australasia*, 219 (March 1996), pp. 16, 13 (p. 13).

significant length of time, has been the Australian Opera's 1974 *Jenůfa* and there are still a number of important centres, such as Brisbane, Perth and Christchurch, which have never seen a professionally staged performance of any of the composer's works. Nevertheless, the catalogue of Janáček productions in Australasia is richer than that of many countries with larger populations and longer opera traditions, and it is disappointing that this performance history has been so little noticed elsewhere. In particular, the significance of the 1974 *Brouček* – the first English-language production of the work – has been almost entirely overlooked.

Until the remaining two operas in the Armfield cycle make their debut it is probably premature to draw final conclusions about the status of Janáček's operas in Australasia. Armfield belongs to a generation of Australian artists who have been able to make their reputations in their own country rather than take their talents abroad. His approach to Janáček owes nothing to overseas tradition. It is possible that, when his four productions can be viewed in retrospect, they will be seen to have brought a uniquely Australasian perspective to the composer's stage works. If they remain in the repertory and are regularly revived in future seasons, they may also create a level of interest which will encourage other Australasian companies to mount Janáček operas more frequently.

In one respect, however, Armfield and Opera Australia have clearly been mindful of overseas trends. The four operas chosen for the cycle are those which are increasingly being regarded as the core works in the Janáček canon. Leaving aside performances in the Czech Republic, a cursory survey of company programmes in 1995 and 1996 shows that *Kát'a* was performed not only in Sydney, Melbourne and Wellington, but in Berlin, Paris and Düsseldorf. The Sydney and subsequent Melbourne performances of *Makropulos* can be set beside others in Chicago and at Glyndebourne, while *Vixen* was seen in London, Belfast and Dresden and *Jenůfa* in Toronto, Dresden, Portland and Vancouver. By comparison, *From the House of the Dead*, *Brouček* and, more understandably, *Fate* make only occasional appearances in the world's opera schedules. This international narrowing of the core repertory should concern lovers of the composer's stage works. Certainly, if it continues, the likelihood of any further Janáček operas being premiered in Australia and New Zealand would seem remote.

Appendix

Janáček Premieres in Australia

11 March 1974: *The Excursions of Mr Brouček* (in English, translation by Norman Tucker); Festival Theatre, Adelaide; New Opera, South Australia

Matěj Brouček, Gregory Dempsey; Mazal/Mazalun/Petřík, Thomas Edmonds; Sacristan/Lunkristan/Domšík, Dean Patterson; Málinka/Etherea/Kunka, Marilyn Richardson; Würfl/Lunobor/The Councillor, Rob Dawe; Piccolo (pot boy at Würfl's inn) /Jasmin/A scholar, Judith Henley; Fanny Nowak [Brouček's Housekeeper]/An artist/Kedruta, Judith James; An artist/An artist/Miroslav, Paul Ferris; A guest/A poet/Vojta, Eric Maddison; A guest/A composer/Vacek, Lyndon Terracini; A guest/An artist/Svatopluk Čech, Noel Robbins; Guests/Artists/ Taborites, Brian Messner, Lyndon Piddington

Director, John Tasker; Set Designer, Stanislaw Ostoja-Kotkowski; Costume Designer, Ross Anderson; New Opera Chorus and The Adelaide Singers; South Australian Symphony Orchestra; Conductor, Patrick Thomas

25 July 1974: *Jenůfa* (in English, translation by Edward Downes and Otakar Kraus); Sydney Opera House; The Australian Opera

Jenůfa, Lone Koppel Winther; Grandmother Buryja, Rosina Raisbeck; Laca Klemeň, Ron Stevens; Jano, Jennifer Bermingham; Barena, Cynthia Johnston; Foreman of the mill, John Germain; The Kostelnička, Elizabeth Connell; Števa Buryja, Robert Gard; A Maid, Mary Hayman; Mayor, Alan Light; His Wife, Miluska Simkova; Karolka, Suzanne Steele; Aunt, Jacqueline Kennsett-Smith

Producer, John Copley; Set Designer, Allan Lees; Costume Designer, Michael Stennett; Lighting Designer, Leslie Bowden; The Australian Opera Chorus; The Elizabethan Trust Sydney Orchestra; Conductor, Edward Downes

17 March 1976: *The Cunning Little Vixen* (in English, translation by Norman Tucker); Princess Theatre, Melbourne; The Australian Opera

The Forester, Robert Allman; The Forester's Wife/The Owl, Elizabeth Fretwell; Pepík, Andrew Dalton; Frantík, Gordon O'Neill; The Parson/The Badger, Grant Dickson; The Schoolmaster/The Dog, Ronald Dowd; Pásek the Innkeeper, Robin Donald; The Innkeeper's Wife, Etela Piha; Harašta the Poacher, Gregory Yurisich; The Vixen, Eilene Hannan; The Cock, William Bamford; The Hen, Dawn Walsh; The Fox, Ron Stevens

Producer, Jonathan Miller; Set Designer, Patrick Robertson; Costume Designer, Rosemary Vercoe; Lighting Designer, Leslie Bowden; The Australian Opera Chorus; The Melbourne Symphony Orchestra; Conductor, Carlo Felice Cillario

28 July 1980: *Katya Kabanová* (in English, translation by Norman Tucker); Sydney Opera House; The Australian Opera

Vanya Kudriash, Ron Stevens; Glasha, Jennifer Bermingham; Dikoy, Neil Warren-Smith; Boris, Gregory Dempsey; Feklusha, Lesley Stender; Kabanicha, Rosina Raisbeck; Tichon, Robert Gard; Katya, Marilyn Richardson; Varvara, Kathleen Moore; Kuligin, John Germain

Producer, David Pountney; Set Designer, Roger Butlin; Costume Designer, Maria Bjørnson; Lighting Designer, Donn Byrnes; The Australian Opera Chorus; The Elizabethan Sydney Orchestra; Conductor, Mark Elder

4 March 1982: *The Makropulos Affair* (in English); Festival Theatre, Adelaide; State Opera of South Australia

Emilia Marty, Elisabeth Söderström; Albert Gregor, Gregory Dempsey; Jaroslav Prus, James Christiansen; Vítek, Thomas Edmonds; Kolenatý, Roger Howell; Janek, William Bamford; Krista, Claire Primrose; Hauk-Šendorf, Geoffrey Harris; Stage Hand, Keith Hempton; Charlady, Isabel Townsend; Chamber Maid, Jolanta Nagajek

Director, Elijah Moshinsky; Set Designer, Brian Thomson; Costume Designer, Luciana Arrighi; Lighting Designer, Rory Dempster; The Adelaide Symphony Orchestra; Conductor, Denis Vaughan

Janáček Premieres in New Zealand

16 October 1976: *Jenůfa* (in English, translation by Edward Downes and Otakar Kraus); Grand Opera House, Wellington; The Australian Opera

Jenůfa, Lone Koppel Winther; Grandmother Buryja, Jacqueline Kennsett-Smith; Laca Klemeň, Ron Stevens; Jano, Jennifer Bermingham; Barena, Cynthia Johnston; Foreman of the mill, John Germain; The Kostelnička, Elizabeth Fretwell; Števa Buryja, Robert Gard; A Maid, Mary Hayman; Mayor, Joseph Grunfelder; His Wife, Miluska Simkova; Karolka, Janice Hill; Aunt, Elizabeth Allen

Producer, John Copley; Set Designer, Allan Lees; Costume Designer, Michael Stennett; Lighting Designer, Leslie Bowden; The Australian Opera Chorus; The New Zealand Symphony Orchestra; Conductor, Georg Tintner

2 March 1996: *Katya Kabanová* (in Czech, with English surtitles); Michael Fowler Centre, Wellington; New Zealand International Festival of the Arts

Vanya Kudriash, Mark Luther; Glasha, Helen Medlyn; Dikoy, Conal Coad; Boris, Peter Kazaras; Feklusha, Virginia-Marie Stack; Kabanicha, Antonie Denygrová; Tichon, Richard Greager; Varvara, Margaret Medlyn; Katya, Eva Jenis; Kuligin, Zane Te Wiremu Jarvis

Director, Gale Edwards; Set Designer, Peter J. Davison; Costume Designer, Guy Cadle; Lighting Designer, Mark McCullough; Wellington City Opera Chorus; The New Zealand Symphony Orchestra; Conductor, David Parry

(For each production, the opera titles and role names are as given in its programme booklet.)

9   Janáček's Moravian publishers

NIGEL SIMEONE

Janáček's first published work was the brief unaccompanied motet *Exaudi Deus,* completed in 1875 and printed as part of a musical supplement to the Prague-based Cecilian movement periodical *Cecilia* in 1877.[1] After this debut, at the age of twenty-three, the publication of Janáček's music was centred for more than three decades on his home town of Brno. The Moravian capital played host to some distinguished musicians in the second half of the nineteenth century. Concerts were given by Clara Schumann (1859), Anton Rubinstein (1867), Brahms and Joachim (1867), the Hellmesberger Quartet (1882), von Bülow as both conductor and soloist with the Meiningen Orchestra (1884), the ten-year-old Josef Hofmann (1886, a concert reviewed by Janáček), the Rosé Quartet (1888), Ysaÿe (1890), Kreisler (1895), Richter conducting the Vienna Philharmonic (1896), Dvořák conducting the Czech Philharmonic (1897), and many others.[2]

Janáček himself was perhaps the most trenchant critic of local musical life in Brno, particularly of Czech-run institutions, compared with the wealthier German-run organisations. He began one of his reviews (*Hudební listy,* 24 February 1886) with the uncompromising assertion that there was 'Complete stagnation at our opera house!', continuing with a vigorous polemic on what was needed to raise standards: better acting, sparing use of the prompter, and the quest for 'perfection' in the chorus and orchestra. Remarkably, Janáček considered it necessary to specify the minimum

---

[1]   A facsimile of this publication is in Nigel Simeone, *The First Editions of Leoš Janáček: A Bibliographical Catalogue* (Tutzing: Hans Schneider, 1991), p. 74.

[2]   For a detailed account of musical visitors to Brno before the First World War see Vojtěch Kyas, *Slavné hudební osobnosti v Brně (1859–1914)* [Famous Musical Personalities in Brno (1859–1914)] (Brno: Opus musicum, 1995).

requirements for such an orchestra: '(a) in the strings four first violins, four second violins, three violas, two cellos and an equal number of double basses, and (b) two flutes, two oboes, two clarinets, two bassoons, two trumpets, two trombones and one timpani'.[3]

Janáček was later to encounter problems of his own with the orchestral forces for the first production of *Její pastorkyňa* (Her Stepdaughter; Jenůfa; 1894–1903; rev. 1906–7) in 1904: the opera was played by 'an orchestra of just twenty-nine which lacked the harp, bass clarinet and English horn that Janáček specified'.[4] Even more disturbing is that the orchestra was depleted still further during the first run, with Janáček writing ruefully to Hana Kvapilová in April or early May 1904:

> Even before now, the orchestra of the local theatre has been incomplete to an
> alarming extent: the new director has given notice to the horn player, the
> trumpet player – they are apparently not needed for the summer season.
>   I myself don't even go to the theatre now – I don't want to hear my own
> work in such a broken-down state.[5]

Music publishing in the Moravian capital at the end of the nineteenth century tended to reflect the somewhat parlous state of music in the city at the time, but the advent of a composer of Janáček's significance ensured that several major works were first published there. The present study will examine this local publication of his music, which continued even after December 1916, when Janáček first signed a contract with Universal Edition in Vienna and, at about the same time, started to develop close ties with the leading Czech music publisher, Hudební matice Umělecké besedy in Prague. The appendix on pp. 178–82 below includes a complete list of Janáček's works published in Moravia during his lifetime, and gives details of plate numbers, engravers, printers and publishers for each work.

There was no major music publisher in Brno at the end of the nineteenth century and the publications discussed here were predominantly issued by very small firms: an unusually high proportion of Janáček's locally published works bear the plate number '1'. During Janáček's lifetime the

---

[3]   Mirka Zemanová, *Leoš Janáček's Uncollected Essays on Music* (London: Marion
    Boyars, 1989), pp. 136–41 (p. 138).
[4]   John Tyrrell, *Janáček's Operas: A Documentary Account* (London: Faber, 1992),
    p. 56.   [5]   Ibid., p. 60.

principal Brno firms were Karl Winkler, Arnošt Píša and Oldřich Pazdírek. It was to be another four years after the publication of *Exaudi Deus* before Janáček's next published musical work. Again it was for a liturgical purpose: Janáček's harmonisations of ten Czech hymns. These were issued in about 1881 by the Brno firm of Karl Winkler as *Deset českých cirkevních zpěvů z Lehnerova mešního kancionálu harmonizoval Leoš Janáček* (Ten Czech Hymns from the Lehner Hymn-book for the Mass Harmonised by Leoš Janáček).[6] This rare and slender publication, bearing the plate number 'W.1', was reissued by the same firm in an expanded and substantially revised edition eight years later. The 1889 edition boasts an emended title, *České církevní zpěvy z Lehnerova mešního kancionálu*, and the plate number '9'. Like the earlier edition it was engraved by the Leipzig firm of Engelmann & Mühlberg, less internationally renowned than C. G. Röder, but the engraver of choice for many smaller German and Austrian music publishers, and for most of the Brno firms of the time.[7]

Winkler's other Janáček publication was to be of greater significance. In 1886, the firm published the score and parts of the four *Mužské sbory* (Male-voice Choruses)[8] with a touching dedication on the title page from Janáček to his friend Antonín Dvořák: 'Slovutnému pánu Antonínu Dvořákovi na důkaz neobmezené úcty věnoval Leoš Janáček' (Dedicated to the esteemed master Mr Antonín Dvořák in token of unbounded respect by Leoš Janáček).[9] The music for this edition was typeset by a local firm, as a note at the foot of the last page of each voice part indicates: 'Tiském papežské knihtiskárny benediktinů rajhradských'

---

[6] This title page is reproduced in Simeone, *The First Editions of Leoš Janáček*, p. 76.

[7] See the Appendix on pp. 178–82 below for details of Janáček editions engraved and printed by Engelmann & Mühlberg.

[8] 'Vyhrůžka' (The Warning), 'O lásko' (Oh Love), 'Ach vojna, vojna' (Alas the War) and 'Krásné oči tvé' (Your Lovely Eyes); the title page is reproduced in Simeone, *The First Editions of Leoš Janáček*, p. 106. The precise publication date was almost certainly at the very end of August 1886. On 30 August of that year Janáček sent a copy to the Hlahol Choral Society in Prague and, at about the same time, to Dvořák.

[9] Dvořák's letter of thanks, acknowledging receipt of the publication is dated 13 September 1886 – see Milan Kuna et al., eds., *Antonín Dvořák: korespondence a dokumenty, kritické vydání: 2. korespondence odeslaná 1885–1889* [Antonín Dvořák: Letters and Documents, Critical Edition: 2. Letters from 1885–9] (Prague: Editio Supraphon, 1988), pp. 177–8.

(Printed by the Papal Printing House of the Benedictines of Rajhrad [on the outskirts of Brno]).

This was an organisation to which Janáček had already turned himself two years previously when he had two organ pieces printed, at his own expense, as *Skladby pro varhany, čís. 1 a 2* (Pieces for Organ, nos. 1 and 2). Printed by the Knihtiskárna rajhradských benediktinů, it is an intriguingly quirky publication, mostly printed on five staves. The music is laid out as follows: Manual II occupies staves 1–2, Manual I staves 3–4, and the Pedals stave 5. The printer is given at the foot of the title page, together with the imprint 'Nákladem vlastním', the Czech equivalent of 'Selbstverlag' or 'Printed for the author'. This was the first publication of any instrumental music by Janáček and, uniquely for his music at this time, the title page and the elaborate preliminary instructions on registration are bilingual, printed in both Czech and German.[10] Here is something of a puzzle: Janáček the militant Czech speaker producing a publication which includes German titles and instructions; the only probable explanation is that the composer was seeking a wider audience with these pieces, though the number of copies printed would not have exceeded more than a few hundred. Much later in his career, Czech and German title pages and preliminaries in Janáček editions were to become the norm once Universal Edition began publication of Janáček's music.

The Winkler edition of the four *Male-voice Choruses* was the first independent publication of Janáček's secular choruses, but a year earlier, in 1885, one chorus, 'Kačena divoká' (The Wild Duck), was issued by Joža Barvič in Brno, printed on pp. 141–9 in Volume 2 of a school songbook: *Zpěvník pro školy střední a měst'anské* (Songbook for Secondary Schools). This was edited by Janáček's friend Berthold Žalud, a musician and critic who had stood in as conductor of the Brno Beseda concerts while Janáček was studying in Leipzig and Vienna, and who died of tuberculosis in 1886, the year after this songbook appeared.

As is well known, the first edition piano-vocal score of *Jenůfa* was published by the Klub přátel umění v Brně (Friends of Art Club in Brno, hereafter 'KPU'), in March 1908. This was the KPU's first and most ambi-

---

[10] The title page is reproduced in Simeone, *The First Editions of Leoš Janáček*, p. 216.

tious venture into music publishing, and the publication of *Jenůfa* was also a major landmark for Janáček himself, as it was by far the most substantial of his compositions to be published by this date. His proposal at a meeting of the KPU on 2 December 1907 that they should begin publishing music was accepted, and *Jenůfa* was proposed for immediate publication by František Veselý.[11] Just how immediate is clear from the remarkable speed with which production went ahead: Janáček received the first set of proofs from Engelmann & Mühlberg by 31 December 1907 and all his own proof corrections to the 281 pages of the score were completed by the middle of February 1908. With great efficiency, Engelmann & Mühlberg completed the printing within a month, enabling Janáček to send out the first copies on 18 March, the date on which wrote to his friend Artuš Rektorys enclosing a copy.[12]

The handsome decorative title page and front wrapper are by an unnamed artist who was, presumably, a member of the KPU. According to the preliminary matter in the score, the publication was given as a gift to members of the KPU for the 1907–8 season, though all copies have a printed price of '15 K.' (15 Czech crowns) at the foot of the title page and front wrapper. In all, 600 copies were printed, of which 300 were put on sale, 227 of these by Mojmír Urbánek in Prague, who is credited on the title page as selling them on commission. The KPU had agreed a realistic budget of 3,000 crowns for printing the score; in fact it cost them a total of 3,684 crowns.[13] To recover these production costs, at least 246 copies needed to be sold, without allowing for Urbánek's agency commission fees. The edition remained on sale for several years, with the important later addition of an inserted sheet containing cuts and corrections made by Janáček. This extra sheet was 'Printed for the author' by the same Benedictine organisation that had printed the *Pieces for Organ, nos. 1 and 2* in 1884 (although its name had now been simplified to 'Benediktinská knihtiskárna v Brně' (The Benedictine Printing House in Brno)).

[11] Jaroslav Vogel, *Leoš Janáček: A Biography*, trans. Geraldine Thomsen-Muchová, rev. 2nd edn (London: Orbis, 1981), p. 223.

[12] Artuš Rektorys, ed., *Korespondence Leoše Janáčka s Artušem Rektorysem*, 2nd rev. edn (Prague: Hudební matice, 1949), pp. 74–5; see also Tyrrell, *Janáček's Operas*, p. 63.

[13] Ludvík Kundera, *Janáček a Klub přátel umění* [Janáček and the Friends of Art Club] (Olomouc: Velehrad, 1948), pp. 56–7.

The KPU continued limited activity as a music publisher, not only of works by Janáček: for instance the gift for the year 1912 was a *Cyklus písní* (Cycle of Songs) by one of Janáček's most gifted pupils, Jaroslav Kvapil. Comprising five songs to texts by Heyduk (nos. 1–2) and Sova (nos. 3–5), Kvapil's song cycle has the plate number '10'; it was engraved and printed in Leipzig by Engelmann & Mühlberg. The following year (1913) saw the publication of Janáček's *V mlhách* (In the Mists) by the KPU, with the confusing plate number '1'. According to Ludvík Kundera, 400 copies were printed 'towards the end of 1913'.[14] Finally, the KPU were responsible for the first publication of Janáček's 'Ballada pro orchestr', *Šumařovo dítě* (Ballad for Orchestra, The Fiddler's Child). This was issued as a study score in 1914, with yet another plate number '1'. Jaroslav Vogel has observed that the score was published 'on the occasion of Janáček's sixtieth birthday' (3 July 1914),[15] but it was almost certainly not printed until November 1914: on 16 November 1914, Janáček sent copies to the dedicatee Vilém Zemánek, along with Artuš Rektorys, and Otakar Ostrčil, who was to conduct the first performance of the work almost exactly three years later, on 14 November 1917, with the Czech Philharmonic Orchestra.

The KPU score bears a dedication to Zemánek, and also a leaf dedicating the publication itself from the KPU to Janáček on his sixtieth birthday. The dedication to Zemánek was omitted in the 1924 edition of the score issued by Hudební matice, incorporating Janáček's revisions. Though this could have been a simple oversight, one possible alternative explanation could be the calamitous early performance history of the work: on 6 October 1912, when Zemánek was chief conductor of the Czech Philharmonic, he conducted the first Prague performance of the cantata *Amarus* (c. 1897; rev. 1901, 1906) and subsequently invited Janáček to write a new orchestral work. This was *The Fiddler's Child*, which Janáček sent to Zemánek on 28 April 1913. Almost a year later, in March 1914, there followed one abortive rehearsal for the piece in Prague, but it lay unperformed until it was taken up by Ostrčil.

From premises at Česká 32, the firm of Oldřich Pazdírek published two substantial works by Janáček during the 1920s: *Zápisník zmizelého*

---

[14] Kundera, *Janáček and the Friends of Art Club*, p. 63.
[15] Vogel, *Leoš Janáček*, p. 193.

(The Diary of One Who Disappeared; 1917–19; rev. 1920) and the early Suite for strings (1877). The *Diary* was published before 23 November 1921 (the date on which Janáček inscribed a copy to Břetislav Bakala, who had extracted the work from the chest where Janáček kept his manu-scripts).[16] It is clear that Pazdírek foresaw some international success for the work, issuing separately printed sheets containing French and German translations of the text, which were inserted into the score.[17] The front wrapper of this edition, designed by Ferdiš Duša, includes a woodcut depicting a couple in an embrace; the woman in this illustration is thought to be a stylised likeness of Kamila Stösslová; since the woman's face is partly obscured, it is difficult to tell, though her long dark hair, untied, was in accordance with the composer's wishes.[18] In 1943, Pazdírek issued an extraordinary separate printing of no. 13 (the piano interlude) with the title *Intermezzo erotico*. This came equipped with a lurid front cover designed by F. Drlík, printed in shades of red, yellow and green, depicting a naked woman.

The 1877 Suite for strings was issued by Pazdírek as a pocket score and parts in 1926, describing the work on the title page as 'Suite pour deux

[16] Janáček's correspondence helps us narrow this date of publication a little further. Janáček wrote to his wife from Luhačovice on 24 July 1921 (Janáček Archive class mark A 988), commenting that the proofs had arrived. On 20 September Max Brod wrote to Janáček saying that he had received two copies of the work and requesting some more to give to friends in Berlin (see Jan Racek and Artuš Rektorys, eds., *Korespondence Leoše Janáčka s Maxem Brodem* (Prague: Státní nakaldatelství krásné literatury, hudby a umění, 1953), p. 84). The crucial letter (Janáček Archive B 1594) is, unfortunately, undated, although its general content suggests that it was written in late August or early September 1921. It is from Janáček to his friend and lawyer Jaroslav Lecián, who also sang tenor and had previously rehearsed the cycle with the composer. In his letter Janáček states that he is sending Lecián the first printed copy, as promised. [ed.]

[17] In the early stages of the *Diary*'s publication history Pazdírek was competing with two other publishers for the right to issue the work: Hudební matice of Prague, and Vladimír Buňata, who operated in the small Moravian town of Bojkovice. Janáček gives his reasons for eventually choosing Pazdírek in a letter to Max Brod dated 30 April 1921 (Racek and Rektorys, eds., *Korespondence Leoše Janáčka s Maxem Brodem*, p. 74): 'I wrote to you about Pazdírek. He wants to publish an edition of the "Diary". I gave him very moderate terms. We need here [in Brno] at least a "bread-and-butter" publisher.' [ed.]

[18] Charles Susskind, *Janáček and Brod* (New Haven: Yale University Press, 1985), p. 57; illustration of the front wrapper on p. 58.

violons, alto, violoncelle et contrebasse',[19] possibly edited by the conductor František Neumann, who conducted a successful performance of the work with the strings of the Czech Philharmonic Orchestra on 24 October 1926. Shortly afterwards, the third movement of the Suite ('Andante con moto') was published in an arrangement by Josef Gregor for three violins with Janáček's approval. This appeared in the periodical *Hudební besídka*, 3 (1926–7), pp. 26–7. A year later, the same periodical issued the first edition of Janáček's *Pochod Modráčků* (March of the Blue Boys; 1924) in an issue dedicated to the composer by Václav Sedláček, flautist at the Brno National Theatre and well known as Janáček's most important copyist. This little piece – a preliminary study for the wind sextet *Mládí* (Youth; 1924) – scored for piccolo with accompaniment for bells and drum or piano, was published in *Hudební besídka*, 4 (1927–8: March–April 1928 issue), pp. 121–7.

The small firm of Boleslav Svoboda, with premises at Křížová 55–7 in Old Brno, was responsible for one significant later Janáček publication: the *Slezské písně (ze sbírky Heleny Salichové)* (Silesian Songs from Helena Salichová's Collection), a group of ten folk-song arrangements for voice and piano composed in January 1918. Svoboda published the thirteen-page score in 1920, with the plate number 'B. 1 S.', presumably this firm's first publication,[20] but just one in a long line of Janáček's Moravian publications bearing the plate number '1'.

[19] The title page is reproduced in Simeone, *The First Editions of Leoš Janáček*, p. 158.

[20] The firm is listed under 'Hudební nakladatelství a obchody hudebninami' [Music Publishers and Sellers of Sheet Music] in the Brno section of Jan Branberger, ed, *Almanach musical pour la république Tchéco-Slovaque, 1922* (Prague: Jan Hoffman, 1922), p. 449.

Appendix: chronological list of Janáček editions published in Moravia during the composer's lifetime

Abbreviations

CGR   C. G. Röder, Leipzig
EM   Engelmann & Mühlberg, Leipzig, followed by the firm's own printer's numbers
FELJ   Nigel Simeone, *The First Editions of Leoš Janáček: A Bibliographical Catalogue* (Tutzing: Hans Schneider, 1991)
JaWo   Nigel Simeone, John Tyrrell and Alena Němcová, *Janáček's Works: A Catalogue of the Music and Writings* (Oxford: Clarendon Press, 1997)
KPU   Klub přátel umění v Brně (Friends of Art Club in Brno)
LN   *Lidové noviny*, Brno
MAK   Moravská akciová knihtiskárny v Brně (Moravian Printing Company in Brno)
min.   miniature
OT   Občanské tiskárny v Brně (Town Printers in Brno)
PKBR   Papežské knihtiskárny benediktinů rajhradských (Papal Printing House of the Benedictines of Rajhrad [near Brno])
suppl.   supplement
VS   Piano-vocal score

Date	Work	Publisher (Brno unless stated)/ Plate Number (PN)[a]	Engraver/Printer
1881	*Deset českých církevních zpěvů z Lehnerova měsíčního kancionálu* II/10[b] (Ten Czech Hymns from the Lehner Hymnbook for the Mass)	Karl Winkler/PN W. 1	EM, 5740[c]
1884	*Skladby pro varhany, čís. 1 a 2* (Pieces for Organ, nos. 1 and 2) VIII/7	Nákladem vlastním (Leoš Janáček)	PKBR
1885	*Kačena divoká* (The Wild Duck) IV/18	Joža Barvič (*Zpěvník pro školy střední a měšťanské*, Vol. 2, pp. 141–9, ed. Berthold Žalud)	

1886 (by 30 August)	Mužské sbory (Male-voice Choruses) IV/17	Karl Winkler	PKBR
1887(?)	Na památku (In memoriam) VIII/9	Beseda Brněnská(?)[d]	
1889	České církevní zpěvy z Lehnerova mešního kancionálu II/10 (rev. edn of 1881 Deset českých církevních zpěvů . . .)	Karl Winkler/PN 9	EM, 12674
1890	Ave Maria IV/16	Emanuel Binko, Brtnice (suppl. in Varyto, Vol. 13/1)/PN 98	
1890	Kytice z národních písní moravských (A Bouquet of Moravian Folk-songs) XIII/1	Emil Šolc, Telč	
1891	Národní tance na Moravě (National Dances of Moravia) VIII/10, Vols. 1 and 2	Nákladem vlastním (Leoš Janáček, Lucie Bakešová, Xavera Běhálková)	MAK
1892	Kytice z národních písní moravských V/2, Vol. 1 (15 songs)	Emil Šolc, Telč/PN 1	EM, 11695
1893	Kytice z národních písní moravských XIII/1, 2nd edn	Emil Šolc, Telč	
1893	Národní tance na Moravě VIII/10, Vol. 3	Nákladem vlastním (Leoš Janáček, Lucie Bakešová, Xavera Běhálková, Martin Zeman)	MAK
1893	Což ta naše bříza (Our Birch Tree) IV/22	Památník spolku Svatopluk	
1895	Hudba ke kroužení kužely (Music for Club Swinging) VIII/13	Tělocvičná jednota Sokol/PN 1	EM, 13471
1899 (25 April)	Návod pro vyučování zpěvu (Singing Teaching Manual) V/5	Arnošt Píša/PN 1	EM, 16190

Date	Work	Publisher (Brno unless stated) / Plate Number (PN)[a]	Engraver/Printer
1899 (January)	Ukvalská lidová poezie v písních (Hukvaldy Folk Poetry in Songs) V/4	Arnošt Píša/PN 2	EM, 16191
1901	Kytice z národních písní moravských, slovenských a českých XIII/2, 3rd edn	Emil Šolc, Telč	Unie, Prague
1901	Kytice z národních písní moravských V/2, Vol. 2 (38 songs)	Emil Šolc, Telč/PN4	EM, 17549
1901	Což ta naše bříza (Our Birch Tree) IV/22, 2nd edn	Joža Barvič	
1901	Po zarostlém chodníčku (On an Overgrown Path) VIII/17, series 1, nos 1, 2 and 10	Emil Kolář, Ivančice (Slovanské melodie, Vol. 5)	F. M. Geidel, Leipzig
1902	Po zarostlém chodníčku VIII/7, series 1, nos. 4 and 7	Emil Kolář, Ivančice (Slovanské melodie, Vol. 6)	F. M. Geidel, Leipzig
1905 (Spring)	Moravské tance (Moravian Dances): 'Čeladenský', 'Pilky' VIII/18	Arnošt Píša/PN 7 and 8	EM, 19206, 19207
1908 (18 March)	Její pastorkyňa (Her Stepdaughter; Jenůfa) I/4, VS	KPU	EM, 20789[e]
1908	Moravská lidová poezie v písních (Moravian Folk Poetry in Songs) V/2 (53 songs = 2nd edn of Kytice z národních písní moravských V/2)	Emil Šolc, Telč	EM(?)
1909 (29 December)	Narodil se Kristus Pán (Lord Christ was Born) VIII/20, in 'Světla jitřní' (Morning Light)	LN	
1911 (30 September)	Po zarostlém chodníčku VIII/17, series 2, no. 1	Večery (suppl. to LN)	

Date	Work	Publisher	Catalogue
1911 (November?)	Po zarostlém chodníčku VIII/17, series 1	Arnošt Píša/PN 9	EM, 22803
1911 (23 December)	Podme, milá, podme (Come, dearest) V/10	Večery (suppl. to LN)	
1912 (17 February)	Krajcpolka (Round Polka) V/6 no. 5	Večery (suppl. to LN)	EM, 23854
1913 (towards end)	V mlhách (In the Mists) VIII/22	KPU/PN 1 (!)	(CGR)[f]
1914 (November)	Šumařovo dítě (The Fiddler's Child) VI/14, min. score	KPU/PN 1 (!)	
1920	Slezské písně (Silesian Songs) VI/13	Bohumil Svoboda/PN B. 1 S.	EM, 25172
1920	Ukolébavka (Lullaby) V/14	Kniha Komenského, ed. František Pražák	
1921 (August?)	Zápisník zmizelého (The Diary of One Who Disappeared), V/12	Oldřich Pazdírek/PN 301	CGR[g]
1922 (17 March)	'Budem tady stat' (We will wait here) VIII/25, in 'Počátek románu' (The Beginning of a Romance)	LN	
1923 (18 March)	Three Folk-song arrangements in 'Starosta Smolík' (Mayor Smolík) V/15 ('Radujte se všichni' (Rejoice, All of You), 'Sklenovské pomezí' (Sklenov Border Country), 'Pod'te, pod'te děvčvatka' (Come Girls)	LN	
1923 (5 July)	'Con moto VIII/26, in 'Ústa' (The Mouth)	LN	
1924 (8 January)	Untitled piece VIII/27, in 'Měl výtečný sluch' (He had an Excellent Ear)	LN	
1926 (4 July)	'Sletové fanfáry' (Sokol Festival Fanfares: Sinfonietta VI/18, movement 1, bar 47 to the end)	LN	

Date	Work	Publisher (Brno unless stated) / Plate Number (PN)[a]	Engraver/Printer
1926	Suite for Strings VI/2	Oldřich Pazdírek/PN 411a (score), 411 (parts)	(CGR)[h]
1926	'Andante con moto' from Suite for Strings VI/2, arr. Josef Gregor for three violins[i]	Hudební besídka, Vol. 3 (1926–7), pp. 26–7	
1927 (16 January)	'Andante' VIII/31, in 'Toulky' (Rambles)	LN	
1928 (March/April)	Pochod Modráčků (March of the Bluebirds) VII/9 and Ukolébavka V/14 (J. A. Komenský)	Hudební besídka, Vol. 4 (1927–8), nos 7–8, pp. 121–7 and 108–9	OT

Notes

a Plate numbers are given when one is present on the publication.

b The work numbers here refer to those in JaWo.

c Engelmann & Mühlberg included an engraver's reference number on publications produced by the firm, usually printed at the foot of the title page.

d For discussion of the possible publisher of Na památku see FELJ, p. 219; JaWo, p. 248.

e The separately printed errata sheet has the printer's mark 'Tiskem benediktinské knihtiskárny v Brně' (a later formulation for the PKBR) – 'Nákladem vlastním'.

f No indication of printer or engraver is given, but the score is printed on Röder paper with the watermark 'CGR * 10'.

g C. G. Röder engraved and printed the large-format edition. The miniature score issued at about the same time has the printer's mark 'Uniotypie (Manul)'.

h Though no printer's mark appears on the parts, they are printed on Röder paper with the watermark 'CGR'.

i This arrangement was approved by Janáček.

10 Janáček, musical analysis, and Debussy's 'Jeux de vagues'

PAUL WINGFIELD

Úvodní slovo

during the past year I have got to work and read all the harmony manuals, beginning with Reicha-Paris up to Schoenberg. I believe that my path is the right one.   (Janáček, 1920)[1]

Most would agree with Michael Beckerman's statement that to Janáček 'theory was both as important as composition and vitally related *to* composition'.[2] There is, however, still widespread confusion about the content of Janáček's 'theoretical' writings, few of which have been translated. Also, the composer's importance within the field of discourse about music is all too often accorded only superficial debate. Commentators are apt summarily to consign Janáček to the periphery, asserting that he is excessively 'metaphysical' and 'incoherent'. Jaroslav Vogel, for example, finds Janáček's 'written deductions unmethodical and hard to understand';[3] and John Tyrrell observes in a blunt one-liner: 'Janáček's theoretical writings had no impact on Czech theoretical thought.'[4] Even those writers more positive about Janáček's theoretical activities tend to eschew reasoned argument. Jaroslav Volek crudely divides all musical theorists into two camps,

[1] ('Voriges Jahr nahm ich mir die Arbeit und las alle Werke, seit Reicha-Paris bis auf Schönberger, über Harmonielehre durch. Ich glaube, daß mein Weg der richtige ist.') From an undated 1920 letter to Universal Edition, quoted in Miloš Štědroň, 'Janáček a Schönberg', *Časopis Moravského musea: vědy společenské*, 49 (1964), pp. 237–58 (p. 239).

[2] Michael Beckerman, *Janáček as Theorist* (Stuyvesant, NY: Pendragon Press, 1994), p. 103.

[3] Jaroslav Vogel, *Leoš Janáček: A Biography*, trans. Geraldine Thomsen-Muchová, rev. 2nd edn (London: Orbis, 1981), p. 163.

[4] John Tyrrell, 'Janáček', in *The New Grove: Turn of the Century Masters*, ed. Stanley Sadie (London: Macmillan, 1985), pp. 1–77 (p. 48).

183

the 'mechanico-materialists' (e.g. Helmholtz) and the 'idealists' (e.g. Hauptmann), and claims that Janáček's achievement lies in his 'middle' stance.[5] Perhaps surprisingly, then, I would like to suggest that Janáček made a 'mainstream' contribution to the field of 'music theory and analysis'. Before pursuing this with reference to the composer's unpublished 1921 analysis of Debussy's *La mer* (1903–5), I shall briefly appraise the literature.

Many scholars have hitherto segregated Janáček's writings on music into rigid categories – feuilletons, criticism, 'speech-melody' theory, ethnographic studies, music theory, pedagogy, musical analysis and so on – and have tended to concentrate on either a single category or one text principally in isolation.[6] The problem here is not merely that there are substantial overlaps between categories, or that many individual texts are interdisciplinary in orientation; it is more that some key ideas are actually developed across several texts of different types. The two broadest and commonest distinctions applied to Janáček's writings – between 'theory as conceptual frame, analysis demonstration',[7] and between musicology and ethnomusicology – are the least helpful. On the face of it, Janáček did favour theory over analysis. His canonical 'theoretical' writings as edited by Zdeněk Blažek fill two substantial volumes,[8] whereas a collected edition of his 'analyses' would constitute a short pamphlet[9] – an apparent imbalance

5 Jaroslav Volek, 'Živelná dialektika a její klady i nedostatky v teoretických názorech Leoše Janáčka' [Elemental Dialectics and their Positive and Negative Repercussions in the Theoretical Opinions of Leoš Janáček], in *Leoš Janáček a soudobá hudba: mezinárodní hudebně vědecký kongres* [Leoš Janáček and Contemporary Music: International Musicological Conference] (Prague: Hudební rozhledy, 1963), pp. 352–60 (p. 352).

6 For a detailed bibliography, see Beckerman, *Janáček as Theorist*, pp. 120–31.

7 Dai Griffiths, review of Anthony Pople, ed., *Theory, Analysis and Meaning in Music* (Cambridge: Cambridge University Press, 1994), in *Music Analysis*, 15 (1996), pp. 381–92 (p. 382).

8 Zdeněk Blažek, ed., *Leoš Janáček: Hudebně teoretické dílo* [Leoš Janáček: Music Theory Works], Janáčkův archív, Second Series/Vol. 2: I *Spisy, studie a dokumenty* [Writings, Studies and Documents] (Prague: Supraphon, 1968); Second Series/Vol. 3: II *Studie, Úplná nauka o harmonii* [Studies, *Complete Harmony Manual*] (Prague: Supraphon, 1974).

9 Apart from the *La mer* analysis, the only other major 'analyses' are of four Dvořák symphonic poems (*Vodník* (The Water Goblin), *Polednice* (The Noon Witch), *Zlatý kolovrat* (The Golden Spinning Wheel) and *Holoubek* (The Wild Dove)), reprinted in *Musikologie*, 5 (Prague: Státní nakladatelství krásné literatury, hudby a umění, 1958), pp. 324–59; English translations by Tatiana

reflected in the *New Grove* work-list for the composer, where the 'analysis' texts are subsumed within 'criticism'.[10] However, as Ian Bent suggests, might not a theorist 'when executing an analysis within the environment of a manual of compositional theory . . . abandon the educational mode of thought for one that is entirely analytical'?[11] Janáček does indeed switch within a single text between many authorial identities (pedagogue, philosopher, analyst, conductor etc.). The distinction between musicology and ethnomusicology is equally misleading. Many of the voluminous 'ethnographic' writings are not in fact restricted to folk music.[12]

According to Blažek, the canon of the 'musical theory' writings comprises seventeen texts (some subdivided) spanning the period 1877–1920; he regards three as seminal: *O skladbě souzvukův a jejich spojův* (The Composition of Chords and Their Connections; 1896; 2nd edn 1897), 'Můj názor o sčasování (rytmu)' (My Opinion about *Sčasování* (Rhythm); 1907), and *Úplná nauka o harmonii* (Complete Harmony Manual; 1912–13; rev. and enlarged 2nd edn 1920).[13] Among the elucidatory literature, Beckerman's 1994 monograph stands out.[14] Beckerman seeks not only to explain Janáček's core concepts but also to evaluate in depth his significance as a theorist. Even this pioneering book raises difficulties, many of which stem from Beckerman's pragmatic adherence to Blažek's canon.[15] As a result of his initial policy decision, Beckerman is encouraged to describe the development of Janáček's theoretical ideas in terms reminiscent of the organicist metaphor of the unified cyclic work whose whole is greater than the sum of the parts. He divides Janáček's theoretical develop-

Firkušný of the third and fourth of these analyses are available in Michael Beckerman, ed., *Dvořák and his World* (Princeton: Princeton University Press, 1993), pp. 262–76.   [10] Tyrrell, 'Janáček', p. 57.

[11] Ian Bent, *Music Analysis in the Nineteenth Century*, I *Fugue, Form and Style* (Cambridge: Cambridge University Press, 1993), p. xiv.

[12] Jan Racek and Jiří Vysloužil, eds., *Leoš Janáček: O lidové písni a lidové hudbě: dokumenty a studie* [Leoš Janáček: On Folk-song and Folk Music: Documents and Studies], Janáčkův archív, Second Series/Vol. 1 (Prague: Státní nakladatelství krásné literatury, hudby a umění, 1955).

[13] There is a list of the canonical theory texts in Beckerman, *Janáček as Theorist*, pp. 119–20; all but one of these is reprinted in Blažek's edition of the music theory works (see note 8).   [14] See note 2.

[15] Beckerman gives his reasons for adopting Blažek's canon on p. xv of *Janáček as Theorist*.

ment into four discrete phases (1884–8, 1894–7, 1907–12 and 1916–20), each influenced by one major extra-musical field (abstract formalism, acoustics, ethnography and experimental psychology), and each culminating in a key text; the final phase witnesses 'a last synthesis of ideas'.[16] This proposition ignores Janáček's continued reformulation of his thoughts up to his death in 1928: the 1926 essay 'O tónině v lidové písni' (On Key in Folk-song) is arguably his definitive statement on tonality *per se*,[17] and the 1921 *La mer* analysis constitutes a much more extensive application of his theories than the analysis of a two-bar snippet from Richard Strauss's *Elektra* that prefaces Part III of the *Complete Harmony Manual* and is promoted by Beckerman as 'a kind of showpiece for [Janáček's] method of analysis'.[18]

Beckerman's evaluation of Janáček's claims as a theorist is ingenious. Having concluded that Janáček neither had much influence nor shed any light on previously unknown or unexplained phenomena, he argues that Janáček's attempt 'to relate all theory both to new artistic developments and to human activity' is intrinsically valuable, and that the composer's theoretical writings can be viewed as a set of secondary, historico-critical texts, which point out the underlying connections between many important, and richly diverse, intellectual trends of his time.[19] To Beckerman, Janáček's theoretical activities ultimately remain 'a stimulus for his compositional work': once his theory had in around 1920 reached its 'definitive' form, he was able to concentrate on composing.[20] But if this is so, one wonders why Janáček continued to write about music for the rest of his life.

It seems worth at least trying another approach to the subject: namely, examining a Janáček analysis of a specific work in the context of his relevant prose writings of whatever category, the reception history of the work, and the history of musical analysis. Since analytical practice shapes theory as much as the other way round, this will allow us to reassess whether the composer's writings contain a conventionally 'valuable' thread of musical thought. The *La mer* analysis is the obvious subject for such an investigation: although it has been published in facsimile, it has been

---

[16] Ibid., p. 57.
[17] Racek and Vysloužil, eds., *Leoš Janáček: O lidové písni a lidové hudbě*, pp. 446–56.
[18] Beckerman, *Janáček as Theorist*, pp. 92–5 (p. 92). [19] Ibid., p. 101.
[20] Ibid., p. 104.

accorded virtually no critical attention.[21] The majority of the material in this analysis pertains to the second movement, 'Jeux de vagues', on which I shall focus. First, I shall examine selectively the critical reception of *La mer*, and of 'Jeux de vagues' in particular, referring to a few other relevant publications about Debussy. Then I shall assess the contents, chronology and context of Janáček's study. After that, I shall examine Janáček's three 'Jeux de vagues' analyses, drawing in some of the remaining sketchy material and consistently comparing Janáček's ideas with those of others. My discourse will be difficult to follow without a score. The 1997 critical edition is recommended;[22] failing that, the Dover score is adequate.[23]

Some remarks on the critical reception of *La mer*

The 1905–8 critical reception of *La mer* – which Debussy subtitled '3 symphonic sketches' after Paul Gilson's *La mer* (1892) – is centred on rather general reviews, mainly of the Paris premiere and the Paris revival.[24] Many reviewers exude nostalgia for the more muted language of *Pelléas et Mélisande* (1893–1902). Pierre Lalo deems *La mer* less spontaneous than 'the grotto scene in *Pelléas*', and complains: 'I neither hear, nor see, nor feel the sea.'[25] The most analytical early review, by Louis Laloy, is strikingly conservative.[26] To Laloy, *La mer* is more 'classical' than any previous Debussy work, above all because of its more 'definite' melody and the arch-like tonal structure of both the first movement (Db–Bb–Db) and the whole work (the outer movements close in Db). Laloy consigns 'Jeux de vagues' to the margins of his discourse.

The period 1908–14 saw a trickle of *La mer* performances in Europe

---

21 The facsimile is printed in Miloš Štědroň, 'Janáček, verismus a impresionismus', *Časopis Moravského musea: vědy společenské*, 53–4 (1968–9), pp. 125–54 (Appendices Ia to IIIb).

22 Marie Rolf, ed., *Œuvres complètes de Claude Debussy*, Séries V, Vol. 5: *La mer* (Paris: Durand, 1997).

23 *Claude Debussy: Three Great Orchestral Works* (New York: Dover, 1983), pp. 143–279 [essentially a reprint of the second edition (Paris: Durand, 1909)].

24 Further details about the early reception of *La mer* are available in: Léon Vallas, *Claude Debussy: His Life and Works*, trans. Maire and Grace O'Brien (London: Oxford University Press, 1933), pp. 171–80; and Simon Trezise, *Debussy: La mer* (Cambridge: Cambridge University Press, 1994), pp. 19–26.

25 Vallas, *Claude Debussy*, p. 172.   26 Ibid., pp. 175–6.

and America (the piece reached Prague in 1910). After the First World War, the work's popularity was still negligible in comparison with that of *Prélude à l'après-midi d'un faune* (1892–4). Renditions increased gradually during the 1920s, Walther Staram doing more than anyone to establish it as a core repertory work. The first two recordings were made in 1928 and 1932, both by French orchestras playing under Piero Coppola. During the 1930s the piece was transformed (partly through dubious editorial changes) by Toscanini and Koussevitsky into a vehicle for the virtuoso conductor.[27] *La mer* is progressively classicised in the musical literature from between the wars. Ladislaus Fábián takes his lead from Laloy, arguing that it inaugurates a 'simplified melodic style' that foreshadows the late 'neoclassical' works, such as the three sonatas.[28] In his 1927 monograph, Léon Vallas still deems it necessary to play down *La mer*'s innovatory aspects, claiming unpersuasively that Laloy's analytical approach had the approval of Debussy himself.[29] This classicising trend is maintained even by some post-1945 authors: in the 1951 revision of his 1936 monograph Edward Lockspeiser declares *La mer* to be the modern equivalent of Beethoven's Fifth and opines that 'The three movements of this great work are not sketches' but unfold a cyclically connected symphonic succession of clear formal prototypes: sonata allegro/arch, 'free' rondo and fantasia.[30]

Of the wartime writers, the American Oscar Thompson distances himself from the European 'battleground' of *La mer*'s reception.[31] He is adamant that 'the unity of the work' is 'beyond dispute' but is disinclined to support this assertion analytically. Instead, he concentrates on the representational dimension, expanding Debussy's titles by means of the following scenario: the sea 'awakening'; the 'awakened sea at play'; and a 'gustier, wilder sea, with a stronger dramatic emphasis and something more closely akin to human quality in the impersonation'. His description of 'Jeux de vagues', 'the scherzo of Debussy's heretical symphony', is especially evocative.

27 The performance history of *La mer* is examined in Trezise, *Debussy: La mer*, pp. 26–31.
28 Ladislaus Fábián, *Claude Debussy und sein Werk* (Munich, 1923).
29 Vallas, *Claude Debussy*, p. 176.
30 Edward Lockspeiser, *Claude Debussy*, rev. 3rd edn (London: Dent, 1951), pp. 193–7.
31 Oscar Thompson, *Debussy: Man and Artist* (New York: Tudor Publishing Co., 1940), pp. 322–5.

The reception of Debussy's music saw a marked change of direction after 1945 in the hands of a younger generation of composers brandishing agenda aplenty. The two most influential commentators of the post-war European *avant-garde* are Pierre Boulez and Herbert Eimert. In a much quoted 1956 article, Boulez claims Debussy as an 'ancestor', 'one of the most isolated of all musicians', who was forced into 'fleeting, feline solutions' as an outlet for his radical impulses.[32] Only Boulez can realise the true potential of Debussy's visionary experiments with *sonority*. In a 1961 study Boulez reappraises Debussy's compositional development, proposing *Jeux* (1912–13) as its pinnacle.[33] Based on the 'constant evolution of thematic ideas', *Jeux* is important particularly for its 'individualization of timbre and acoustic conception of the orchestral ensemble', the 'logical outcome of experiments made in *La mer* and *Images*'. Once again *La mer* is classified as a transitional work, but it is now 'Jeux de vagues' – whose very title indicates a link with *Jeux* – that is given special commendation. Boulez praises its 'bold and radical conception of timbre', as well as its 'elegant, condensed, and elliptical syntax'.[34]

Herbert Eimert's 1959 analysis of *Jeux* has a different emphasis: Debussy is recast as a precursor of the electro-acoustic music that Eimert and others were writing in Cologne in the 1950s.[35] Eimert embraces the conventional notion that all the motivic material grows from a single 'kernel'. But his organic motivic metaphor has a twist. Variants may, through a chain of metonymical associations, be related only syntagmatically to the original model. (This idea is an offshoot of Schoenberg's concept of 'developing variation', even if many later motivic analysts sideline it.) The resulting 'endless variation' evokes the 'organic inexactness of vegetation' and the biological process of 'mutation'. Also, 'in the vegetative circulation of the form there is no development, no intensification or return of themes'; instead, dynamics, density, tempo and timbre combine

---

32 Pierre Boulez, 'Corruption in the Censers', in *Notes of an Apprenticeship* (New York: Knopf, 1978), pp. 27–34.

33 Pierre Boulez, 'Items for a Musical Encyclopedia', in *Notes of an Apprenticeship*, pp. 334–57 (p. 353).

34 Quoted in Roger Nichols, *Debussy* (London: Oxford University Press, 1973), p. 57.

35 Herbert Eimert, 'Debussy's "Jeux"', trans. Leo Black, *Die Reihe*, 5 (Bryn Mawr: Theodore Presser Co., 1959), pp. 3–20.

with phrase structure and motivic variation to create a 'kinetic' process comprising 'a whole system of waves' governed by quasi-electrical patterns of acceleration and deceleration. If Eimert is exaggerating, he seems justified in his claim that, in 'Jeux de vagues' as well as *Jeux*, there is a remarkable level of motivic transformation.

The first detailed analysis of the whole of *La mer* was completed by Jean Barraqué in 1962 (but not published until 1988).[36] Barraqué's title presumably alludes to Debussy's famous remark that he designed the ending of 'Jeux de vagues' (revised very late in the compositional process) to be 'neither open nor closed'.[37] Yet again, *La mer* is viewed as a transitional work that inaugurates new procedures attaining full 'bloom' in *Jeux*. In essence, Barraqué's argument is that in *La mer* 'the very notions of exposition and development co-exist in an uninterrupted outpouring'. It is therefore puzzling that he divides 'Jeux de vagues' into seven conventionally labelled parts ('Introduction', 'Exposition', 'Développement' etc.). Overall, he identifies four structural levels: five of the seven parts subdivide, the resulting sections delineating miniature binary, ternary and bar forms, the subsections of which break down into similarly arranged phrase units. Barraqué's detailed comments cover a large range of parameters: motives and themes, structural pacing, tonality, texture, timbre, articulation, dynamics, 'orchestrated silence' (a concept presumably derived from Barraqué's studies with Messiaen) etc.

Within Barraqué's bar-by-bar analysis of 'Jeux de vagues', individual parameters are pursued, temporarily abandoned, and then taken up again, in a manner analogous to his view of the movement's motivic processes. Naturally, the elements are not accorded equal weight. Only design, motives and thematic structure are dealt with in depth. Barraqué identifies an impressive array of motivic cross-references. Additionally, he argues persuasively that from bb. 102–3 the first movement's opening pentatonic gesture is alluded to increasingly overtly. Most illuminating of all is Barraqué's evaluation of phrase structure. He analyses with great precision matters of internal accent, patterns of momentum and dissolution, hyper-

---

[36] Jean Barraqué, '*La mer* de Debussy, ou la naissance des formes ouvertes', *Analyse musicale*, 12 (1988), pp. 15–62 [posthumous publication].

[37] Jacques Durand, *Lettres de Claude Debussy à son éditeur* (Paris: Durand, 1927), p. 24.

metre, fluctuations in motivic density and competing priorities between textural levels. James Briscoe summarises: 'Debussy worked with traditional boundaries while revitalizing these at lower levels of form. "Forming" is seen within "form".'[38] However, Barraqué also suggests a first-order structural process. This comprises: (1) increasing frustration of momentum leading to 'complete petrification' in bb. 153–62; (2) a watershed (bb. 163–70) and a 'repart' (b. 171) accelerating towards a powerful climax (bb. 215–18); and (3) a dissolution. Later analyses of 'Jeux de vagues' reformulate this blueprint.

In context, Barraqué's concentration on *La mer*, as opposed to *L'après-midi* or *Jeux*, is unusual. William Austin opens his 1966 history of twentieth-century music by suggesting that Debussy had a greater influence on the course of musical history than any other turn-of-the-century composer, yet he ignores *La mer* in favour of *L'après-midi*.[39] Similarly, Stefan Jarocinski's influential 1966 book (not published in English until 1976) barely mentions *La mer*.[40] Jarocinski (who is beholden to Boulez) posits that Debussy developed a 'new form of Symbolism', which 'freed music from the semantic approach' and purged it of 'all its stale rules and abstract rhetoric which destroyed any feeling for the true significance of sound'. He concentrates on vocal pieces, in which, he claims, the textual frame allows Debussy's music more freely to adumbrate post-Webernian sonorial experiments.

Not all 1960s publications evaluating *La mer* are as imaginative as Barraqué's analysis. Lockspeiser proclaims *La mer* to be 'the greatest example of an Impressionist orchestral work', influenced in particular by Turner, Monet and Hokusai (whose painting *The Hollow of the Wave off Kanagawa* Debussy chose for the front cover of the first edition), and an analogue in terms of sound to Monet's paintings, with their loosening of representation and innovatory approaches to colour and perspective.[41] Lockspeiser steadfastly refuses to be any more specific. A 1967 article by

---

[38] James Briscoe, *Debussy: A Guide to Research* (New York: Garland, 1990), p. 398.

[39] William Austin, *Music in the 20th Century: From Debussy through Stravinsky* (New York: Norton, 1966).

[40] Stefan Jarocinski, *Debussy: Impressionism and Symbolism*, trans. Rollo Myers (London: Eulenburg, 1976).

[41] Edward Lockspeiser, *Debussy: His Life and Mind*, II: *1902–18* (London: Cassell, 1965).

Hellmuth Wolff lamely reduces *La mer* to a static 'unity', claiming that the work is founded on the paradigmatic derivation of all its thematic material from a single six-note *Urmotiv* introduced in the first two bars.[42]

Most 1970s writers on *La mer* follow Boulez by focussing on 'Jeux de vagues'. Noteworthy are two subsequently frequently cited but unpublished papers given at the A.M.S. general meeting in 1974. Douglass Green appraised Debussy's 'neither open nor closed' remark about 'Jeux de vagues' in relation to the Sibley manuscript, suggesting vaguely that we 'abandon the traditional concepts of statement, development and restatement [and listen] to the work as a coherent flow of short moments from one to the next'.[43] In his response to Green, Laurence Berman proposed an overlying process for this movement similar to that advocated by Barraqué. Roy Howat summarises:

> Noting the dominance of the final climax at *38* [b. 215] over the movement's shape and form, Berman pointed out how various events on the way there set up an alternation of impediments and forward impulses, before the final sweep towards *38* gets properly underway. He singled out the passage between *26* [b. 104] and bar 117 ... as representative of forward motion, in contrast to the surrounding [passages beginning] at *25* [b. 92] and bar 118, both of which obstruct forward impetus, pulling the tempo back to $\sature = 112$ after prior spurts of increased speed.[44]

Although Berman's structural turning-point (b. 130) is earlier than Barraqué's (bb. 163–70), both men invoke a model of progressive frustration then release of momentum encompassing bb. 1–218. Moreover, Berman does apparently regard the acceleration as having two phases, the first from b. 130 and the second (the breakthrough) from b. 163, which he describes as 'a rebeginning' and the start of 'a huge consequent phrase'.[45]

Of the British writers at this time, Roger Nichols toes the Boulez line, asserting: 'viewed as a part of his total output, the outer movements of *La*

---

[42] Hellmuth Wolff, 'Melodische Urform und Gestaltvariation bei Debussy', *Deutsches Jahrbuch der Musikwissenschaft für 1966*, 11 (1967), pp. 95–106.

[43] Quoted in Marie Rolf, 'Debussy's *La mer*: A Critical Analysis in the Light of Early Sketches and Editions', Ph.D. dissertation (University of Rochester, Eastman School of Music, 1976), p. 157.

[44] Roy Howat, *Debussy in Proportion: A Musical Analysis* (Cambridge: Cambridge University Press, 1983), p. 114.

[45] Recalled in Rolf, 'Debussy's *La mer*', p. 219.

mer . . . figure rather as rogue specimens. More representative and, for a study of Debussy's later style, more interesting is . . . "Jeux de vagues".[46] Nichols selects bb. 72–82[1] for scrutiny, arguing that this passage can be explained only through examination of texture, density and, above all, timbre – the horns are 'the centre around which the other parts revolve'. Unfortunately, Nichols merely affirms the primacy of motive: the horns in this section unfold at pitch a variant of the movement's principal motive (the Cor anglais's C–D–E–F♯ tetrachord in bb. 9–10, which derives from the bass C–F♯ tritone in bb. 7–8). Nichols's brief remarks about *La mer* in his *New Grove* article on Debussy are also predominantly concerned with timbre.[47]

David Cox patronisingly acclaims *La mer* 'the best symphony ever written by a Frenchman', 'an organic whole' unified by motives introduced in the first section.[48] He then echoes Boulez. After remarking that 'Jeux de vagues' ('a kind of scherzo') foreshadows *Jeux*, he continues: 'textures . . . change and overlap too quickly for development in the traditional sense and therefore become fragmented, decorative, moment to moment in a way that is new and prophetic. Add to that a use of timbre as an *essential* element in the construction.' His strongest observation is redolent of Barraqué and Berman: he detects an interplay between superficial rapid textural shifts (changes on 'the surface of the water') and deeper structural forces, notably the 'unmoving pedal note (G♯)' in bb. 171–214 ('the sea's unchanging depth and stillness'). The 1970s Anglo-American intensification of the post-War predilection for suggesting overlying structural processes for 'Jeux de vagues' was pithily summed up in a 1980 BBC broadcast by Roger Nichols: '[motives] are signposts, not the road itself'.[49]

In the light of all this, two 1970s German analyses make peculiar reading. Max Pommer takes the fact that Debussy altered his original movement titles ('Mer belle aux Îles Sanguinaires', 'Jeu de vagues' and 'Le vent fait danser la mer') as proof that 'the music of *La mer* . . . does not slavishly obey

---

[46] Nichols, *Debussy*, pp. 57–61 (p. 57).
[47] Roger Nichols, 'Claude Debussy', in Stanley Sadie, ed., *The New Grove: Twentieth-century French Masters* (London: Macmillan, 1986), pp. 41–125 (pp. 63–4).
[48] David Cox, *Debussy Orchestral Music* (London: BBC Music Guides, 1974), pp. 24–32.   [49] Quoted in Howat, *Debussy in Proportion*, p. 115.

PAUL WINGFIELD

its poeticising titles but its own musical laws'.[50] These 'laws' are those of the nineteenth-century *Formenlehre*. Pommer classifies 'Jeux de vagues' as ternary with introduction and coda, the introduction containing a preliminary development of the 'Hauptthema' (introduced definitively at b. 36) and 'A' material twice returning during the 'B' section (!). Wolfgang Dömling is another devotee of *Formenlehre* models.[51] His ternary-based analysis of 'Jeux de vagues' (a 'scherzo', naturally) identifies five main themes and an additional important 'chromatic motive' (bb. 134–5). Any material not related to one of these paradigms he terms simply 'Nebenthema'. His improbably short 'B' section (bb. 130–62) is made up of material that either derives from the 'A' section or recurs throughout the 'A¹' section. Dömling's penultimate sentence raises an issue later to be pursued in depth by Roy Howat. He remarks that the patterns of dynamics in the movement outline 'wave' forms whose high points tend not to coincide with clear structural divisions, giving bb. 28, 72 and 126 as examples of such high points (but oddly not bb. 153 and 215).

A further 1970s German book about Debussy, by Albert Jakobik, contains a bizarre analysis of *La mer*.[52] Jakobik's central proposition is that Debussy's 'silent revolution' is based on a new approach to 'Klang' (i.e. harmonic colour). The principal constructional unit is the 'Klanglicher Dreitakt', which contains a 'Grundfarbe' (in its pure form, a single transposition of the diatonic collection), a 'Vermittlungsfarbe' (the whole-tone collection), and a 'Gegenfarbe' (a contrasting key or group of related keys employing the pitch classes absent from the 'Grundfarbe'). Form is created through sequences of variants of this basic pattern ('Klangbewegungen'); themes are merely 'linear and rhythmic' manifestations of the underlying changes of harmonic colour. 'Jeux de vagues' itself begins with an eight-bar motto fusing all the elements of the three-part model within a musical representation of Hokusai's *The Hollow of the Wave Off Kanagawa*. There follow five *Klangbewegungen*. The *Grundfarbe* is E major with an added

---

[50] Max Pommer, Preface to the Peters Edition of *La mer* (Leipzig, 1972), pp. xvii–xxii.

[51] Wolfgang Dömling, *Claude Debussy: La mer* (Munich: Wilhelm Fink Verlag, 1976), pp. 15–20.

[52] Albert Jakobik, *Claude Debussy oder Die lautlose Revolution in der Musik* (Würzburg: Konrad Triltsch Verlag, 1977), pp. 108–16.

194

sharpened fourth, the principal *Gegenfarbe* C major. Each type of harmonic colour allegedly has its own melodic and rhythmic character. Unsurprisingly, Jakobik rapidly concedes that harmonic colours are constantly mixed, and that melodic and rhythmic *topoi* transfer allegiances incessantly.

In the early 1980s, Jann Pasler takes on *Jeux* from an ostensibly different angle.[53] Previous attempts to uncover unity 'have skirted half of the central problem: *Jeux* concerns not just sound but also time'. What gives the piece 'its formal coherence is its overall rhythmic organization'. Specifically, the work is bound together by 'a common pulse', the quaver; all tempo fluctuations are 'eventually compensated for'. Pasler's conclusions are supported by quotations from Debussy himself and references to the contemporary cultural context. She clearly has a case, although it is only the starting point for an analysis and is not entirely new, given that Boulez remarks in a much earlier article: 'the general organization of [*Jeux*] is as changeable instant by instant as it is homogeneous in development. A single basic tempo is needed to regulate the evolution of the thematic ideas.'[54]

A useful 1981 piece by Jean-François Monnard details mistakes in the Durand editions of *La mer* and attacks the near-universal tendency of conductors to ignore Debussy's performance instructions.[55] He calls for Debussy's proportional relationships to be respected and exaggerated ritardandos to be avoided. Temporal issues also preoccupy Roy Howat.[56] Howat's premise is that in many of Debussy's works the deployment of key structural events is determined by symmetrical and Golden Section proportions. Briefly, the Golden Section (hereafter 'GS') is 'the way of dividing a fixed length in two so that the ratio of the shorter portion to the longer portion equals the ratio of the longer portion to the entire length'. (To six decimal places, the two measurements are 0.618034 and 0.381966.) Howat further distinguishes between 'primary' (long–short) and 'secondary'

53 Jann Pasler, 'Debussy's *Jeux*: Playing with Time and Form', *Nineteenth-century Music*, 6 (1982–3), pp. 60–75.

54 Boulez, 'Items for a Musical Encyclopedia', p. 354.

55 Jean-François Monnard, 'Claude Debussy: "La mer": Des fautes de copie à l'interprétation', *Schweizerische Musikzeitung*, 121 (1981), pp. 11–16.

56 Howat, *Debussy in Proportion*, pp. 110–35.

(short–long) GS divisions. In this scheme of things, *La mer* has pride of place: its complex proportional arrays are not surpassed in Debussy's oeuvre.

Howat maintains the post-War tradition of problematising 'Jeux de vagues'. He initially suggests 'a type of architectural counterpoint' in which the principal thematic and tonal events are bifurcated. He then pinpoints a second hierarchical level consisting of twelve primarily motivically defined segments, many of which overlap texturally. Discerning no 'consistent purpose', he turns to dynamics, finding that the movement 'breathes in a series of [nine] dynamic paragraphs'. The model paragraph comprises: fluctuation around '*p*' or '*pp*'; build-up; peak; diminuendo. Through this interpretation, the final two peaks (bb. 153–60 and 215–18) – the loudest and most prolonged – emerge as the movement's main focal points. There are some irregularities: the dynamic paragraph starting at b. 92 'cuts in to prevent an incipient culmination' and the peak at b. 104 is not prepared. These anomalies are the result of a binary process in which dynamics have a surface role up to b. 130, thereafter transferring to a fundamental structural level. The dynamic process is mirrored by the sequence of tempos, which decelerate to b. 130 and then accelerate. This whole plan is redolent of Berman's, which Howat deftly amplifies.

Turning to proportions, Howat prefers counting beats to measuring clock time, searching, like Pasler, for a common pulse. From b. 36 'Jeux de vagues' is all in 3/4; but the opening requires thought. Howat opts for the following sequence of notional equality: $\downarrow. = 77\frac{1}{3}$ (bb. 1–8) / $\downarrow. = 72$ (bb. 9–35) / $\downarrow. = 46$ (b. 36). The movement has 261 bars but now comprises 269 'units', each of the first eight bars counting double. Howat scours the movement for symmetrical and GS sequences involving mainly motivic, textural and dynamic parameters. He constructs two principal proportional frames, 'Sequence A' and 'Sequence B', which cover up to b. 215, the start of the final peak. There is a consistent trend: 'focal points of tension . . . form predominantly GS divisions'; small-scale structural events are connected through symmetry. With reference to the movement as a whole, Howat contends that the penultimate peak – the most prolonged of all – 'lies aptly over the movement's primary GS after 166 units [b. 159[1]]'. In reality, by b. 159[1] the peak in question is nearly over, and in any case bb. 157–60 are a minimally emended repeat of bb. 153–6. Equally problematically, the movement's secondary GS (b. 96^1) has no structural significance and bb. 215–61 have no proportional connections with Sequences A and B.

Howat negotiates this impasse by unveiling a 'synthesis' between 'Jeux de vagues' and the finale. One can find further (predominantly symmetrical) proportional sequences by measuring from b. 215 of the former to various structural highpoints of the latter. Howat justifies this by pointing out the similarity of tempo between the end of the second movement and the start of the third, and by citing Debussy's 'neither open nor closed' remark about 'Jeux de vagues'. The result is a plan for the entire work:

> If the first movement has all the weight of the sea's tidal pulls, and if the
> second movement's airier waves can be associated with the action of the
> wind, the structuring of the finale provides a dialogue of the two, combining
> a recapitulation of structures from the first movement with a completion of
> the dynamic sequences from the central movement.[57]

This prompts an analogy between the three movements and the three parts of a sonata allegro, where 'defined shapes and structures' replace 'subjects and motives'. A notable forerunner of this scheme is Schumann's Fourth Symphony, and Debussy is know to have admired Schumann. All of a sudden, the reader – battered by a whirlwind of measurements – is deposited abruptly in the comforting surroundings of the nineteenth-century symphony.

Despite some striking results for the outer movements, Howat's explanation of 'Jeux de vagues' fails to convince. No proportional scheme works for the whole movement, Sequences A and B are rather thin in concrete proportional relationships, and the 'synthesis' fails to land the knockout punch. A spin-off article from Howat's book is worth brief mention because of the seminal position it accords to 'Jeux de vagues', whose 'dramatic shape' is asserted to be a 'structural template' for 'Rondes de printemps' (1905–9), 'Gigues' (1909–12) and *Jeux* (which 'pushes' the basic format to its 'utmost').[58] Proportional calculations here matter less than the relative weights of the 'wave' forms produced by the dynamic paragraphs.

Arthur Wenk's 1983 Debussy book examines 'Jeux de vagues' briefly

---

[57] Ibid., p. 132.
[58] Roy Howat, 'Dramatic Shape and Form in "Jeux de vagues" and its Relationship to *Pelléas, Jeux* and Other Scores', *Cahiers Debussy*, 7 (1983), pp. 7–23.

as a prelude to ten pages on *Jeux* (Wenk has begun by quoting Boulez).[59] We are informed that in 'Jeux de vagues' the 'formal impulse of the music depends on a continually changing mosaic of melodic fragments while harmonic progression in the traditional sense has been arrested, sometimes nearly to the point of stasis'. But recurring melodic fragments are not responsible for defining musical structure; rather, Wenk pontificates nebulously, 'they form a musical matrix out of the complex psychological, artistic and literary associates that constitute the "program" for the work'. Wenk's supporting 'analysis' inspires little confidence in his pronouncements. For example, he posits that the bass progression in bb. 1–47 (F♯–C–G♯–B♭–E) is a whole-tone version of ii–vi–IV–V–I, failing to appreciate the complex interplay between diatonic, chromatic and whole-tone sonorities in these bars, and omitting to explain how a non-symmetrical and a symmetrical collection might be regarded as equivalent. As regards motive, Wenk merely invokes Eimert's notion of 'vegetative' transformation, contending airily that this process is employed to a limited extent in 'Jeux de vagues' and becomes the norm in *Jeux*.

Bruno Gousset attempts to reinstate timbre as an analytical priority: in *La mer*, for the first time in music history timbre 'becomes the unifying element in the work'.[60] Naturally, 'Jeux de vagues' is the most radical movement, its timbral experiments reaching their apex in *Jeux*. Gousset's two principal concepts are the 'note-son' – the essential connection between a melodic motive and an instrument – and the 'accord-timbre', the linking of a chord to a specific sonority. However, all that he really demonstrates is that motives and harmonies tend towards developmental and recapitulatory processes in their instrumentation. This point could be made about a Mozart symphony; and, surprisingly, Gousset admits precisely that in relation to one of his secondary areas of examination: the association of certain rhythms with particular instruments.

A rare excursion into narrativity is made by Marie Rolf.[61] The dis-

---

[59] Arthur Wenk, *Claude Debussy and Twentieth-century Music* (Boston: Twayne Publishers, 1983), pp. 68–73.

[60] Bruno Gousset, 'Le prééminence du timbre dans le langage musical de *La mer* de Debussy', *Analyse musicale*, 3 (1986), pp. 37–45.

[61] Marie Rolf, 'Mauclair and Debussy: The Decade from "Mer belle aux Îles Sanguinaires" to *La mer*', *Cahiers Debussy*, 11 (1987), pp. 9–23.

carded title of the opening movement derives from a short story by Camille Mauclair. Rolf posits a parallel between the three principal sections of the first movement and the three stages of Mauclair's story, also contending that both works 'display a quality of gradual progression or continuous transformation from their beginnings to their ends'. This is all extremely general, although her examination of another potential literary source – 'Escale en rade de Nemours' from Pierre Louÿs's *Sanguines*, which Debussy seems to have read in 1903 – is even more vague.

Richard Parks exposes Debussy's output to the full rigours of modern post-tonal analytical technique (including the notion of pitch-class set genera).[62] With regard to *La mer*, he bucks the post-war trend of isolating 'Jeux de vagues', concentrating instead on 'De l'aube à midi sur la mer'. He puts forward the idea that Debussy's 'advanced' music embodies complex interactions between 'morphological' (architectural, 'static') and 'kinetic' ('locomotive') forms. Morphologically, 'De l'aube à midi' has four hier-archical levels, which Parks depicts graphically by vertical lines of differing lengths connected to a horizontal axis. (Parks's cause is aided by the unusu-ally clear-cut outlines of this movement: virtually all commentators divide it into the same five main sections.) The movement's principal kinetic aspects are cycles of expansion and compression and vice versa at the higher levels, 'a rhythmic counterpoint' created by the contradictory tendencies between one level and another, and the maintaining of 'constants . . . to "hide the seams"' between formal units. This crude binary opposition would not be of much use in relation to 'Jeux de vagues'. Parks draws on the ideas of Barraqué, Eimert and Howat. Timbre even makes an appearance, although Parks is wary about making large claims on this parameter's behalf. One is just beginning to anticipate a synthesis of post-war trends in Debussy analysis when Parks terminates suddenly with a truism: 'Nothing is ever regular for long; no pattern or tendency is truly uniform. In its pro-portions and means of partitioning, the musical surface resembles and emulates natural surfaces – such as the sea.'

In a 1991 survey of twentieth-century music Robert Morgan remarks about Debussy: 'The "surface" of the music – its texture, color, dynamic

---

62 Richard Parks, *The Music of Claude Debussy* (New Haven: Yale University Press, 1989), pp. 233–40.

nuances, etc. – assumes an unprecedented prominence and importance.'[63] He then homes in on bb. 1–4 of 'Jeux de vagues' as self-evident justification of this. The tenacity of Boulez's influence is striking. In contrast, Craig Ayrey propounds a revision of the 'received view' of Debussy as 'predecessor': '[Debussy's] originality is doubly centred, conservative (Wagner and Mallarmé) and iconoclastic (the early Stravinsky). Debussy's modernism . . . depends on this thoroughly questioning subversive duality.'[64] To demonstrate this, Ayrey tests discourse 'as a model for musical structure', selecting the tropes of metaphor and metonymy as a basis for examining that old warhorse of semiotic analysis, the Prelude to *Pelléas*. He destabilises the simple notion of metaphor as paradigmatic and metonymy as syntagmatic, showing that there is a tendency for 'metaphor to resolve into metonymy'. This state of affairs concurs with Paul de Man's assessment of rhetoric in Proust, whose 'typical strategy is to collapse the aspect of "necessity" in metaphor ("the inference of identity and totality" inherent in resemblance) into contiguous metonymic relations of "chance" '. In the Prelude to *Pelléas*, there is a pervasive tendency for 'a "chance" metonymic relation' (e.g. the melodic succession G–A) to masquerade 'as a figure of necessity' through subsequent repetition. In sum, Debussy's quintessentially modernist 'discourse', like Proust's, is 'assertively metaphorical'. The disparity between the broad sweep of Ayrey's proposed re-evaluation of Debussy and the narrowness of his analytical demonstration is rather off-putting. However, there is no questioning the sophistication of his problematisation of the metaphor/metonymy opposition.

A major recent contribution to *La mer* scholarship is Simon Trezise's 1994 handbook.[65] Trezise is impatient with '-isms'; he considers *La mer* 'both subversive of, and responsive to, Debussy's diverse cultural inheritance', exhibiting an 'ambivalent rapprochement with the nineteenth-century symphony'. His revisionary stance extends to the matter of *La mer*'s place in Debussy's compositional evolution. He asserts that it is the orchestral *Images* (1905–12) rather than *La mer* which embody the stylistic break. In Trezise's opinion, *La mer* represents a severe challenge to the analyst. His

---

[63] Robert Morgan, *Twentieth-century Music* (New York: Norton, 1991), pp. 46–8.

[64] Craig Ayrey, 'Debussy's Significant Connections: Metaphor and Metonymy in Analytical Method', in Pople, ed., *Theory, Analysis and Meaning in Music*, pp. 127–51.   [65] See note 24.

approach is to examine 'Design', 'Rhythm and rhythmicised time', 'Motif and arabesque' and 'Tonality'. 'Design' turns out to denote synoptic accounts of all three movements. He pronounces 'Jeux de vagues' to be 'the most complex and rewarding movement to study in detail'. His ensuing analysis is hierarchical: there are four parts, the second of which subdivides, and the last of which is more a 'coda' than the first is an 'introduction'. In addition, parts I and II contain respectively three and ten smaller sections, many of which delineate miniature 'bar', 'strophic' and 'rondo' forms; part III is a series of 'strophic variations' of a four-bar unit, part IV a 'rondo'. This approach is similar to Barraqué's. Trezise's large-scale plan for the movement recalls Barraqué, Berman and Howat: initial fragmentation and instability cede to 'greater flow', leading first to 'a metamorphosis of time' (at b. 147) and afterwards (from b. 163) to an 'all-consuming forward motion that reaches an *fff* climax and then rapidly subsides'.

Trezise deals with rhythm, motive and tonality primarily in terms of their evolution across all three movements. He inadvisedly terms these processes 'narratives', the four principal of which are: (1) a progression from fragmentary phrase structure to regular periodicity; (2) a progression from motivic fragmentation to sustained development (saliently from b. 163 of 'Jeux de vagues') and then to a 'growing degree of motivic unanimity' in the finale, all culminating in the 'melting pot' of the closing bars; (3) a curious, pseudo-Schenkerian voice-leading 'narrative' comprising the prolongation and resolution of an 'A♭–B♭ conflict'; and (4) a process of evolution from initial harmonic informality to a closing 'definitive cadential progression'. As with Barraqué, perhaps the strongest part of Trezise's analysis of 'Jeux de vagues' is his examination of phrase structure. The transformation from 'discontinuity' to 'an expansive, continuous flow' at b. 163 is, he suggests, particularly evident in this dimension. In bb. 1–162 there is a tendency for phrase units to be linked at best by 'passive' or 'tangential' continuation. From b. 163, more 'active' continuation predominates. The result is a 'single, long-breathed melody' made up of groups of two four-bar units connected by sequence and other traditional means of development. Although lacking precise definitions of types of continuation, this ground plan has some obvious merits. However, the combined teleological impact of Trezise's 'narratives' is overwhelming. Having begun by proposing a modernist duality in *La mer*, he concludes by endorsing Laloy's and Lockspeiser's view of the work as a post-Beethovenian masterpiece.

Janáček's *La mer* analysis: contents, chronology, background

Janáček's *La mer* study is written on both sides of three loose folios: two of these measure 225 × 290 mm; the third is half a piece of the same paper-type (145 × 225 mm).[66] All six sides are in oblong format bar fol. 1v. The main text is written in brown ink. Most pages also have ink corrections and jottings in pencil. Only the rectos of the first two sheets are numbered. The final layers of fols. 1r–2v are transcribed in Appendices 10.1 to 10.3. Readers may check my transcriptions against the published facsimile, which cuts off some of the material at the edges.[67] Folios 1r and 2r contain two tabular analyses of the whole of 'Jeux de vagues'. The first (Analysis A; Appendix 10.1), on fols. 1r and 2r (upper half), comprises four horizontal columns laid out in four systems; the second (Analysis B; Appendix 10.1), on fol. 2r (lower half), has four columns (one of which is blank) spanning a single system. The first column of Analysis A contains a continuous straight horizontal line interrupted by system and page breaks and by various types of vertical strokes. It quotes some metronome marks, some rehearsal numbers and one page number (from the Durand score), as well as all changes of time-signature. These elements combine to divide the piece into segments, which are timed, Janáček sometimes indicating briefly how he calculated the timing for an individual segment.

Analysis A's second column contains what Janáček terms 'key [i.e. tonal-centre] motives', the third column shows 'harmonic motives'. 'Key motives' are represented by conventional letter-names (upper case for major, lower-case for minor), and their sequence is represented by lower-case letters, many of which are modified by quasi-algebraic symbols. 'Harmonic motives' are emblemised more variously: Janáček mixes letter-names, Roman numerals, accidentals, figured-bass symbols and musical reductions of some passages. A few of them are also allotted lower-case letters. The fourth column is devoted to 'melodic motives', which are mainly

---

[66] This manuscript is housed in the Janáček Archive (which forms part of the Music History Division of the Moravian Museum in Brno) under the class mark S64.   [67] See note 21.

written out in musical notation on at least their first appearance, and whose pattern of recurrence is once more shown by lower-case letters, modified by an expanded range of quasi-algebraic symbols. Lastly, Analysis A incorporates a few pseudo-mathematical formulae and verbal remarks, which elucidate matters of design and motivic transformation. Analysis B summarises Analysis A. Column 1, labelled 'Time elapsed', is reduced to timed segments and a total timing only. Columns 2 and 3 reduce and slightly emend their equivalents in Analysis A; totals are once more supplied. The 'harmonic motives' column is blank. Six motivic symbols in column 3 are ringed, connected by curved lines and labelled 'Pivotal m[otives]'.

Fol. 2v (Appendix 10.3) is also concerned with 'Jeux de vagues'. This untidy page has four constituent elements (Analyses C1–C4). In order roughly from top to bottom they are: (C1) a narrative plot written in prose captions numbered according to their related musical motives; (C2) a very brief diagrammatic summary of the movement mixing text, numbers, letters and graphic symbols; (C3) 'Pivotal motives', written out (not in their correct sequence) in musical notation, numbered, and annotated; and (C4) a second, more detailed diagrammatic summary of motivic structure, which again mixes different types of graphic apparatus. The page as a whole has two principal layers. Clearly, there were only four 'pivotal motives' to begin with (what is now no. 3 was omitted initially), the later expansion to five initiating substantial revision of C1, C3 and C4. Since C2 – which is squeezed in between C1 and C3 – has no such changes, it may be an afterthought. Analysis C1's prose captions have been crammed in too, this time at the top of the page. This all indicates the following order of composition: C3, C4, C1, C2.

The chronological relationships between the three pages of 'Jeux de vagues' material are most likely as follows. Obviously, the uncharacteristically neat fols. 1r and 2r go together. Also, Janáček appears to have completed fols. 1r and 2r before fol. 2v: he identified ten different motives (fol. 2r), ringed six of them, and then began to write 'Pivotal m[otives]'; he then appears to have turned over the sheet (fol. 2v), written 'Pivotal motives' in full and copied out four of the six ringed motives (abandoning the two least prominent ones), later deciding to add a new motive (no. '3'). Folio 1v (Appendix 10.2) comprises prose notes about words and music. Since some

203

of these concern programme music, they probably relate in at least some way to Analysis C1. Unlike fol. 1r, this page is in upright format (about the top two-fifths of it are blank). Four lines of supplementary remarks appear above the main text at an angle of 180 degrees. This is the only portion of the entire manuscript to bear a date: 11 March 1921. The layout of fol. 1v suggests that it postdates fol. 1r, so the additional four lines were probably the last material pertaining to 'Jeux de vagues' to be written. Folio 3r is an extremely sketchy diagrammatic analysis of 'Dialogue du vent et de la mer', along with captions outlining a further narrative plot. Although just legible, this analysis is no more than a few initial ideas. The final page (fol. 3v), written in ink with added illegible pencil scribbles, is an aphoristic explanation of how *La mer* may be related to Janáček's theory of 'složité reakce' (complex reactions) and the 'komplikační skladba' (complicated work). Folio 3 probably postdates fols. 1r, 2r and 2v, although it might predate fol. 1v.

In early 1921 Janáček was revising *Káťa Kabanová* (1920–1). On 6 March he wrote to Kamila Stösslová announcing that he had finished the opera,[68] although revisions seem to have continued until 17 April.[69] Consequently, Janáček probably wrote the *La mer* analysis in the period around 7–11 March 1921, during a brief lull in the final stages of his revision of *Káťa*. Previous critical comment is limited to a few sentences by Miloš Štědroň in an article about broader stylistic issues.[70] Štědroň provides a brief commentary and a transcript of some of the text. His main critical comment is that the graphic presentation of much of the analysis is 'reminiscent of contemporary methods'. This is not a particularly helpful remark, for even if one excludes Schenker as a special case, many of Janáček's contemporaries (e.g. Lorenz)[71] employed elaborate graphic techniques.

Little scholarly attention has been paid to Janáček's knowledge of

68 John Tyrrell, *Janáček's Operas: A Documentary Account* (London: Faber, 1992), pp. 254–5.

69 John Tyrrell, *Leoš Janáček: Káťa Kabanová* (Cambridge: Cambridge University Press, 1982), pp. 4–5.

70 Štědroň, 'Janáček, verismus a impresionismus' (see note 21), pp. 147–9.

71 Part of Lorenz's analysis of the *Ring* is reproduced in Ian Bent with William Drabkin, *The New Grove Handbooks in Music: Analysis* (London: Macmillan, 1987), pp. 47–9.

Debussy's music in general. Jan Racek highlights early Prague performances of (unspecified) Debussy piano works (1908), *Pelléas et Mélisande* (1908) and *Ibéria* (1911), although he does not provide evidence that Janáček attended any of these.[72] He also singles out 1909 correspondence between Janáček and Jan Branberger about some of Debussy's songs, and he observes that editions of both the *Deux arabesques* (Durand, 1904) and *Children's Corner* (Durand, 1908) are preserved in Janáček's personal library, the latter with annotations. Additionally, Janáček allegedly studied the String Quartet and the *Suite bergamasque*. Concerning *La mer* itself, Racek notes that it was performed by the Czech Philharmonic in Prague in 1910. Štědroň is a little more systematic.[73] He cites the *La mer* analysis and lists fourteen concerts in Brno and Prague between 1912 and 1927 of a wide variety of Debussy's works for which programmes have survived amongst Janáček's papers. The highlights are: *Pelléas* (Prague, 6 February 1921),[74] a selection of the preludes played by Alfredo Casella (Prague, 4 November 1922), *La mer* (Prague, 9 March 1924) and 'Nuages' and 'Fêtes' from *Nocturnes* (Brno, 19 May 1927, played by the Berlin Philharmonic Orchestra under Wilhelm Furtwängler).

The Czech Philharmonic in fact played *La mer* at least four times in Prague in the period 1910–24: on 30 January 1910 under Vilém Zemánek, 8 December 1918 (Ludvík Čelanský), 27 February 1921 (Walther Staram) and 9 March 1924 (Václav Talich).[75] There is no evidence that Janáček attended any of the first three of these performances. The surviving programme suggests that he might have gone to the 1924 Prague concert, although he does not mention it in two letters written the very next day from Brno to Kamila Stösslová and Max Brod.[76] Whether Janáček heard *La*

---

[72] Jan Racek, 'Der Dramatiker Janáček', *Deutsches Jahrbuch der Musikwissenschaft für 1960*, 5 (1961), pp. 37–57 (p. 49).

[73] Štědroň, 'Janáček, verismus a impresionismus', pp. 146–7.

[74] The opera was also performed in Prague on 1 November 1921.

[75] Richard Veselý, *Dějiny České Filharmonie v letech 1901–1924* [The History of the Czech Philharmonic in the Years 1901–24] (Prague, 1935), pp. 192, 228, xv, xxvii.

[76] John Tyrrell, ed. and trans., *Intimate Letters: Leoš Janáček to Kamila Stösslová* (London: Faber, 1994), p. 45; Jan Racek and Artuš Rektorys, eds., *Korespondence Leoše Janáčka s Maxem Brodem* [The Correspondence of Leoš Janáček with Max Brod] (Prague: Státní nakladatelství krásné literatury, hudby a umění, 1953), pp. 151–2.

mer is less important than his possession of a score, apparently of the 1909 Durand revised edition, when writing his analysis. Unfortunately, no score now survives in the composer's *Nachlass*; neither is there any reference to one in the available correspondence. We do know that Janáček habitually borrowed scores of recent works from friends, and that Brod often drew new works to his attention: for example, a letter from Janáček to Brod dated 11 June 1921 testifies that Brod had recently lent the composer a score of Nielsen's Fourth Symphony.[77] Janáček may well have borrowed the *La mer* score from Brod as well. *La mer* is not the only Debussy work that Janáček analysed. The annotations in his 1908 Durand edition of *Children's Corner* evaluate the motivic structure of nos. 2 ('Jimbo's Lullaby') and 4 ('The Snow is Dancing') by means of quasi-algebraic symbols identical to those employed in the *La mer* analysis.[78]

Oddly, neither Racek nor Štědroň records that Janáček quotes the piano part of bb. 26–9 of 'En sourdine' from *Fêtes galantes*, set 1 (1891) in part II of the first version (and in part III of the revision) of his *Complete Harmony Manual*. The accompanying text in both editions directly associates Debussy's music with the sea: 'Further, Fr[anz] Liszt And Cl[aude] Debussy bestow harmony with such luminous chordal colours, as if the sun were playing them while setting on the surface of the sea.'[79] Debussy is one of only three then living composers to be quoted in this book (the others are Richard Strauss and Max Reger, who died in between editions in 1916). The choice of composers is not mere personal predilection: it seems to have been *de rigueur* for Czech writers on modern music at the time to single out Debussy and Strauss. One of the most illuminating such articles – which examines the harmonic languages of *Pelléas* and *Elektra* – was probably known to Janáček, as it was published in a volume of a periodical to which he also contributed a piece on Dvořák.[80]

---

[77] Racek and Rektorys, eds., *Korespondence Leoše Janáčka s Maxem Brodem*, p. 79.

[78] What remains of Janáček's personal library is housed in the Janáček Archive.

[79] ('Fr. Lisztem a Cl. Debussym se ještě dostává harmonii takových zářivých akordických barev, jak by slunce je vyhrálo při svém západu na hladině mořské.') Blažek, ed., *Leoš Janáček: Hudebně teoretické dílo*, II (see note 8), p. 317.

[80] Karel Stecker, 'O moderní harmonii' [About Modern Harmony], and Leoš Janáček, 'Za Antonínem Dvořákem', both in *Hudební revue*, 4 (1911), pp. 512–27 and 432–3.

Janáček's selection of *La mer* as opposed to *Pelléas* is more individual. One possible reason for his choice is that he was contemplating writing a symphonic work and was seeking guidance from a contemporary whose music he valued. It should be remembered that in 1921, despite having recently written *Ballada blanická* (The Ballad of Blaník) (probably in late 1919), Janáček was relatively inexperienced as an orchestral composer – his most substantial orchestral work to date, *Taras Bulba* (1915–18), had caused him an inordinate amount of endeavour. The most plausible candidate for the planned orchestral piece is the unfinished *Dunaj* (The Danube; 1923–5?). This water work has a 'symphonic sketches' format, and Janáček referred to it variously as 'symphony', 'symphonic cycle' etc. The first concrete evidence of his having begun to compose *The Danube* is afforded by the first draft of the second movement (dated 18 June 1923).[81] Possibly then, Janáček – having just finished *Kát'a* – briefly intended starting his 'symphonic cycle', analysing *La mer* in preparation, but then shelving the project until he had finished *Příhody Lišky Bystroušky* (The Adventures of the Vixen Bystrouška; 1922–3). Alternatively, having just revised his *Complete Harmony Manual*, Janáček may have decided to try out some of his theoretical ideas on an extended piece of music, and he may have used the analysis as an *aide-memoire* for one of the composition master classes he gave (in Brno) for the Prague Conservatory in 1920–5 – the analysis's sketchy textual portions resemble other surviving lecture notes.[82]

'Jeux de vagues': Analysis A

By focussing on the middle of *La mer*'s three movements, Janáček not only displays his customary predilection for the unorthodox but also adumbrates standard practice from Boulez to Trezise. Analysis A can be divided under four broad headings: design; rhythm and time; motive;

---

[81] Alena Němcová, 'Was Janáček Satisfied with his Symphony "The Danube"?', in Michael Beckerman and Glen Bauer, eds., *Janáček and Czech Music: Proceedings of the International Conference (St. Louis, 1988)* (Stuyvesant, NY: Pendragon Press, 1995), pp. 311–20 (p. 314).

[82] Some of Janáček's lecture notes are reproduced in translation in Němcová, 'Was Janáček Satisfied with his Symphony "The Danube"?', pp. 318–19.

harmony and tonality.[83] These headings are virtually identical with those of Trezise.[84]

Design
What I would like to create is something ... inorganic in appearance yet
ordered deep down.   (Debussy, 1907)[85]

'There are some points on which writers on *La mer* will never reach agreement; of them all, the form of "Jeux de vagues" is probably the most vexing', announces Trezise.[86] Table 10.1 tests this contention, summarising the views of nine analysts. Pommer's ternary scheme is inadequate: his unbalanced proportions, suggestion of identity between two different motives (introduced in bb. 9–10 and 36–9 respectively) and failure to account for obvious thematic returns undermine his case. Dömling's ternary straitjacket does equally little justice to the movement. He is more coherent at the sectional level, but he still omits to label the clarinet motive at b. 76, to explain this motive's clear relationship with the 'chromatic motive' (bb. 134–5 etc.), to include the horn motive in bb. 50–1, and so forth.

Table 10.1 contains Barraqué's two highest structural layers (he describes the lower two incompletely). The movement's 'découpage global' is a modified sonata allegro, which has a secondary development with its own 'Section conclusive' added after the reprise. There are obvious problems with this arrangement: e.g. it ignores the movement's first 'motivic returns' (b. 92), and bb. 104–17 seem more like a modified reprise than a development of bb. 60–71. Barraqué's subsections – defined by motivic and/or textural shifts – are largely uncontroversial, although that at b. 44 is odd. The only other analysis with textbook allegiances is Howat's column 1a, an irregular sonata structure staggering motivic and tonal events as well as conflating development and reprise. This scheme allows Howat to account for the later reprises of the material introduced at both b. 9 and b. 36; and it accords due weight to the 'motivic returns' at b. 92. Howat agrees

---

[83] An obvious omission is timbre, which clearly interested Janáček (see pp. 37 and
      40 above of Macdonald's article in this volume). Had Janáček completed his
      analysis, he may have gone on to examine this aspect of the movement.

[84] Trezise, *Debussy: La mer*, pp. 51–95.

[85] ('Ce que je voudrais faire, c'est quelque chose d'inorganique en apparence et
      pourtant d'ordonné dans le fonds.') Quoted in Jean Barraqué, *Debussy* (Paris:
      Editions du Seuil, 1962), p. 159.   [86] Trezise, *Debussy: La mer*, p. 60.

with Barraqué that bb. 163–225 contain a secondary development and reprise, although Howat does not subdivide this section (what is to Barraqué the start of the 'Section conclusive' is to Howat the beginning of a structural overlap spanning bb. 219–25). On the whole, Howat's plan is the more coherent, but there is little to be gained by applying the sonata principle to this movement. Howat's 'tonal exposition' has its motivic dimension; the two parameters cannot so glibly be separated. In Rolf's rudimentary textually determined frame, her divisions (at bb. 36, 92 and 163) correspond to three of Howat's four, but she strangely ignores bb. 219–25. Nor is her 'continual transformation' plan persuasive.

The remaining analyses are more empirical. Jakobik's is unquestionably the weakest. Four of his five *Klangbewegungen* begin with harmonies belonging to the *Gegenfarbe* constellation (bb. 8, 72, 104 and 153), but the fifth does not; moreover, there are many other possible divisions that he might have chosen (notably bb. 28 and 215). Cox's motivically oriented analysis operates at Barraqué's subsectional level. Up to b. 118 the two men are in close agreement, even if Cox's labelling of a single rhythmic motive ('e') seems pointless (in any case, this figure is foregrounded first at b. 60 rather than b. 76). Cox ignores bb. 118–62, but is back on track from b. 163, reducing Barraqué's fussy plethora of subdivisions to just three, presumably to reflect the greater flow of the music (cf. Howat, column 1b, and Trezise).

Howat's motivic segments (column 1b) propose several (largely textural) overlaps. This is the most consistent analysis so far: changes of motivic orientation (usually supported by tempo markings) take priority; textural factors mainly support this scheme, but they create bifurcation close to many motivic boundaries. There is only one issue requiring comment: the overlap starting at b. 126[2]. Here the introduction of repeated A♯s/B♭s in the harps is certainly a prominent textural event, but the all-important trumpet motive (not labelled by Howat) has already begun two bars earlier. Howat's dynamic paragraphs are shown in column 2. These conflate two groups of motivic segments (nos. 1–2 and 3–5) but otherwise the divisions here are the same as in column 1b. One can, however, quibble about some details. First, bb. 48–59 delineate a subsidiary dynamic paragraph in their own right, with a peak of *mf* + at b. 57[3]. Moreover, each of the segments in bb. 1–8, 9–17, 36–47 and 76–87 concludes with a crescendo that is abruptly cut off by a return to a lower dynamic level. This all means that paragraphs 1 to 5 are complex structures expanding the four-part

Table 10.1 *Nine analyses of design in 'Jeux de vagues'*

Bars	Barraqué 1962	Pommer 1972	Berman 1974	Cox 1974	Dömling 1976	Rolf 1976	Jakobik 1977	Howat 1983	Trezise 1994	motivic returns
1	Intro.: 1a	Intro.:	Ia: i	Intro.	Intro. 1:	Intro.	I: i	Intro.:	I: A	(aab)
8										
9	1b	a		ai	Intro. 2: VII		ii	Thematic Exp.:	B	(aa¹)
18				aiii						
28									C	(aab)
30									Ps	
32									Pc Pe 1	
36	Exp.: 2a	A: a¹	Ib: i	bi	VIII	I	iii	Tonal Exp.:	II: D 2 (H)	
44	2b		ii				iv			
48		B: b	iii	bii					E 3 (J)	
56									4	
60	2c			c	IX		v		F 5	(aab)
62									III: (K)	
72	Dev. 1: 3a		iv	d		II	II: i		G	
73									Ps	
74									Pc	
76	3b		v	e/f	N1				Pe	
82					N2		ii		6 (L¹)	
86					N3		iii			
92	3c	a	Ic: i	a	VII		iv	Thematic Reprise and Dev.:	IV: H 7 (H)	
99³					N4				A[/B]/F/I P	
100										

Bar	Label	Hierarchy	Letter	Sub	Roman (chr.)	Roman (diat.)	Section	Theme	Group	Form	Notes
104	3d	Id: i	c/e	b	IX	III: i	8 (K)	V: P	F	(aab)	motivic returns
106		ii		b		ii					
112											
115											
118	3e	iii	a	a	VII	III: iii	9 (H)	VI: P	A/B/I J	(rondo)	motivic returns; turning point
124	3f	iv				III: iv					
126²				B:	X/XVII Chr.			VII: P			build up
130											
134								10 (L²)			
142	3g	ii									
147		iii							K		
153	3h	iv									
157											
161	A¹:				VIII	IV: i	11 (J)	VIII: Ps Pc Pe	D/L	(strophic variation)	tonal and motivic return
163	Reprise: 4a a¹	IIa: i	b		IX/X	ii	(M)				
171	4b	ii	g								
187	Dev. 2: 5a	iii			(+VII)	iii	(H)				
191		iv									
199	5b	v			X/Chr.	iv		(L) Ps Pc Pe			
207		vi									
215								Pe			
217					Coda:	Coda:		IX		(rondo)	coda
219	Coda 1: 6	Coda	Coda (a)		VII	V: i	12 (H)		B/E/M		
225	Coda 2: 7a	IIb			X	ii			IV:		
227						iii					
231	7b										
234											
237	7c										
245											

dynamic paragraph model; it is only paragraphs 6 and 7 that present the core pattern without any distortions (the apparently orthodox paragraph 4 is destabilised by the unprepared peak at the start of paragraph 5). The prominent aborted build-up in bb. 88–91 (cancelled by the '*pp*' markings in b. 92) can now be seen as the outcome of several earlier and increasingly insistent frustrations of dynamic momentum.

In Howat's elaboration of Berman's ground plan, events move slowly to begin with: after the opening's motivic, harmonic and metrical ambiguity the principal theme arrives (b. 9), followed by the main tempo (♩ = 138) in conjunction with a 'tonic' pedal in the bass (b. 36). Thematic continuity is frustrated at b. 48, and the tempo is pulled back at b. 62. In bb. 62–75, an attempted acceleration is repressed, leading to an even slower tempo (♩ = 112) at b. 76.[87] The forward propulsion of bb. 76–91 is thwarted by a return to ♩ = 112 in bb. 92–103. This whole process is repeated by bb. 104–17 and 118–29. Bar 130 is the turning-point. Momentum is stepped up at bb. 142, 147 and 153, breaking through at b. 163. More pronounced increases in dynamism at bb. 171, 187 and 199 culminate in a '*fff*' highpoint at b. 215. The tension dissipates in bb. 219–24, leading to a motivically fragmented coda.

Trezise's four-part plan largely follows Berman's analysis, as does his higher-order binary division at b. 163. Also, like Berman, Trezise detects an earlier preparation of the shift of priorities at b. 163, describing b. 147 as 'the beginning of the metamorphosis of time in "Jeux de vagues"'.[88] Indeed, his differences with Howat too prove to be trivial. The main disparities between the divisions in Howat's column 1a and Trezise's four-part schema concern bb. 92, 219 and 225. Trezise deems the start of the 'motivic returns' at b. 92 a secondary matter when compared with the 'broader scale' of events from b. 163. Nevertheless, the layout of his formal table suggests that b. 92 constitutes the major subdivision of part II, and of course Howat's critique of Berman accords the greater weight to b. 163. As regards the start of the coda, Trezise favours b. 219 because of the bass line's continuity in bb. 219–61, whereas in opting for b. 225 Howat accords priority to dynamics, tempo, texture and motives; but since Howat stresses that there is an overlap in bb. 219–25, there is no real disagreement here either.

[87] This marking was inadvertently omitted from the 1905 and 1909 editions; it is reinstated in Rolf, ed., *Œuvres complètes de Claude Debussy; La mer* (see note 22).

[88] Trezise, *Debussy: La mer*, p. 66.

There are only a few differences between Trezise and Howat (column 1b) at the sectional level: Trezise divides bb. 60–91 twice at bb. 72 and 82, Howat does so only once at b. 76; similarly, Trezise splits bb. 92–153 twice at bb. 124 and 147, Howat has a single division at b. 130. These minor divergences are partly accounted for by Howat's structural overlaps in bb. 72–6 and 126^2–30, all the more so if the latter is modified to begin at b. 124. The remaining discrepancies are easily explained. For bb. 1–162, Howat chooses principally divisions accentuated in at least three musical dimensions (motives, dynamics and tempo). Many of these divisions also coincide with textural changes. For bb. 163 onwards, he accords tempo and dynamics the greatest weight, because motivic changes have little impact on other structural parameters. Trezise privileges textural changes. He too is largely consistent; only his interpretation of b. 219 is at all problematic. Furthermore, there are only two passages in the movement in which the priorities of different musical dimensions are in enough conflict for the two men to disagree. Significantly, the first of these (bb. 60–91) intensifies the impact of the abrupt cessation of dynamic momentum that accompanies the start of the 'motivic returns' (b. 92), and the second (bb. 118–62) highlights the 'tonal and motivic return' (b. 163). Trezise's sectional structural patterns are more convincing than Barraqué's, who embraces a disconcertingly wide variety of proportions. However, Trezise possibly needs to rethink bb. 1–35. Here, he identifies two 'bar' forms (bb. 1–8 and 28–35) comprising $2+2+4$ bars, yet he classifies bb. 9–27 as a binary structure with the much larger proportions of $9+10$ bars, even though each of these sections (bb. 9–17 and 18–27) has its own aa^1a^2 plan ($2+3+4$ and $2+4+4$ bars).

In sum, Berman, Howat and Trezise concur so closely about the 'design' of 'Jeux de vagues' that it is possible to reconcile their views: see columns 2a and 2b of Table 10.2. This table acknowledges the slight differences of opinion about bb. 60–91 and 118–62 by including both interpretations of these bars. Also, it prefers the Berman/Howat positioning of the start of the 'coda', but it adapts Trezise's motivic labels in preference to those of Howat, who ignores the trumpet motive at b. 123^3 (Trezise's omission of 'B' from bb. 92–103 is presumably a simple error). For the last two parts of the movement, subsidiary changes of motivic orientation are shown in round brackets. This composite view takes into account many of the opinions of Barraqué, Cox and Dömling as well. Most importantly of all, there is widespread agreement about the tendency in the movement for

Table 10.2 *A reconciliation of Janáčeks, Berman's, Howat's and Trezise's views on design in 'Jeux de vagues'*

	Janáček		Berman/Howat/Trezise	
Bars	1a	1b	2a	2b
1	A: I	1 (A)	A: I	1 (A)
9		2a (B)		2a (B)
18		2b (B)		2b (B)
28		2c (A/B)		2c (B/C)
36	IIa: i	3 (C)	IIa	3 (D)
48		4 (D)		4 (E)
60	ii	5 (D/E): i		5 (F)
68		ii		
72	iii	6 (F): i		6a (G): i [+
76		ii		ii 6 (G) i
82		iii		6b (G) ii]
86		iv		
92	IIb/IIIa	7 (B/G/H)	IIb/IIIa	7 (A/B/H)
104		8 (D)		8 (F)
118		9 (B/H)		9 (A/B/H)
124			IIc/IIIb	10a (I): i [+
126²	IIc/IIIb	10a (I): i		
130				ii 10a (I): i
134		ii		iii
136				iv
140				v
142				vi ii
147		10b (J): i		10b (J): i iii
153		ii		ii 10b (B/J)]
163	B: III/IV	11 (C/D/I): i	B: III/IV	11 (B/D/I/K): i
171		ii		ii
179		iii		iii
187		iv		iv
199				v
211		v		
215		vi		vi
219				vii
225	Coda: IV/V	12 (B/C): i	Coda: IV/V	12 (B/E/L): i
231				ii
237		ii		iii
245		iii		iv

motivic and/or textural changes to articulate sectional divisions up to b. 163 and to be absorbed into larger patterns of continuity thereafter. There is even agreement that this process is gradual, the turning-point occurring around b. 130.

Affinity amongst the analysts extends to the functions of the outer parts. Most of the analysts label it 'introduction'. Trezise understandably has misgivings, since the term fails to account for either the expository elements of bb. 1–35 or the fact that the passage's concluding structural 'upbeat' (bb. 28–35) prefigures the expanded version of this gesture (bb. 153–62) that precedes the start of part III.[89] However, most of the other analysts also use the label reluctantly. Barraqué, for example, quickly emends it to 'preparation', suggesting that bb. 1–35 contain elements in 'subterranean' form that are foregrounded in the exposition and delineate their own microcosmic preparation–exposition–reprise–coda pattern.[90] Howat finds expository elements in these bars, which, he proposes, establish the movement's core dynamic paragraph model. Everyone seems convinced that the first part embodies a matrix of material for the entire movement. Equally pervasive is the concept of bb. 1–8 as in a sense pre-thematic, a 'gestation embryonnaire' in Barraqué's words. Concerning the 'coda', most seem to concur with Green that Debussy's 'neither open nor closed' remark is pertinent: there is motivic fragmentation yet continuity of phrase lengths, and the ostensibly new tremolo motive in bb. 231–7 adumbrates the 'storm' that erupts at the start of the finale. Barraqué is particularly expansive on this topic, implying that the clear 'cyclical' return at b. 237 of the opening gesture of the first movement has as much a disruptive as a 'unifying' effect.

Janáček's views on textbook forms are as forthright as Debussy's. In an 1886 article he takes Smetana to task for preaching suspicion of 'staré' (traditional) forms whilst relying on them in his operas.[91] Janáček promotes instead what he terms 'čisté hudební formy' (pure musical forms), arising from a piece's musical materials. Unsurprisingly then, his analysis of 'Jeux de vagues' eschews all-embracing conventional formal prototypes. Table 10.3 reformulates Janáček's markings pertaining to design in Analysis A. Janáček's view of this aspect of structure is also hierarchical. His page break indicates the largest structural division (Table 10.3, column 1): he has

[89] Ibid., p. 61.   [90] Barraqué, 'La mer de Debussy' (see note 36), pp. 29–31.
[91] 'Bedřich Smetana o formách hudebních' [Bedřich Smetana on Musical Forms], in Blažek, ed., Leoš Janáček: Hudebně teoretické dílo, I, pp. 99–103.

Table 10.3 *Summary of Janáček's 'Analysis A' of 'Jeux de vagues'*

Bars	(1) Page break	(2) System breaks	(3) Verbal remarks	(4) Paragraphs	(5) Vertical lines	(6) Rehearsal and page numbers	(7) Time segments	(8) 'Key motives'	(9) 'Harmonic motives'	(10) 'Melodic motives'
1				1)			1	a	a (c♯)	a
5										a
8									b (C)	b
9					type b		2	b	c (C♯)	b
18					type b		3	c	d (F♯)	b
28					type b		4	d (E)	♯IV	a, b
36		x		2)	type a		5	d (E)		c
48									V; HR	d²
50										d²
54										d
60				3)	type c	21	6		e (E♭⁷)	d
62										e
64									[E♭:] III⁷	=d
66										d
68				4)	type c	22	7	?	F♯: II⁷	d
72					type c	p. 44	8	e (F)		f̄
76										
82									HR	f̄
86									HR	(f)
92		x		5)	types a+b	25	9	f (A)		b, g
95										h

measure	marker	no.	chord	HR	
104		26			=d
106					=b
118					=h
122			e (F)	F♯:V	ch
126²	salient point 6)				
134		30			
136			f (A)		+k
147	type c	32			
153	7)	33			c
163	x		g (c♯)	E♭:V	d̄
171					=c
179					d̄
187	x	35	g		
211				HR	
215				E♭:V	ch
225	8) (Coda)	39	√d (E)	HR	+b
227					+b
237				HR	c

Note:
HR = harmonic reduction

left blank around two-fifths of the third system of fol. 1r. This division is at
b. 163, Berman's 'rebeginning'. The next level is partly defined by system
breaks (column 2). These two subdivisions (at bb. 36 and 92) are familiar
too, marking respectively the end of the 'introduction', and the start of the
'motivic returns'. Two additional subdivisions are indicated by verbal
remarks: 'salient point' (b. 126^2) and 'coda' (b. 225). The first of these annotations is reinforced by musical quotation of the start (bb. 126^{2-3}) of the
harps' repeated A♯/B♭s (bb. 126^2–35 and 138–41); this is Janáček's only
musical example that is neither a melodic motive nor a harmonic reduction. The second beat of b. 126 is of course the peak underlining the first
stage (bb. 124–9) of Trezise's turning-point (bb. 124–46), also forming the
highpoint of Howat's sixth dynamic paragraph (bb. 118–29) and concluding the first statement of the trumpet motive (bb. 123^3–26). Furthermore,
Janáček agrees with Trezise that the final section is the only one warranting
a conventional label, though he concurs with Howat that this section begins
at b. 225. What we have already is a higher-order frame remarkably similar
to the Berman/Howat/Trezise composite: compare columns 1a and 2a of
Table 10.2. Janáček seems undecided about the structural weight of b. 92;
the dual numeration in column 1a of Table 10.2 reflects this. As yet, there is
no evidence that Janáček is positing a structural process encompassing the
entire movement; such evidence emerges at the lower hierarchical levels.

Superficially, Janáček's eight bracketed arabic numerals (Table 10.3,
column 4) merely further subdivide bb. 36–91 at bb. 60 and 72 (six of these
numbers confirm divisions in columns 1 to 3). Both these subdivisions are
popular choices: b. 60 marks the start of the rapidly repeated wind chords
that accompany the movement's first sustained melody (bb. 62–7), nick-
named by Berman the 'smooth-sailing' motive;[92] b. 72 is the beginning of
the second major dynamic peak. (Janáček additionally marked b. 72 by a
page reference from the 1909 edition of the full score.) The principal focus
of Janáček's bracketed numerals seems to be dynamic sequences rather than
thematic structure: subdivisions nos. '(1)', '(7)' and '(8)' encompass whole
dynamic paragraphs; nos. '(3)' and '(5)' conclude at peaks; nos. '(4)' and
'(6)' both start at a peak and include at least one additional complete
dynamic paragraph; and subdivision no. '(2)' delineates the subsidiary

dynamic paragraph in bb. 36–59 (see p. 209 above). As a rule, Janáček seems to start a new subdivision at the beginning of a dynamic paragraph, unless textural and harmonic shifts assume overriding prominence at a peak: b. 72 brings a sudden change to swirling demi-semiquaver movement and the arrival of an F bass pedal that is not superseded until b. 92; b. 126^2 introduces repeated A♯s in the harps over a C♯ pedal.

That Janáček is conveying an overlying process is suggested by the remaining columns of Table 10.3, all of which supplement the ground plan outlined by the bracketed numbers. At the top of each system in Analysis A Janáček has drawn a horizontal axis, which he divides at certain points by vertical lines (Table 10.3, column 5). This layout indicates a privileging of syntagmatic analytical strategies over paradigmatic ones. It also recalls Parks's diagrammatic summary of 'De l'aube à midi'. Both men employ different types of vertical lines to convey hierarchical relationships. Janáček's order of precedence is: (a) double lines crossing the horizontal axis (bb. 36 and 92); (b) single lines crossing the axis (bb. 9, 18 and 28, and b. 92 again); and (c) single lines joining the axis from above or below (bb. 60, 68, 72 and 147). Five of these subdivisions are new. The type (b) lines at bb. 9 and 18 emphasise the tendency within the 'introduction' towards rapid and decisive changes of tempo and harmonic focus, and that in b. 28 segregates the movement's first peak. The type (c) lines in bb. 68 and 147 mark the beginning of the sustained build-ups to the peaks at bb. 72 and 153. More important is the actual disposition of the lines. Parks refers to the 'seamlessness' of the boundaries in *La mer*.[93] However, for 'Jeux de vagues' Janáček seems to be suggesting progressive 'seamlessness'. Up to b. 92 vertical lines are common, but after that there is only a single type (c) line (at b. 147). Moreover, Janáček's most decisive break seems to be at b. 36, since he obviously vacillated about whether to put a single or a double line at b. 92.

Janáček has inserted some rehearsal numbers (Table 10.3, column 6), all but four of which confirm subdivisions specified by other means. Those that create new subdivisions seem to refine his analysis of climactic structure. He singles out bb. 104 (Fig. *26*) and 153 (Fig. *32*), both peaks. Also, he draws attention to b. 130 (Fig. *30*), the start of a dynamic paragraph, and b. 187 (Fig. *35*), in which the expanded 'reprise' of bb. 36–47 gives way to the

---

[93] Parks, *The Music of Debussy* (see note 62), p. 299.

build-up proper to the final peak. Janáček's time segments (Table 10.3, column 7) confirm all the subdivisions so far except b. 104, and they add a new one – b. 215, the beginning of the final peak. All the main events in the movement's dynamic structure are accounted for by the layout of the top horizontal column of Analysis A; the principal changes of tempo are also included.

The 'key motives' are shown in Table 10.3, column 8. Altogether, they add a solitary extra subdivision (at b. 118) to Janáček's structural plan. To begin with, Janáček gave 'harmonic motives' (Table 10.3, column 9) their own identifying labels, but he abandoned this practice after b. 60; some others were allotted roman numerals; the remainder were simply written out in harmonic reduction ('HR'). The main point to note here is the distribution of 'harmonic motives', which are concentrated particularly in the passage leading up to b. 92 and rather sparse thereafter. Indeed, the second system and the start of the third in Analysis A are in general very crowded, suggesting increasing structural density towards the movement's half-way point. Janáček's motivic paragraphs (Table 10.3, column 10) are straightforward: essentially, they add subdivisions at bb. 48, 76 and 134. As columns 1b and 2b of Table 10.2 show, there are few differences between Janáček's motivic analysis and those of Howat and Trezise. Concerning the more complex passages (bb. 60–91 and 118–62), Janáček agrees with Trezise about the subdivisions at bb. 72 and 147, but he is closer to Howat in his additional singling out of bb. 126² and 134. Overall, Janáček's Analysis A clearly adumbrates the post-war view of motives as 'signposts' rather than 'the road itself'.

Janáček has written 'most homogeneous part' below b. 118, presumably suggesting that bb. 118–62 are the most 'seamless' part of the movement (there are few major divisions on the third system of the analysis: bb. 92–162). He has also inserted an arrow above bb. 163–214, the passage of sustained melodic development pointed out by virtually all other analysts. Furthermore, he initially went as far as to suggest that a 'great rondo' (by which he seems to mean 'large-scale ternary') pattern with its own 'tonally unified architectonic construction' spans bb. 163–261 (dividing at bb. 187 and 225). This scheme is rather contrived in both tonal and motivic terms, and Janáček wisely deleted it. But he did allow to stand his labelling of bb. 163–86 as a 'miniature rondo' (i.e. small-scale ternary arrangement). This contention is much less dubious, as bb. 163–70 and 179–86 do employ thematic material not used in bb. 171–8 (even if 'a' and 'b' material are actually combined in the last of these sections). What really matters, however, is that Janáček is, like Trezise et al., overtly proposing greater flow and thematic regularity from b. 163. In short, Analysis A today preempts mainstream 'Jeux de vagues' reception by more than forty years, a contention supported by Janáček's timings for the movement.

Time and rhythm

A musically gifted man measures time by music.   (Janáček, 1903)[94]

I am more and more persuaded that music, by its very essence, is not something that can be cast in a rigorous, traditional form; it consists of (rhythmicised?) colours and rhythmicised.   (Debussy, 1907)[95]

The timings in Analysis A relate to the core concept of Janáček's theory of music: 'sčasování'. This noun is derived from the invented verb 'sčasovat' (to put into time). From the verb are also derived an adjective, 'sčasovací', and a further noun, 'sčasovka' (a unit of rhythmicised time). Beckerman's postage-stamp definition of *sčasování* is: 'The word used by Janáček to describe musical events in time, especially as related to psychological phenomena'.[96] Janáček's own explanation is distributed amongst four main texts that straddle the conventional demarcation line between 'music theory' and 'ethnography': 'Sčasování v lidové písni' (*Sčasování* in Folksong; 1901), 'Základy hudebního sčasování' (The Bases of Musical *Sčasování*; c. 1905–8), 'My Opinion about *Sčasování*', and the *Complete Harmony Manual*.[97] Since the composer's views changed over the years, I will consider mainly the last of these texts.[98]

---

[94] Quoted from 'How Musical Talent Manifests Itself', in Mirka Zemanová, ed. and trans., *Janáček's Uncollected Essays on Music* (London: Marion Boyars, 1989), pp. 76–9 (p. 78).

[95] ('... je me persuade, de plus en plus, que la musique n'est pas, par son essence, une chose qui puisse se couler dans une forme rigoureuse et traditionnelle. Elle est de couleurs et de temps rhythmés.') Quoted from François Lesure, ed., *Claude Debussy: lettres 1884–1918* (Paris: Hermann, 1980), p. 166.

[96] Beckerman, *Janáček as Theorist*, p. 134.

[97] Racek and Vysoužil, eds., *Leoš Janáček: O lidové písni a lidové hudbě*, pp. 244–81; Blažek, ed., *Leoš Janáček: Hudebně teoretické dílo*, II, pp. 63–86, 15–61, 169–328.

[98] For an alternative explanation of Janáček's theory of *sčasování* see Beckerman, *Janáček as Theorist*, pp. 81–95.

Example 10.1a and 10.1b A 'sčasování' analysis of bb. 26–7 of 'Jeux de vagues'

A time-signature implies a consistently reiterated note-value and higher-order grouping of that basic unit of pulse. Metre thus arises from interaction between 'sčasovací vrstvy' (*sčasovací* layers). The minimum number of layers is two. Example 10.1a contains a short-score version of bb. 26–7 of 'Jeux de vagues'; Example 10.1b shows the *sčasovací* layers of these two bars. To Janáček, the fundamental temporal unit in a piece of music is the 'dno sčasovací' (*sčasovací* base). The duration of this basic unit falls within the spectrum of $1-1\frac{1}{2}$ seconds (between 60 and 40 per minute).

222

Janáček's suggested tempo for the music in Example 10.1a is ♩. = 60. There are two *sčasovací* bases here, each a dotted crotchet in length. Both are activated by two upper *sčasovací* layers (quavers and semiquavers), each of which contains duple and triple subdivisions of the layer immediately below (i.e. structurally more significant) in the hierarchy. Janáček terms the interaction between two or more different subdivisions of a *sčasovací* layer the 'náporový spoj' (impact connection). He contends that the mind apprehends a *sčasovací* base as a rhythmic composite ('sčasovka výsledná' (resultant *sčasovka*)) conflating all the attack points of the various voices, which it breaks down into hierarchical layers. The resultant *sčasovky* of both the bars in Example 10.1a are shown at the top of Example 10.1b. In accord with Janáček's usual practice, I have not included the tremolos in Example 10.1b, although he certainly viewed tremolos as a foreground rhythmic phenomenon.

Janáček selects the time span $1–1\frac{1}{2}$ seconds for *sčasovací* bases because he considers this fundamental temporal unit to be defined by its *harmonic* as well as its rhythmic content, and because in his view the mind requires at least a second in which to perceive a sonority as a harmonic entity in its own right.[99] In the simplest type of *sčasovací* base, the core element is a single chord ('souzvuk prostný' (simple chord)) held or reiterated throughout. Another sort of *sčasovací* base consists of a progression – labelled by Janáček 'souzvuk výsledný' (resultant chord) – in which two chords are connected by at least one sustained or restated common tone, and in which one of the sonorities (likely to incorporate non-harmonic tones, or 'melodické disonance' (melodic dissonances)) is an elaboration ('souzvuk vztažný' (subordinate chord)) of the other. A *sčasovací* base may also contain two overlapping or simultaneously sounded harmonies, one of which enriches the other ('prolínání' (percolation)). Additionally, a controlling harmony might not be sustained throughout a *sčasovací* base but may be implied by, for example, compound melodic structuring.[100] And since Janáček consistently rejects the viability of atonality (see p. 246 below), we can further assume that a *sčasovací* base might comprise a succession of two or more

---

[99]   In Janáček's early theory, $\frac{3}{4}$ second (bar = 80) is the crucial duration: see 'My Opinion', in Blažek, ed., *Leoš Janáček: Hudebně teoretické dílo*, II, pp. 15–61.

[100]   Clear instances of this type can be found in the *Complete Harmony Manual*; see for example, Blažek, ed., *Leoš Janáček: Hudebně teoretické dílo*, II, p. 293.

vertical sonorities not connected by common tones, of which one sonority is clearly the structural harmony.

Janáček labels various common sorts of *sčasovací* base 'taktové typy' (bar types). He examines, for instance, four bar types common in triple time, the three most important of which for present purposes are: type A – a bar filled by a single chord; type B – a bar divided unequally into 2 + 1 or 1 + 2 beats by a resultant chord comprising either a structural harmony embellished by a sonority containing mainly non-harmonic tones (e.g. I_{4-3}^{7-8}) or a progression from one inversion of a sonority to another (e.g. $I–I^6$); type D – a bar divided into 2 + 1 or 1 + 2 beats by a resultant chord comprising two different consonant harmonies, one if which has the more important structural role (e.g. $I–V^6$). Any of these bar types may be decorated by additional non-harmonic notes. Where there is a clear 2 + 1 subdivision of a bar in triple time, Janáček views the larger division as the *sčasovací* base proper and terms the smaller 'připojené dno sčasovací' (attached *sčasovací* base). As regards perception, whereas type A and type B bars can easily be apprehended by the mind at bar = 60, type D bars ideally need a slower tempo of around bar = 40 to be assimilated fully. Type D bars are thus in effect subdivided into units of 2/4 and 2/8. More generally, if the tempo of a piece is substantially faster than bar = 60, the listener will tend to interpret units larger than a bar as *sčasovací* bases. Conversely, if the tempo of a bar is substantially slower than 40 per minute, the listener will be encouraged to interpret a note-value smaller than the duration of the whole bar as the *sčasovací* base.

To return to Example 10.1a, Janáček would classify both of these bars as type B: each contains a resultant chord and extra melodic dissonances. At a deeper hierarchical level, bb. 26–7 form a single phrase unit (indicated by the dotted minim in square brackets at the bottom of Example 10.1b), which is in turn part of a four-bar **aa**[1] unit encompassing bb. 24–7, and so on. Janáček constantly raises hypermetrical issues in his musical examples, although he does not theorise such matters systematically.[101] The most important aspect of the two-bar level in Example 10.1b is that it allows duple and triple subdivision of the *sčasovací* bases themselves, placing hemiolas within the ambit of the impact connection. (This rhythmic

---

[101] Hypermetrical issues are introduced by, for example, Janáček's analysis of a passage from Richard Strauss's *Symphonia Domestica* in 'My Opinion' (Blažek, ed., *Leoš Janáček: Hudebně teoretické dílo*, II, pp. 37–9).

element is only weakly articulated in Example 10.1a, so it appears in square brackets in Example 10.1b.)

To summarise, in Janáček's view, metre can only be inferred from the combination of rhythmic strata and the interaction of these layers with pitch elements. He outlines his position on this in an article published as early as 1884, in which he remarks that, although rhythm and 'takt' (literally 'bar'; frequently used by Janáček to denote 'metre') are interrelated, 'Rhythm is a superior concept, takt a subordinate concept.'[102] Janáček's theory is evidently an eclectic mixture of ideas. His 'sčasovací base' and fundamental pulse of around 60 per minute are founded on the much older notions of *tempus* and *tactus*; his 'resultant sčasovka' equates to Riemann's 'rhythmic resultant'; his pronouncements on cognition derive from Helmholtz; and so on.[103] There are problems. For instance, Janáček's explanation of his criteria for determining the hierarchical significance of pitches is incomplete, and his 'bar types' scarcely seem to exhaust all possible rhythmic and harmonic configurations. More broadly, Janáček's scientific evidence is now out of date. The affective aspects of *sčasování* are even more difficult to accept. Janáček suggests that *sčasovací* layers are 'an expression and faithful reflection of certain fixed elemental moods': each layer has its own harmonic structure and affective character; in combination, different layers create 'a texture rich in emotional possibilities'.[104] The 'impact connection' has a particularly powerful affective quality, constituting a 'frustration of emotional assimilation'.[105]

Despite these problems, we should remember that many other turn-of-the-century theories of rhythm appear yet more peculiar to the modern reader. As Maury Yeston notes, nineteenth-century theorists are apt to view 'rhythm as a self-enclosed system of organizing time' and to ignore the interaction between rhythm and pitch.[106] Rudolph Westphal, for example, strangely revives the metrical concepts of the Ancient Greek thinker

---

[102] ('Rytmus je pojem nadřaděný, takt pojem podřaděný.') Quoted from 'Stati z teorie hudební' [Studies in Music Theory], in Blažek, ed., *Leoš Janáček: Hudebně teoretické dílo*, I, pp. 59–73 (p. 60).

[103] Janáček frequently cites the writings of both Riemann and Helmholtz.

[104] Beckerman, *Janáček as Theorist*, p. 84.

[105] ('... hatění asimilace citové'.) See Blažek, ed., *Leoš Janáček: Hudebně teoretické dílo*, II, p. 303.

[106] Maury Yeston, *The Stratification of Musical Rhythm* (New Haven: Yale University Press, 1976), p. 19.

PAUL WINGFIELD

Aristoxenus (c. 350 BC), who saw music in terms of 'a succession of syllabic modules' that can be classified according to 'a vocabulary of archetypal patterns (iambs, trochees, etc.)'.[107] Moritz Hauptmann draws on Hegelian dialectics, and in particular on Hegel's view (propounded in the third part of his *Ästhetik*) that rhythm derives its meaning from metre.[108] To Hauptmann, the fundamental metrical form is duple time (thesis), triple time represents an intersection of two units of duple time (antithesis) and quadruple time is made up of the intersection of two triple units (i.e. it synthesises duple and triple units). Hugo Riemann's model differs from Hauptmann's, but it is also dialectic: 'an undifferentiated duration is the thesis, a divided one is the antithesis, and groupings within the division form the synthesis'.[109] The basic synthetic unit of all music is the pattern weak–strong, or the 'Motiv', 'a single unit of energy passing from growth to decay by way of a central stress point'.[110] Two successive such units form a *Motiv* at a higher structural level, which in turn is the first part of a *Motiv* at a yet higher level, and so on. Thus 'metre' denotes the combining of single units to create larger structures, 'rhythm' applies to the internal workings of units.

In general then, late nineteenth-century theorists see rhythm as animated metre. Even Schenker, who does consider the interaction of rhythm and pitch, advances this view:

> Meter and rhythm play the same role in music as in language. The basis of meter is the division of time itself; the basis of rhythm is the organization of specific word- and tone-successions which occur within time. Meter is absolute – the time-pattern itself; rhythm is relative – the particular play of successions of words or tones within this time-pattern.[111]

---

[107] Rudolph Westphal, *Allgemeine Theorie der musikalischen Rhythmik seit J. S. Bach auf Grundlage der Antiken* (Leipzig, 1880); Aristoxenus's and Westphal's views are summarised in Yeston, *The Stratification of Musical Rhythm*, pp. 1–3 and 28–9.

[108] Moritz Hauptmann, *Die Natur der Harmonik und der Metrik: zur Theorie der Musik*, 2nd rev. edn (Leipzig, 1873); Hauptmann's ideas are examined in detail in Yeston, *The Stratification of Musical Rhythm*, pp. 20–4.

[109] Hugo Riemann, *Musikalische Dynamik und Agogik: Lehrbuch der musikalischen Phrasierung* (Hamburg, 1884), and *System der musikalischen Rhythmik und Metrik* (Leipzig, 1903); summarised in Yeston, *The Stratification of Musical Rhythm*, pp. 24–7 (p. 24).

[110] Bent with Drabkin, *The New Grove Handbooks in Music: Analysis* (see note 71), p. 90.

[111] Heinrich Schenker, *Free Composition*, ed. and trans. Ernst Oster (New York: Longman, 1979), p. 118.

226

The twentieth century has witnessed increasing divergence from this fundamental standpoint. Dissent became mainstream after the First World War, Rudolf Steglich, for example, defining rhythm as a 'meaningfully formed line of force' that is 'free of fixed models'.[112] As H. W. Fowler puts it with reference to language: 'Metre is measurement; rhythm is flow, a flow with pulsations as infinitely various as the shape and size and speed of the waves.'[113] Since then, the idea that rhythm is a subcategory of metre has died out. Grosvenor Cooper and Leonard Meyer put forward an interactive view: metre is projected by the elements that make up rhythm; equally, metre is the 'matrix out of which rhythm arises';[114] however, they are still peculiarly reliant on Aristoxenian metrics.

In 1976, Maury Yeston, Wallace Berry and Carl Schachter all published major contributions to the debate.[115] Yeston is firmly at the rhythm-as-organising-force end of the spectrum. His theoretical observations primarily concern regularly barred tonal music, and he adopts a mainly 'pitch-to-rhythm' approach. He argues that in this repertory rhythm is a hierarchical phenomenon. The rhythmic strata of a piece are created by pitch levels, which can be determined by application of the voice-leading principles of Schenkerian analysis. Metre is not an 'independent force' but arises in the rhythmic 'middleground' as the result of interaction between different layers. Moreover, although in many instances easy enough to infer, metre may at times be ambiguous or impossible to determine. Yeston's theory has its unconvincing aspects: most obviously, it fails to acknowledge that durational patterns and pitch structure are not hierarchical to the same extent or in the same way.

In Berry's opinion, rhythm is 'a generic class of *pacing, patterning, and partitioning events in music*; a facet of rhythm is grouping, a subcategory of which is represented as meter'; at the same time, metre is not 'of subsidiary

---

112 Rudolf Steglich, 'Über Dualismus der Taktqualität im Sonatensatz', *Beethoven-Zentenarfeier: Wien 1927*, p. 104.

113 Henry Fowler, *A Dictionary of Modern English Usage* (Oxford: Oxford University Press, 1926), p. 504.

114 Grosvenor Cooper and Leonard Meyer, *The Rhythmic Structure of Music* (Chicago: University of Chicago Press, 1960), p. 96.

115 Yeston, *The Stratification of Musical Rhythm*; Wallace Berry, *Structural Functions in Music* (Englewood Cliffs, NJ: Prentice Hall, 1976), pp. 301–424; Carl Schachter, 'Rhythm and Linear Analysis', *The Music Forum*, 4 (1976), pp. 281–334.

importance', because it can be 'felt at various structural levels, perhaps even at the ultimate macrolevel'; furthermore, 'metric fluctuation, however extreme, is not "meterlessness"'. Another of Berry's key notions is that each structural parameter in a piece of music has its own rhythm, and that inter-action between parameters may produce recognisable processes, such as a '*succession toward metric resolution*'. Berry's definition of metre seems unhelpfully broad. His notion of higher-order rhythm aligns him with Edward Cone, who coins the term 'structural downbeat' in connection with this concept.[116] Cone is equally sweeping: he comes near to equating a 'structural downbeat' with any clearly articulated tonal resolution.

Schachter's is the most lucid of the three 1976 texts. Like Yeston, he believes that 'Rhythm is so bound up with tonal organization that the analysis of rhythm must be compatible with our clearest and deepest insights into tonal structure', as provided, of course, by Schenker. Central to his thought is the idea that the tonal system has its own rhythmic prop-erties, such as the strong–weak–strong pattern of an *Ursatz* founded on a descent from the third degree to the tonic. This leads him to distinguish between 'tonal' and 'durational' rhythm. Metre is closer to the latter, but durational change cannot produce either steady pulse or metre. Conversely, though tonal rhythm has a high degree of independence, it can help to express metre. As a result, neither duration nor metrical accent is entirely congruent with tonal stability, and patterns of 'durational' rhythm are hierarchical only up to a point: higher-order patterns are shaped by 'tonal' rhythm.

Fred Lerdahl and Roy Jackendoff censure the 1976 texts for avoiding 'psychology'.[117] Their 1983 book is nothing less than an attempt 'to eluci-date the organization which the listener imposes mentally on the physical signals of tonal music'.[118] In the section on rhythm and metre, they argue that it 'is the interaction of different levels of beats . . . that produces the sen-sation of metre'; a piece may not have a metrical structure at all. As regards cognition,

---

[116] Edward Cone, 'Analysis Today', *The Musical Quarterly*, 46 (1960), pp. 172–88 (pp. 182–3).

[117] Fred Lerdahl and Roy Jackendoff, *A Generative Theory of Tonal Music* (Cambridge, MA: MIT Press, 1983), p. 1.

[118] Bent with Drabkin, *The New Grove Handbooks in Music: Analysis*, p. 73.

The listener tends to focus primarily on one (or two) intermediate level(s) in which the beats pass by at a moderate rate. This is the level at which the conductor waves his baton, the listener taps his foot ... The regularities of metrical structure are most stringent at this level. As the listener progresses away by level from the tactus in either direction, the acuity of his mental perception fades.[119]

Hence, unlike pitch, metre is not a significant organising force at the 'global' level. Lerdahl and Jackendoff go on to observe that each beat of the tactus as a rule has only 'a single functional harmony'.

It should now be apparent that Janáček is closer than many of his celebrated contemporaries to later twentieth-century thought on rhythm. His rejection of the prevailing turn-of-the-century idea of rhythm as animated metre allies him with Yeston, Schachter et al. (His musical examples showing rhythmic layers are actually extraordinarily similar in conception and layout to Yeston's.) Equally importantly, the centrality of psychology to his thought aligns him with relatively recent research, such as that of Lerdahl and Jackendoff. Like them, Janáček is concerned with the way the listener/analyst infers metre from 'different levels of beats' and tends to focus principally on a small number of 'intermediate' levels, even if he permits a narrower range for the tactus (40 to 60 per minute) than do Lerdahl and Jackendoff (40 to 160 per minute). All three of them even share the notion that there is one structural harmony per beat of the tactus as a rule. Naturally, Janáček's emphasis on cognition is a problem as well as a strength: there has been a rapid turnover of ideas in that area of research since the 1920s. But at worst, he must be regarded as a precursor of modern trends. Moreover, as Schachter writes about Schenker, 'if [he] never arrived at a comprehensive theory of rhythm, neither ... has anyone else'.[120] As a preliminary excursion into the field, Janáček's theory of sčasování is notable.

Table 10.4 contains the information necessary for an evaluation of Janáček's segmental timings in 'Jeux de vagues'. The first column shows Debussy's metronome markings and other tempo indications. The symbol '<' denotes an accelerando, '>' a ritardando, '+' and '−' an immediate

---

119 Lerdahl and Jackendoff, *A Generative Theory of Tonal Music*, p. 21.
120 Schachter, 'Rhythm and Linear Analysis' (see note 115), p. 299.

Table 10.4 Summary of Debussy's and Janáček's sectional timings for 'Jeux de vagues'

Bars	Debussy				Janáček			
	Time signatures	Metronome markings	Implied sectional timings	Running total	Time segments	Running total	Implied metronome markings	Seconds per bar
1	3/4	♩=116	12.41	0:00	12	0:00	♩=120	$1\frac{1}{2}$
9	3/8	♩.=72	20	0:12	12	0:12	♩.=45	$1\frac{1}{3}$
18					10[a]	0:24	♩.=60	1
28					8	0:34		
33		> [♩.=48]	3.75	0:32				
36	3/4	♩.=138	33.91	0:36	30[a]	0:42	♩=144	$1\frac{1}{4}$
60		— [♩.=120]	9	1:10	14	1:12	♩=$102\frac{6}{7}$	$1\frac{3}{4}$
62		< [♩.=128]	5.59	1:19				
68		— [♩.=120]	6	1:24	7	1:26		
72		♩.=112	19.29	1:30	35	1:33		
76		< [♩.=120]	6	1:49				
88		♩=112	32.14	1:55				
92		< [♩.=116]	9.31	2:28	66	2:08	♩=120	$1\frac{1}{2}$
112		♩.=112	9.64	2:37				
118		< [♩.=124]	5.81	2:47				
124		> [♩.=110]	3.27	2:52				
128		♩=112	27.32	2:56				
130								

136				25.5[a]	3:14		
147	< [♩=124]	8.71	3:23	12	3:39	♩=150	1⅕
153	♩=138	13.04	3:32	24	3:51	♩=180	1
163	♩=138	31.3	3:45	38	4:15		
187	< [♩=148]	24.32	4:16				
207	+ [♩=158]	13.66	4:40				
219	> [♩=148]	7.27	4:54				
225	♩=138	48.26	5:01	37	4:53		
End		(350)	(5:50)	(330.5)	(5:30.5)		

[a] = adjusted for error

Table 10.5 *Comparison of Debussy's implied sectional timings with seven recorded performances of 'Jeux de vagues'*

Bars	Debussy	Koussevitsky 1938–9	Toscanini 1942	Karajan 1964	Ansermet 1964	Ashkenazy 1986	Solti 1991	Boulez 1995
1	0:00	0:00	0:00	0:00	0:00	0:00	0:00	0:00
9	0:12	0:13	0:13	0:13	0:15	0:11	0:14	0:16
18	0:19	0:24	0:23	0:23	0:25	0:22	0:24	0:28
28	0:28	0:35	0:33	0:35	0:36	0:34	0:36	0:39
33	0:32	0:42	0:39	0:41	0:42	0:40	0:42	0:46
36	0:36	0:46	0:43	0:45	0:47	0:44	0:47	0:50
60	1:07	1:15	1:17	1:16	1:21	1:17	1:22	1:25
62	1:10	1:18	1:20	1:20	1:24	1:20	1:25	1:29
68	1:19	1:26	1:31	1:29	1:34	1:29	1:36	1:40
72	1:24	1:31	1:37	1:36	1:41	1:34	1:43	1:48
76	1:30	1:37	1:45	1:42	1:49	1:40	1:50	1:54
88	1:49	1:54	2:06	2:00	2:12	1:59	2:14	2:17
92	1:55	1:59	2:13	2:07	2:19	2:04	2:21	2:24
112	2:28	2:28	2:47	2:40	2:58	2:39	3:01	3:05
118	2:37	2:36	2:57	2:49	3:09	2:48	3:13	3:17
124	2:47	2:43	3:07	2:58	3:19	2:57	3:23	3:28
128	2:52	2:48	3:10	3:05	3:25	3:03	3:30	3:35
130	2:56	2:51	3:13	3:08	3:28	3:06	3:33	3:38
136	3:05	3:00	3:26	3:17	3:38	3:14	3:43	3:49
147	3:23	3:15	3:44	3:33	3:57	3:29	4:01	4:08
153	3:32	3:22	3:53	3:41	4:07	3:37	4:10	4:18
163	3:45	3:34	4:06	3:55	4:22	3:52	4:27	4:37
187	4:16	4:02	4:35	4:24	4:52	4:23	4:58	5:10
207	4:40	4:25	4:56	4:47	5:15	4:48	5:23	5:33
219	4:54	4:39	5:09	5:00	5:28	5:03	5:39	5:47
225	5:01	4:48	5:16	5:07	5:35	5:11	5:47	5:54
End	(5:50)	(5:42)	(6:21)	(6:10)	(6:29)	(6:24)	(6:57)	(7:05)

switch to a faster tempo and a slower tempo respectively. Column 2 gives the implied timings; where there are accelerandos etc., the notional markings on which I have based my calculations are shown in square brackets; Column 3 contains the running total. Janáček's timings for individual segments are in column 4, and his running total is in column 5; column 6 shows his implied metronome markings, and column 7 gives the duration in seconds of one bar at each of the specified tempos.

Only one of Debussy's metronome markings allows straightforward durational calculations: ♩. = 72 (= $\frac{5}{6}$ second). However, relatively close manageable fractional equivalents are available for the other three tempos (♩ = 116, ♩ = 112 and ♩ = 138): ♩ = 120 (= $\frac{1}{2}$ second), ♩ = 110 (= $\frac{6}{11}$ second) and ♩ = 144 (= $\frac{5}{12}$ second). Janáček did in fact choose ♩ = 120 for bb. 1–8. His timing of 12 seconds for bb. 9–17 implies a metronome marking (♩. = 45) less than two-thirds of the speed of Debussy's. The discrepancy is perhaps explained by Table 10.5, which gives the sectional timings for 'Jeux de vagues' from seven major recordings of *La mer*. The average timing for bb. 9–17 is $10\frac{1}{2}$ seconds, much closer to Janáček's 12 seconds than to Debussy's $7\frac{1}{2}$ seconds. It is easy to appreciate why: there are hemiolas in bb. 14–17, and there is heterophonic interplay between cor anglais and first flute in bb. 16–17; Debussy's metronome marking seems too fast. On one level, Janáček thus seems to be assuming the role of conductor here.

For bb. 18–27, Janáček writes '♩. = 1‴' (i. e. ♩. = 60) and calculates the duration as 19 seconds (!). He has erroneously added the preceding nine bars (bb. 9–17) to the ten of this section. The correct duration should be 10 seconds, close to Debussy's 9 seconds, but out of step with our seven conductors, who average more than 11 seconds. For bb. 28–35, Janáček maintains the same speed, ignoring the 'En retenant' of bb. 33–5, which would please Monnard (see p. 195 above). This brings him into both exact congruence with Debussy (8 seconds) and sharper disagreement with our conductors, who wallow for an average of $10\frac{1}{2}$ seconds. Janáček's general policy hereafter seems to be to ignore temporary tempo fluctuations, a decision that makes very little difference to his overall timing: as Pasler notes about *Jeux* (see p. 195 above), minor fluctuations in the movement tend to balance each other out.

Janáček's overall plan for bb. 1–35, proposing a tiered acceleration, is more elaborate than Debussy's. This scheme is immediately striking in the light of Janáček's theoretical pronouncements: the durations for bb. 1–8 ($1\frac{1}{2}$ seconds per bar) and bb. 18–35 (1 second per bar) are exactly those he specifies for type D bars (2/4 + 2/8) and types A and B (3/4) bars respectively. Clearly, Janáček's segmental timings are primarily an analysis of the music. His reasoning seems straightforward. In bb. 1–17 hemiola patterns become increasingly prominent, whereas in bb. 18–27 triple-time groupings are accorded priority. Bars 28–35 summarise the entire process: in bb. 28–32 the horns, cor anglais and harps twice propose a return to duplet groupings but are both times thwarted by superior forces; the passage concludes with a single line unfolding a succession of undivided dotted crotchets (bb. 33–5). Janáček's reading of bb. 1–35 of 'Jeux de vagues' establishes a blueprint for the entire movement. It should be noted that, although Janáček posits a foreground accelerando, the switch of prevailing groupings from duplets to triplets means that his fundamental unit of pulse is a more or less constant tactus ($\downarrow = 1$ second / $\downarrow. = \frac{8}{9}$ second / $\downarrow. = 1$ second).

Janáček apparently selects as his tempo for bb. 36–59 $\downarrow = 144$ ($= \frac{5}{12}$ second) – the nearest practical equivalent to Debussy's $\downarrow = 138$ – but has miscalculated the total timing for the segment. The correct calculation for these twenty-four bars (72 beats) is: $\frac{5}{12}$ second $\times$ 72 = 30 seconds. Janáček has seemingly transposed the two components of the initial fraction and then erroneously multiplied by the number of bars instead of beats: $\frac{12}{5}$ seconds $\times$ 24 = $57\frac{2}{3}$ seconds (rounded up to 58 seconds), or roughly 'three bars = 7 seconds'. While Janáček's deceleration at b. 36 is less precipitous than Debussy's, he moves the one at b. 62 forward to b. 60 and exaggerates it by choosing a seemingly very slow $\downarrow = 102\frac{6}{7}$ ($= \frac{7}{12}$ second). (Table 10.4 follows his rounding down of this timing to 14 seconds in Analysis B.) One reason for the slower tempo of these bars may be proportional elegance: the bar lengths of bb. 36–59 ($1\frac{1}{4}$ seconds per bar) and 60–91 ($1\frac{3}{4}$ seconds) are respectively minus and plus $\frac{1}{4}$ seconds in relation to that of the opening segment ($1\frac{1}{2}$ seconds). However, his 56 seconds for bb. 60–91 is also congruent with available recordings: those in Table 10.5 average 55 seconds. In fact, only Karajan (51 seconds) and Koussevitsky (44 seconds) are near to Debussy's implied 48 seconds. Once again, Janáček seems to be basing his calculations on both analytical and performance considerations: e.g. the relatively fast harmonic rhythm of bb. 82–91, and the triple-tonguing for the wind in bb. 62–7 etc.

Bars 92–142 fluctuate around ♩ = 112, then there is an acceleration up to the highpoint at b. 153. Janáček's '♩ = 120' for bb. 92–152 altogether is a satisfactory compromise, producing a total duration ($66 + 25\frac{1}{2} = 91\frac{1}{2}$) not implausibly shorter than Debussy's (97 seconds) – Karajan (94 seconds) splits the difference between them. (Janáček seems to have counted one bar too many for bb. 136–52, so Table 10.4 reduces his 27 seconds to $25\frac{1}{2}$ seconds.) This speed also results neatly in the reinstatement of Janáček's suggested opening tempo for the movement at the point where the motivic returns begin. Debussy's tempo marking at b. 147 is, in contrast, messy. He inserts 'Peu à peu animé pour arriver à 138 = ♩ au No. 32 [b. 153]' but places no new marking at b. 153 and superfluously repeats '138 = ♪' at b. 163. Superficially, this anomaly seems perhaps responsible for Janáček's assigning an intermediate tempo to bb. 153–62 (♩ = 150) and proposing that the accelerando be completed at b. 163 (♩ = 180, or '♩ = $\frac{1}{3}$'''). But the enormous disparity between Janáček's and the composer's suggested speeds at b. 163 demands that we seek another solution.

No conductor even approaches Janáček's timings of 62 seconds for bb. 163–224 and 37 seconds for bb. 225–61 (Debussy's implied timings are 76 seconds and 49 seconds): Toscanini (70 seconds) clocks the fastest time for the first of these sections, Koussevitsky and Ansermet (both 54 seconds) do so for the second; the averages are 75 seconds and a huge 64+ seconds. The average for the coda is so high because of the universal tendency (decried by Monnard) for conductors to indulge in extravagant ritardandos (not a single one is marked here by Debussy). Even Karajan succumbs to this temptation, despite the fact that one of the reasons why his 1964 recording has been so widely admired is that he adheres very closely indeed to Debussy's markings for the body of the movement (bb. 36–225) – see Table 10.5. Janáček's unwavering ♩ = 180 marking for bb. 163–261 is thus a useful corrective. It has yet more significant analytical implications. At b. 163 he returns to the tempo he proposes for bb. 18–35. This creates an overall plan in which an introductory tiered acceleration based on the proportional relationship 2:3 (bar = 40 to bar = 60) is retraced within the main part of the movement (bb. 92–152, 153–62 and 163–261), the intervening bars delaying the second accelerando.

Janáček's schema is congruent with the introduction-as-blueprint model of, for example, Barraqué, and with Berman's process of increasing frustration then accumulation of momentum. It also constitutes the most extensive application that Janáček ever made of his theory of *sčasování*. He argues that 'Jeux de vagues' embodies a large-scale progression from type D bars to types A and B. This proposition adds valuable insights about how the greater 'flow' of bb. 163 onwards is effected. It has, for instance, already been established that 2 + 1 bar divisions and hemiolas are common in the first half of the movement. The switch from patterns of 3 × 2 beats in bb. 14–17 to ones of 2 × 3 beats at b. 18 is clear-cut. Bars 118–63 are more elaborate. At first, 3 × 2 patterns (bb. 118–21, 130–1 and 138–9) and bars containing two or three different harmonies predominate. At b. 147 (the 'Peu à peu animé') 2 + 1 bar divisions become the norm, bars 153–62 containing no more than one chord per bar and emphasising the two-bar unit. The whole procedure culminates at b. 163, where the four-bar unit with no more than one chord per bar becomes the principal element of construction.

Altogether, Janáček views the rhythmic structure of 'Jeux de vagues' in terms of a higher-order process that is rendered perceptible to the listener at the tactus level of the movement's nodal points. If he distorts a few of Debussy's individual metronome markings along the way, his approach is nevertheless in keeping with the spirit of Debussy's overall tempo patterning, and it recalls a remark made by Marie Rolf in her preface to the *La mer* volume of the Complete Debussy Edition: 'While Debussy's tempo indications may allow for some flexibility in interpretation ... their proportional relationships are notated precisely by the composer, and these indications should be fully respected in performance.'[121] Lastly, Janáček's segmental timings have some important implications for the work of Roy Howat (see pp. 195–7 above). There is no question that Janáček was aware of the existence of the Golden Section,[122] and that this proportion has no bearing on his analysis of 'Jeux de vagues', which is based on the ratio 2:3. However, had

---

[121] Rolf, *Œuvres complètes de Claude Debussy; La mer* (see note 22), p. xvii.

[122] Coincidentally, Janáček actually mentions the Golden Section in some lecture notes dated 25 February, 10 March and 24 March 1924 – see Němcová, 'Was Janáček Satisfied with his Symphony the "Danube"?' (see note 81), p. 319; 10 March 1924 is the day after the *La mer* concert in Prague for which the programme has survived amongst his papers.

Howat followed Janáček's example and measured the movement by clock time instead of beats, he would have achieved much more convincing results. The primary GS according to time is 350 seconds $\times$ 0.618034 = 216.31 seconds, which is, according to Debussy's tempo markings, b. 156^1, the centre of the movement's penultimate dynamic peak. This is far more satisfactory than Howat's b. 159^1. Moreover, the secondary GS according to time occurs after 133.69 seconds, just before b. 104, where a sudden eruption inaugurates the fifth dynamic paragraph. (Howat draws a blank regarding the secondary GS.) Lower-order clock-time GS divisions net most of the remaining dynamic highpoints before b. 155. Astonishingly, Boulez's 1995 recording – despite its leisurely approach to tempo – positions the primary GS according to time (after 262.8 seconds) at b. 155 (see Table 10.5).

The calculation of simple proportions is just as rewarding. The movement's half-way point is b. 130 (also roughly the half-way point in terms of bars). This is the start of the sixth dynamic paragraph and Berman's structural turning-point. The first statement of the 'smooth-sailing' motive occurs after a fifth of the movement (b. 62), the reprise after two-fifths (b. 106); and the motivic returns (b. 92) start a third of the way through. Additionally, the centre of the final peak (at b. 217) is after five-sixths of the movement. None of these calculations involves an inaccuracy of the magnitude permitted by Howat (plus or minus 5 per cent). And, for all its brevity, this analysis has already identified a structure in which dynamic highpoints articulate GS divisions before b. 163 and simple proportional divisions thereafter. Clock-time proportions in Debussy's music obviously merit further investigation.

Motive

Motives are the shadows which do not fade in the sun, they can neither be talked away, nor shouted down – until they mature.   (Janáček, 1897)[123]

---

[123] ('[Motivy] jsou stínem, který ani sluncem nebledne, který ani odmluvit, překřičet se nedá – až doroste.') Quoted from Leoš Janáček, 'Jak napadly myšlenky' [How Ideas Came About] (1897); printed posthumously in *Opus musicum*, 6, nos. 5–6 (1974), pp. 199–202 (p. 200); Eng. trans. in Zemanová, *Janáček's Uncollected Essays*, pp. 69–75 (p. 72).

In Analysis A, Janáček labels ten 'melodic motives' with lower-case letters.[124] His conception of what constitutes a 'melodic motive' is orthodox: all but one are sharply defined gestures spanning one to two bars (the four-bar 'c' is the exception), and the majority are monophonic. He incorporates extra voices if these double the top line at an interval other than the unison or octave (see 'k', for example), apparently deeming such doublings essential to a motive's identity – scarcely a controversial viewpoint in relation to *La mer*. In a single instance ('h'; b. 95), he includes the vertical sonority that the motive arpeggiates. On another occasion – the first appearance of 'c' (bb. 36–9) – he writes out two textural strands (played by the violins and first oboe), possibly also inferring the inclusion of the additional gesture in bb. 38–9 (flutes, second oboe and cor anglais). He seems here to be making the reasonable point that 'c' embodies a larger number of melodic components than any other motive.

The quasi-mathematical symbols designating motivic categories are identical to those Janáček employs in many 'ethnographic' articles and in his *Children's Corner* marginalia (see p. 206 above). He explains these symbols most clearly in two articles written in 1923 and 1927.[125] He uses a separate letter for each distinct motivic paradigm, and he classifies five principal types of manipulation:

x^2 *rozlišování* (differentiation);

$\bar{x}$ *výběr* (selection);

$\sqrt{x}$ *nadřazení* (lit. 'superiorisation');

$= x$ *opětné poznávání/opět poznat* (re-recognition; to re-recognise);

$+ x$ *přidat* (to add).

Straightforwardly, 'rozlišování' denotes modification of a paradigm by transposition, inversion, expansion, contraction etc.; 'nadřazení' refers to the definitive form of a motive, which ends on the tonic or final; 'opětné poznávání' identifies a clear reprise of a motive; and 'přidat' designates the

---

[124] It is worth pointing out to avoid confusion that Janáček uses the Czech alphabet: a, b, c, d, e, f, g, h, ch (a separate letter in Czech), k.

[125] 'Skladebná práce v lidové písni' [Compositional Work in Folk-song] (1923) and 'Úvod ke sbírce "Moravské písně milostné"' [Introduction to the Collection *Moravian Love Songs*] (1927); both printed posthumously in Racek and Vysloužil, eds., *Leoš Janáček: O lidové písni a lidové hudbě*, pp. 442–5 and 475–84.

Example 10.2a and 10.2b Two motives related by 'selection' in 'Jeux de vagues'

insertion of an introductory or closing figure that forms an adjunct to a motive proper.

Whereas 'rozlišování' proposes a metaphorical relationship between two units, 'výběr' implies a metonymical connection. In other words, 'výběr' implies that some *sčasování* elements (i.e. features of either pitch and/or rhythm) of one motive are 'selected' by the composer (through a combination of conscious and unconscious mental processes, Janáček contends) to form the basis of another. Examples 10.2a and 10.2b show (at sounding pitch) Janáček's motives 'd' and 'f'. In his transcription of motive 'f', Janáček has bracketed the descending trichord e^2–d^2–$c\#^2$ and actually written 'výběr', indicating that he deems the motive to have 'selected' (presumably by transposition, retrogression and inversion) this component from 'd' (which opens with the trichord $b\flat^1$–a^1–g^1). A sixth category elucidated in Janáček's 1923 article (but not given its own symbol) is 'ujednocení' (consolidation) – the derivation of a superficially new motive from elements of two or more previously distinct paradigms. Janáček's principal contention in relation to (Moravian) folk music is that his six motivic categories account for all melodic material, and that individual songs are based on a small core of archetypes, which he represents by pseudo-formulae such as '$(a^2 b^2)$, $(a^2 b^2) + c$, $(a^2 b^2)$'. These archetypes are in turn constructed from a restricted number of mainly bi- and tripartite motivic chains, of which the 'drobounké rondo' (miniature rondo; i.e. aba^1) is one of the most common. Moreover, he repeatedly insists that folk music is essentially a 'primitive'

239

microcosm of 'art' music, a contention that his *La mer* analysis is clearly partly designed to exemplify.

A final category of motivic transformation pertaining to the 'Jeux de vagues' analysis as a whole – 'vyspělost' (maturity; ripening) – is alluded to by Janáček as early as 1897 in an article about the compositional process (see the epigraph to this subsection on p. 237 above). Janáček employs this term twice in connection with Analysis C, but conceptually it underpins many of his pronouncements concerning *výběr* in Analysis A. Briefly, it advances an overtly organicist conception of motive. The moment of a motive's 'maturity' is also, dialectically, the start of its process of decay, or in Schoenbergian terms, its 'liquidation'. Bars 112–18 of 'Jeux de vagues' are a good example. This passage opens with what is to most analysts the penultimate full statement of the 'smooth-sailing' motive (bb. 62–3; see Example 10.2a). Although the 'smooth-sailing' motive's characteristic ♩. ♪ ♪ ♪ rhythm is retained in b. 112, its contour is reversed, its interval span is expanded from a perfect fourth to a tritone, and in b. 113 the pitch content is condensed, the rhythm modified. Having 'matured', the motive now liquidates. On repetition in bb. 114–15 its second bar now becomes a rhythmic simplification of what was previously an accompanying ostinato (flutes and oboes, bb. 112–13). Bars 116–17 complete the liquidation process, combining only the ostinato with material derived from both bb. 100–3 of this movement and the opening of 'De l'aube à midi'. The result is a return at b. 118 of the cor anglais's tritone motive (b. 9), this time opening with the whole-tone tetrachord A–B–C♯–D♯. In effect, by 'maturing' the 'smooth-sailing' motive cedes its identity to the cor anglais motive: the last two variants of the former, like the latter, begin with an ascending [0, 2, 4, 6] tetrachord, and the ♩. ♪ ♪ ♪ rhythm that begins the former is shown to be an augmented inversion of the latter's first bar. Furthermore, the relationship between b. 114 and b. 118 is one of *výběr*. It is as though the initial tritone of the oboe variant of Janáček's 'b' at b. 118 is 'selected' from the final version of the 'smooth-sailing' motive; that the oboe brings in at b. 118 a varied reprise of the cor anglais motive (b. 9) thus renders the 'smooth-sailing' motive retrospectively its variant; or so Janáček seems to postulate.

Janáček's thoughts on motive (see Table 10.3, column 10) are more detailed than those of everyone except Barraqué and Trezise. None of his choices of paradigm is eccentric. The sole major lacuna is his omission of

Barraqué's 'motif triomphale' (first trumpet, bb. 123–6). This oversight – also made by Cox, Dömling and Howat – strongly supports the argument that Janáček had not heard *La mer* when he compiled his 1921 analysis (see p. 205 above): one could hardly miss the trumpet motive in performance but might do so if one had access only to a score. Janáček apparently singles out four motives not isolated by anyone else ('e', 'g', 'h' and 'k'). However, the '+' symbol in front of 'k' denotes *přidat* and hence suggests that this motive is subsidiary, and Janáček seems to have labelled 'g' and 'h' primarily to convey the increased motivic density of the passage (bb. 92–6) containing the first large-scale return of the cor anglais motive he labels 'b'. Moreover, he does not in fact propose that 'e' is a motive in its own right: the representation of bb. 62–7 as 'd e = d' simply classifies this passage as a *drobounké rondo*, and in fact he reduces this 'formula' to '= d' for bb. 106–11 (a varied reprise of bb. 62–7).

Janáček's main observation about bb. 1–36 is that elements from motives 'a' and 'b' are combined at the highpoint (bb. 28–36) of this introductory section. Motive 'b' is of course reiterated in bb. 28–31 by the cor anglais, and a variant in augmentation and inversion is stated by the cellos in bb. 31–6. As regards 'a', Janáček evidently considers the flute and clarinet parts in bb. 29 and 31 to relate to the flute parts in bb. 5^3–6^1, and he views the chromatically descending horn and oboe parts in bb. 28–31 to derive from not only the violin and viola lines in bb. 24–7 but also the flute parts at b. 5^2. The motivic element of Janáček's analysis is thus yet another dimension in which he deems the opening section to act as a blueprint for the entire movement, in this instance adumbrating the tendency for motivic superimposition to proliferate at major structural junctures. Turning to bb. 36–9, Janáček appears to view 'c' as a composite motive, comprising three main melodic strands. His reason for highlighting this may be the fact that textural priorities change constantly in subsequent statements of 'c'. For example, in bb. 44–5 what initially appeared to be the primary component (violins, bb. 36–9; flutes, bb. 44–5) is subordinated to a previously secondary figure (flutes, second oboe and cor anglais, bb. 38–9; violins, bb. 44–7).

At this early stage, Janáček evidently espouses the view held widely by later analysts that the harps' whole-tone glissandos in bb. 48–9 are coloration of the cellos' B pedal. It is the ensuing horn figure in bb. 50–1 that he singles out, labelling this as a variant ('d²') of the 'smooth-sailing' motive (bb. 62–3). This interpretation, implying that Janáček considers the rhythm of motivic units as important as their pitch structure, has much to recommend it. Indeed, Trezise describes Janáček's 'd²' as 'the first of a family of motives based on a ♪♩♪♪♪ or a ♩.♪♪♪ [rhythm], moving away from and back to the starting point in mainly conjunct motion'; Trezise also declares it to have 'a more assertive style of melodic construction than the trills and arabesques up to now', a characteristic that the 'smooth-sailing' motive intensifies.[126] Turning to bb. 72–91, Janáček concurs with Trezise that the clarinet motive in bb. 76–7 (his 'f') gives rise to two principal 'offshoots': solo violin, bb. 86–7; and horns 1 and 3, bb. 86–7.[127] Apparently, Janáček omits to highlight the obvious derivation of e.g. bb. 72 (flutes etc.) and bb. 77–8 (horns) from the cor anglais's tritonal 'b', but he may simply have taken this connection as read. (His derivation of 'f' from 'd' by výběr is explained on p. 239 above.)

Janáček's pinpointing of a return of motive 'b' along with an increase in motivic density in bb. 92–103 and of further motivic returns in bb. 104–17 and 118–23 are standard observations. More questionably, he singles out the harp part in bb. 95–6 instead of the much more obviously significant motivic component stated here by the violins, violas and first horn. Also, he ignores the return at b. 92 to the evanescent textures of bb. 1–2, and he allots no separate label(s) to bb. 97–103. The sketchiest part of Janáček's motivic analysis concerns bb. 123–62: as well as omitting the 'motif triomphale' (first trumpet, bb. 123–6), he neglects the wind and horn figures introduced at b. 149, and he ignores bb. 153–62, whose 'treble line', Trezise argues plausibly, 'traces the figure F♯–E–D–C, an inversion of the tritone motif of bar 9 [Janáček's 'b']'.[128]

After suggesting uncontentiously that 'c' (b. 36) returns at b. 163, Janáček dissents from the usual view of the cellos' (and second violins') gesture in bb. 171–2 as a 'new melody' (Trezise's description),[129] instead interpreting this as a derivative of 'd' (b. 62) and a relative through výběr of 'c' (b. 36). His proposal merits respect. The cello gesture and 'd' have the same basic contour centred on a [0, 2, 3] trichord (G–A–B♭ in bb. 62–3), a

126 Simon Trezise, *Debussy: La mer*, p. 64.   127 Ibid., p. 65.
128 Ibid., p. 67.   129 Ibid.

similarity highlighted through comparison of the cello line in bb. 171–2 and the first violins' variant of 'd' in bb. 68–9, where both times the framing minor third is D♯–F♯. Also, the sequence of intervals delineated by the last three notes of 'd' (rising minor third then falling semitone) provides the starting point for the cellos' alleged new motive (b. 171), and the ♩ ♩. ♪ rhythm of b. 171 can be traced back to the violas' and cellos' variant of 'd' in bb. 112–13. Moreover, on a local scale the cello gesture in bb. 171–2 grows out of the $d♯^2$–$f♯^2$ dyad framing the flute and oboe 'arabesques' beginning at b. 163 and b. 167, and the first violins' figure in bb. 171–2 both begins with a transposed heterophonic variant of the cello line and elaborates the immediately preceding oboe 'arabesque' (bb. 169–70). Motive 'd^2' (horns, bb. 50–1) even presages the more robust melodic style initiated by bb. 171–2.

Janáček is more orthodox in his designation of bb. 187–8 as a major variant of bb. 171–2 (cellos and second violins) that gives rise to its own sub-variants, which include bb. 211–14. Similarly conventional is his observation of the return of 'ch' (b. 134) at b. 215. He ignores the returns of 'b' in rhythmic augmentation at b. 191 and b. 195. (His failure to acknowledge the fragmentary reprises of the 'motif triomphale' at b. 185, b. 193, b. 197 and b. 215 is consistent with his earlier spurning of this motive.) Nevertheless, his priorities here coincide with those of, for example, Trezise, who remarks that none of the fragmentary recalls of earlier motives in his Part 3 (bb. 163–218) 'possesses the capacity to break the new-found phraseology so securely rooted in four-bar units'.[130] As regards bb. 225–61, Janáček justifiably seems concerned primarily with the section's fragmented motivic profile; hence he interprets the returns of 'b' at b. 227 etc. as *přidat*. His proposal that 'c' (b. 36) returns in bb. 237–44 is less convincing. As Barraqué demonstrates, these bars derive from the opening of the first movement and the 'motif triomphale'.[131]

Janáček's observations on motive in 'Jeux de vagues', as incisive as those of any later analysts, reveal some highly individual and valuable insights. That neither Janáček's nor anyone else's motivic analysis is in any sense definitive is surely a consequence of the movement's problematisation of the binary opposition between metaphor and metonym, as Ayrey would have it (see p. 200 above), and the tendency within 'Jeux de vagues'

---

[130] Ibid.   [131] Barraqué, '*La mer* de Debussy', pp. 44–5.

for initially apparently transient secondary textural strands to emerge later as key motivic gestures. More broadly, Janáček's ideas about motive are saturated with turn-of-the-century organicist notions. His mixture of architectural and biological vocabulary throughout Analyses A and C is commonplace in historical context, and there can be little doubt that his investigations seek to uncover in the movement a web of motivic interconnections that is greater than the sum of its parts. However, two further general points need to be made.

First, a comparison between Janáček and his more famous analyst successor Rudolf Réti is instructive.[132] Réti views music as a linear compositional process of thematic 'evolution' and resolution, a notion that has had an undeniably powerful impact on analysis in Britain.[133] Many of Réti's ideas derive from Schoenberg's writings,[134] even if Réti substantially modifies, and arguably coarsens, Schoenberg's 'two-dimensional view of formal construction' centred on 'motivic expansion, and division and demarcation' by attempting to reconcile these two dimensions. Réti wholeheartedly embraces the intentional fallacy, deeming his linear process a conscious compositional act.[135] Strikingly, Janáček is more circumspect, distinguishing as soon as 1896 between 'vymyšlené motivy' (fabricated motives: i.e. conscious manipulation of motivic connections by the composer) and 'vycítěné motivy' ('felt' motives: the creation of motivic interrelationships by subconscious mental processes).[136] Also, unlike Réti, Janáček deems a motive's rhythmic profile as integral to its identity: he constantly takes into account rhythmic variation, diminution and augmentation. Most importantly of all, whereas Réti's method reduces 'evolution' to a teleological process, Janáček's metaphor resembles more what is usually understood as 'evolution'. In Janáček's musical world, motivic species with a

132 Rudolf Réti, *The Thematic Process in Music* (New York: Macmillan, 1951) and *Thematic Patterns in Sonatas of Beethoven*, ed. Deryck Cooke (London: Faber, 1967).

133 See Bent with Drabkin, *The New Grove Handbooks in Music: Analysis*, pp. 60 and 85–8.

134 See, in particular, Arnold Schoenberg, *Fundamentals of Musical Composition*, ed. Gerald Strang and Leonard Stein (London: Faber, 1967).

135 Bent with Drabkin, *The New Grove Handbooks in Music: Analysis*, p. 60.

136 See Janáček's 1896 review of Tchaikovsky's *Queen of Spades*, reproduced in English trans. in Zemanová, *Janáček's Uncollected Essays*, pp. 176–9 (p. 178).

common ancestry struggle to assert their identities in competition with others; individual species 'mature' by both small adaptive increments and more abrupt mutations; they may hybridise; and, ultimately, they diversify, decay and become extinct. The common ancestry of motives is not determined by an initial *Grundgestalt* but can only be inferred by the listener or analyst from a piece's unfolding through time. A musical work does not embody a single linear motivic process but contains interaction between many such processes. In fact, Janáček's concept of *výběr* is somewhat akin to de Man's/Ayrey's 'contiguous metonymic relationships of chance' (see p. 200 above), suggesting with respect to 'Jeux de vagues' a genuinely modernist duality. In short, Janáček's approach to motive seems more resourceful than that of Réti or his followers.

My second general point relates to the analysis of Janáček's motivic procedures by others. Here are some of John Tyrrell's remarks on the *Vixen*:

> [Janáček's] approach was to build up sections – often a whole scene – on a single motif, with other themes and usually forming a type of loose rondo. The second half of Act 2 of the *Vixen* is bonded by the structural arch of the offstage chorus; the first half consists of a set of variations on the theme of the opening prelude. The success of the scheme depended almost entirely on his imaginative treatment of the theme, out of which he was able to coax a wide range of moods and emotions without sacrificing its identity.[137]

Tyrrell's *Formenlehre* models, his Lisztian conception of thematic transformation, and his pseudo-Rétian notions about thematic unity (unlike Réti, Tyrrell posits no thematic *process*) seem inadequate alongside Janáček's more imaginative ideas. Zdeněk Skoumal actually proposes the fossilisation of Janáček's motivic technique.[138] Skoumal's starting point appears to be two articles written by Allen Forte in the mid-1980s about Brahms and Mahler.[139] In these articles, 'the motif is seen to operate not only on the

---

137 Tyrrell, 'Janáček' (see note 4), p. 42.

138 Zdeněk Skoumal, 'Janáček's First String Quartet: Motive and Structure of the First Movement', in Beckerman and Bauer, eds., *Janáček and Czech Music*, pp. 93–105.

139 Allen Forte, 'Motivic Design and Structural Levels in the First Movement of Brahms's String Quartet in C minor', *Musical Quarterly*, 69 (1983), pp. 471–502, and 'Middleground Motives in the Adagietto of Mahler's Fifth Symphony', *Nineteenth-century Music*, 8 (1984–5), pp. 153–63.

surface but also – as Schenker had recognized – at middleground level';
Forte thus brings 'Schenkerian graphing techniques into the service of
motivic analysis',[140] even if his graphs bend conventional paradigms.
Skoumal adopts a similar quasi-Schenkerian approach to the opening
movement of Janáček's First String Quartet. To him, the 'generating idea'
for the movement is a [4, 6, 7, 11] 'cell complex' that divides into an e minor
triad and three 'three-note cells' ('x': [4, 6, 11]; 'y': [6, 7, 11]; and 'z': [4, 6, 7]),
each of which generates further motives through inversion, retrogression,
chromatic alteration, what Réti terms 'interversion' (re-ordering of the
pitches), and so on. These motives also govern the various substrata of the
middleground, resulting in 'motivic nesting on several levels' and impart-
ing 'profound order and unity' to the music. Clearly, motivic analysis of
Janáček needs fresh impetus and, though consulting the oracle is problematic, Janáček's own writings are undeniably an untapped source of potential stimuli.

Harmony and tonality

Without key there is no music. (Janáček, 1926)[141]

Janáček maintains even in late articles that tonality is essential. What precisely he means by 'tonality' is a thorny issue. Certainly, he would have dismissed a narrow (neo-)Schenkerian definition such as that proposed by
James Baker: 'Under no circumstances does the mere pointing out of tonal-
like configurations, gestures or progressions constitute a valid analysis
establishing the tonality of a composition. Rather, in order to demonstrate
that such components fulfill tonal functions, their precise roles within a
conventional hierarchical tonal structure must always be specified.'[142] In
his formative years, Janáček immersed himself in the theory and practice of
late-nineteenth-century chromatic tonality. He was rapidly persuaded 'that

---

[140] Bent with Drabkin, *The New Grove Handbooks in Music: Analysis*, p. 61.
[141] ('Bez tóniny není hudby.') Quoted from Leoš Janáček, 'O tónině v lidové písni'
[On Key in Folk-song] (1926), in Racek and Vysloužil, eds., *Leoš Janáček: O
lidové písni a lidové hudbě*, pp. 446–56 (p. 451).
[142] James Baker, 'Schenkerian Analysis and Post-tonal Music', in David Beach, ed.,
Aspects of Schenkerian Theory (New Haven: Yale University Press, 1983), pp.
153–86 (p. 186).

it was impossible to endeavour to understand recent developments in musical composition, on the basis of a diatonic system, that one must consider all twelve tones'.[143] Janáček's earliest articles on harmony and tonality thus insist that any theory of 'modern' harmony must be based on equal temperament. He writes in an 1886 essay: 'Let us distinguish, in terms of content, between chromatic key, altered diatonic, diatonic, untempered diatonic, and key derived from melodic relations [i.e. modally inflected].'[144]

If Janáček's views on tonality are at odds with Schenker's, they are not easy to reconcile with Schoenberg's either. Granted, Janáček's ideas concur with Schoenberg's general contention that 'new chords arose through the chromatic alteration of old ones, from the diatonic church modes or the whole-tone scale, or were built in fourths (rather than the more conventional thirds)'.[145] But he does not adhere to Schoenberg's notions of 'schwebende Tonalität' (floating tonality) and 'aufgehobene Tonalität' (suspended tonality). Schoenberg is unable to explain the former in full, merely citing the *Tristan* Prelude, because 'although [A minor] is to be inferred from every passage, [it] is scarcely ever sounded in the whole piece'.[146] Amongst the 'rich resources' of 'floating tonality' are 'vagrant' chords (e.g. the diminished seventh), whose 'multiple meaning' gives rise to 'roving' harmonic progressions.[147] 'Suspended tonality' is altogether more radical, involving 'almost exclusive use of explicitly vagrant chords'.[148]

To Janáček, in contrast, a 'successful' piece will eventually consolidate a tonal goal, which – even if unclear at the outset – will emerge through the

---

[143] Beckerman, *Janáček as Theorist*, p. 6.

[144] ('Rozeznáváme obsahem tóninu chromatickou, diatonicko-alteravanou, diatonickou, diatonicko-netemperovanou a tóninu z melodických poměrů.') Leoš Janáček, 'O představě tóniny' [On the Concept of Key] (1886), in Blažek, ed., *Leoš Janáček: Hudebně teoretické dílo*, I, 105–25 (p. 109).

[145] Anthony Pople, *Berg: Violin Concerto* (Cambridge: Cambridge University Press, 1991), p. 71.

[146] Arnold Schoenberg, *Theory of Harmony*, trans. Roy Carter (London: Faber, 1978), pp. 383–4 (p. 384); Janáček did single out this passage of Schoenberg's book, which he read in 1920 in the original German – *Harmonielehre* (Vienna: Universal Edition, 1911). However, Janáček's annotations throughout his copy are sceptical – see Štědroň, 'Janáček a Schönberg' (see note 1), pp. 242–50.

[147] Arnold Schoenberg, *Structural Functions of Harmony*, ed. Leonard Stein (London: Faber, 1983), pp. 164–5.

[148] Schoenberg, *Theory of Harmony*, p. 384.

tendency for large-scale harmonic progression to be centred on recognisable patterns of consonance and dissonance. In his own terms, a 'successful' piece will ultimately privilege the triadic 'jádro' (kernel) of its constituent chords, despite frequent modifications through chromatic alteration, or the addition of either extra notes ('zhušťování') or entire chords ('prolínání' (percolation)).[149] He declares forthrightly in his *Complete Harmony Manual*: 'The theory of thickening must not obscure the chordal kernel; thus the harmonic superiority with regard to the first degree, its corporeality, is evident in each chord, the certainty of closure and modulation is not lost.'[150]

Janáček would probably have been more favourably disposed towards a third concept of tonality suggested by Schoenberg, 'extended tonality', which 'may contain roving segments, though, on the other hand, various regions may occasionally be firmly established'.[151] As Anthony Pople observes, this leads 'beyond [Schoenberg's] description of suspended and floating tonality, finding a new accommodation for broadly spaced references'. Pople's own exploration of 'extended tonality' as the basis for an analysis of Berg's Violin concerto offers a useful framework for an examination of Janáček's harmonic analysis of 'Jeux de vagues'.[152] Admittedly, this concept does not provide 'a systematic means for the structural analysis' of Berg's Violin Concerto or any other work. But it does highlight 'the central role of recognition in musical understanding'; and so,

> In this context, the role of analysis is to show how such recognitions may be made via a range of models, comprising linear resources, individual harmonic types, schematic progressions ... Just how the 'tonality' is extended will be seen from the ways in which they interact in the interpretation of specific musical passages.[153]

Pople's starting point is Schoenberg's suggestions that the [0, 3, 6, 10] half-diminished seventh and chords of the ninth and thirteenth are 'less rigidly

---

[149] For further details see Beckerman, *Janáček as Theorist*, pp. 72–9.

[150] ('Teorie zhušťovací neukrývá jádra souzvukového, proto povýšenost harmonická vzhledem k I. stupni, plastičnost, je zjevná v každém souzvuku, jistota závěrová a modulační se neztrácí.') Leoš Janáček, *Complete Harmony Manual*, in Blažek, ed., *Leoš Janáček: Hudebně teoretické dílo*, II, pp. 169–328 (p. 248).   [151] Schoenberg, *Structural Functions of Harmony*, p. 164.

[152] Pople, *Berg: Violin Concerto*, pp. 65–90.   [153] Ibid., p. 72.

"functional"' than 'triads and 6–5 chords', and that, conversely, the dominant seventh's cadential quality can be applied to, for instance, the diminished seventh and whole-tone sonorities. Most pertinently as regards 'Jeux de vagues', the [0, 4, 10] dominant-seventh outline (e.g. B♭–D–A♭) can be expanded to [0, 4, 6, 10] (B♭–D–E–A♭), thereby combining the original with its tritone transposition (E–G♯–D) and 'drawing the associated diatonic scales into a "vagrant" harmonic complex'. In his analysis of bb. 200–7 of the Violin Concerto, Pople contends that in bb. 200–3 'schemata of function harmonic progression are recognisable', and that a comparison between bb. 202–3 and bb. 206–7 'illustrates how the "applied dominant" root progression by ascending fourth may be correlated with a parallel semitonal descent of dominant-quality chords through the tritone substitution routine in 1930s jazz harmony'. Additionally, 'the contrapuntal motion within the duration of each chord may frequently be aligned with an established linear resource, such as the diatonic scale, the dominant-quality [0, 2, 4, 6, 7, 9, 10] "acoustic" scale, the whole-tone scale' etc. Pople goes on to observe a 'tritone link between tonal orientations in connection with the musical *objets trouvés*' (the Carinthian folk-song and Bach's 'Es ist genug'), and to argue that this link 'is involved in the alignment of the concerto's series with the chromatic expansion of diatonic scalar resources'. Nevertheless, the work's 'constant stream of tonal configurations both invites and fails to secure an integrated tonal reading'. In sum, 'The music is not organically, self-referentially coherent, but "makes sense" because at every point *something* in it is always recognisable through an active cognitive framework.'[154]

Returning to Janáček's Analysis A, his treatment of harmony is more fragmentary than that of other parameters. This is true of 'Jeux de vagues' reception in general. However, what Janáček has written does outline a penetrating harmonic approach to the whole movement. Example 10.3 presents an amplified summary of his views: his 'key motive' labels, conventional key designations and roman numerals appear below each system; passages apparently not accounted for in his analysis are shown in square brackets. Janáček identifies seven different 'key motives', labelled 'a' to 'g'. Four of these recur, and at b. 68 he writes an additional '?'. Hence,

---

[154] Ibid., p. 89.

Example 10.3   An amplification of Janáček's harmonic analysis of 'Jeux de vagues'

Example 10.3   (*cont.*)

superficially, he partitions the movement into thirteen segments, each of which is also articulated by clear divisions in other structural dimensions (see Table 10.3). The starts of eight of the thirteen segments simply coincide with new key-signatures (bb. 1, 9, 18, 28, 36, 72, 92 and 163). But common-practice criteria are obviously not solely responsible for Janáček's decisions: the bass C in bb. 9–17 is approached via F♯, the sharpened fourth in bb. 9–13 renders these bars entirely referential to the diatonic collection on G, the repeated movement of B to A♯ in bb. 14–17 implies a reference to the [0, 2, 4, 6, 7, 9, 10] acoustic scale on C, and so on. Janáček's analysis evidently inhabits the domain of 'extended tonality'.

Closer scrutiny of Janáček's partitioning unearths some further complications. Both b. 18 and b. 36 are designated 'd (E)', which suggests that he is proposing that bb. 28–35 are a structural upbeat to b. 36. Similarly, bb. 163 and 187 are both labelled 'g', this time presumably because the G♯ pedal underpinning bb. 171–214 is at b. 187 (the 'En animant beaucoup') once again sustained by the double basses, as it was in bb. 171–8 (in bb. 179–86 it is merely reiterated on the first crotchet of each bar). Hence there are actually only eleven segments, two of which subdivide, and a criterion for segmentation that is more important than a change of key-signature is the arrival, or start of a clear progression towards, a new bass pedal. As Example

251

PAUL WINGFIELD

10.3 shows, the eleven segments are centred on the following pedals: F♯ (bb. 1–7), C (bb. 8–17), G♯ (bb. 18–27), E (bb. 36–46), G♯ (bb. 68–71), F (bb. 72–3), A (bb. 92–7^1), C (bb. 104–11), A (bb. 118–24^2), E (bb. 163–70) then G♯ (bb. 171–214), and E (bb. 225–61). This scheme seemingly ignores seven prolonged bass pedals in the movement: B (bb. 48–57), D♯ (bb. 60–7), C♯ (bb. 126^2–9), G (bb. 131–9), and B♭ (bb. 155–62, 215–18 and 237–44). However, Janáček includes all but one of these at the next hierarchical level ('harmonic motives'), apparently viewing each of them as subsidiary to an adjacent pedal because, together with these neighbouring pedals, they form progressions that can be regarded as quasi-functional. The exception is the G of bb. 131–9, a clear omission on Janáček's part that is in keeping with his patchy analysis of motive in bb. 130–62 (see p. 242 above).

Yet another criterion for segmentation is revealed by Janáček's marking with *výběr* symbols (see p. 238 above) of two 'key motives' at b. 104 and b. 118. In his 1923 'ethnographic' article detailing categories of motivic transformation, Janáček also applies some of these categories to tonal procedure.[155] In this context, 'rozlišování' denotes either the restatement of a body of material in another key or, more broadly, a structurally significant modulation, and 'výběr' is applied to both the reiteration of material with chromatic alteration of some of its scale degrees and the introduction of a new collection based around the tonic or a previously tonicised scale degree. A comparison of bb. 72–3 and bb. 104–11 of 'Jeux de vagues' exemplifies this. The former passage, based on an F major triad and labelled 'e (F)' by Janáček, refers to the diatonic collection on C. The resulting [5, 7, 9, 11, 0, 2, 4] scale would be designated 'Lydian mode on F' by many analysts, but to avoid confusing full-blown modal writing and mere modal inflection I shall prefer the more neutral alternative label 'F scale on F'. Bars 104–5 – 'ē (F)' – contain a dominant major ninth on C, which is expanded in bb. 106–7 to the dominant-quality [0, 2, 4, 6, 7, 9, 10] acoustic scale on C. In short, the core chords of the two passages are I and V^9 of F respectively, but the linear elaborations of the two chords are different. There are similar divergences between bb. 92–6 and bb. 118–24^2. Bars 95–6 – 'f (A)' – are entirely referable to the [9, 11, 1, 3, 4, 6, 7] acoustic scale on A, distilled from the larger [9, 11, 1, 3, 4, 5, 6, 7, 8] collection in bb. 92–4. On the other hand, bb. 118–21 – 'f̄

[155] See note 125.

252

(A)' – outline a six-note collection, [9, 11, 1, 3, 4, 6], that is a subset of both the acoustic and the F scales on A. This passage is framed by bb. 111–17, referable to the F scale on D, and bb. 122–4^2, which circumscribe the acoustic scale on A. The change of scalar orientation that Janáček proposes for bb. 118–21 is thus immediately perceptible in context. (The apparent minor inconsistency in Janáček's labelling – for bb. 104–11 he acknowledges the V^{13} quality of the acoustic scale but does not seem to do so for bb. 92–6 and 122–4^2 – is simply the result of the A major key signature at b. 92.) To summarise, Janáček's 'key motives' are recognisable tonal centres, defined most saliently by prolonged bass pedals supporting the principal chords of schemata of established harmonic progressions; also, the return of a 'key motive' may be marked by a change in its type of linear elaboration.

Janáček's actual key designations for 'Jeux de vagues' are mainly familiar. Entirely orthodox are his choices of E for bb. 28–43 and 225–61, F for bb. 72–3 and 104–11, and A for bb. 92–6 and 118–24^2. He disagrees with Trezise about bb. 163–70, the latter viewing the core E–G♯–B♯–D♯ sonority of bb. 163–5 and 167–9 as 'a version of the tonic harmony'.[156] But Janáček's reading of the passage as centred on C♯ is more coherent (see Example 10.3). The E pedal in bb. 163–5 and 167–9 is each time undermined by the B♯, which is stated in three different octaves and twice moves up a semitone to C♯ in bb. 166 and 170, rather than down a semitone to B, as the C♮ does in bb. 36–43: Debussy's orthography says it all. The result in bb. 166 and 170 is a root-position C♯ minor triad that progresses to one on G♯ and thereafter to V^9 of C♯. Finally on the topic of 'key motives', Janáček appends to the label 'd' applying to bb. 225–61 the symbol he uses for motivic *nadřazení* (see p. 238 above). In tonal terms, this symbol denotes the point where a tonal centre is established unequivocally.

By drawing attention through *výběr* symbols to salient changes of contrapuntal motion around two temporary tonal centres, Janáček seems to identify a major element of the pitch structure of 'Jeux de vagues'. Around three-quarters of the movement consists of passages either purely referential to a familiar collection (diatonic, acoustic, whole-tone and harmonic minor, in order of frequency of occurrence) or predominantly referential to such a collection, in that the extra pitches are grace notes or are deployed

---

[156] Trezise, *Debussy: La mer*, p. 93.

both rhythmically and gesturally in the manner of passing notes, neighbour notes and appoggiaturas. And, in fact, such passages account for all of Janáček's 'harmonic motives' (see Table 10.3, column 10). The exception is bb. 82–4[5], whose string parts he quotes. Although this passage contains all twelve pitches of the chromatic collection, C^9 is the core harmony, and in b. 83 the solo violin refers to the acoustic collection, arranged as a [4, 6, 7, 9, 10, 0, 2] scale.[157] Janáček's reasons for designating these bars a 'harmonic motive' thus seem clear. Equally strikingly, few of the passages purely or predominantly referential to familiar collections are not covered by Janáček's 'tonal' and 'harmonic' labels. There are only two major discrepancies: Janáček apparently ignores bb. 112–17 (F scale on D) and bb. 130–3 (D scale on G), although he may have deemed bb. 112–17 to have been covered by the tonal designation ('A') at b. 118. The sections of 'Jeux de vagues' not accounted for by Janáček's 'tonal' and 'harmonic' motives involve more rapid chromatic motion and less obviously functional chords (see Example 10.3), and they normally occur during build-ups (e.g. bb. 24–7 and 97–9) or just before major structural junctures (e.g. bb. 56–9 and 219–24).

When he was writing Analysis A, Janáček initially allotted individual lower-case letters to both 'tonal' and 'harmonic' motives. Also, he seems to have been slightly confused to begin with about what he meant by each of these terms: the first four 'harmonic motives' (at bb. 1, 8, 9 and 18) have key designations in brackets. From b. 68 he consistently gives only 'tonal motives' individual tags, and from b. 28 he labels only salient non-tonic chords within a key area 'hm'. (The anomalies concerning bb. 1–27 are rectified in Analysis B.) His choice of C♯ minor for the ambiguous opening of the movement – though in accord with, for instance, Barraqué's views[158] – is highly debatable. Janáček's reasoning here seems essentially to be retrospective: bb. 1–35 lead to the movement's first significant E pedal at b. 36, and he sees bb. 163–225 as embodying a large-scale progression from C♯ minor to E major. Once again, he promotes the 'introduction-as-blueprint' idea.

---

[157] This ordering of the acoustic collection is common in Eastern European folk music: for further information, see Elliot Antokoletz, 'Transformations of a Special Non-diatonic Mode in Twentieth-century Music: Bartók, Stravinsky, Scriabin and Albrecht', *Music Analysis*, 12 (1993), pp. 25–46.

[158] Barraqué, '*La mer* de Debussy', p. 29.

Janáček assigns the incomplete diatonic collection in b. 8 its own label and key designation ('C'), presumably in recognition of the structural overlap in bb. 8–9. At b. 9 – where the main theme is introduced and the diatonic collection completed – he shows the F scale on C affiliation by writing 'C #IV' (i. e. C major with a sharpened fourth). He labels bb. 18–27 'F#', ignoring the C# major key-signature, reasonably according priority to the F scale on F# transposition of the main theme in the flute. From b. 28, Janáček puts the hierarchisation of 'tonal' and 'harmonic' motives fully into effect. He sees the next 'harmonic motive', the $B\flat^9$ of bb. 28–31, as an altered dominant of E. This is the first of four such progressions in the movement. As Trezise observes, 'The "dominant" that functions against the tonic in "Jeux de vagues" is not founded on B♮ until the coda; it is usually called a "dominant major ninth on B♭".'[159] Nevertheless, B does appear in the bass at b. 48 as the root of an [11, 1, 3, 5, 7, 9] whole-tone scale. Janáček has no hesitation in labelling this 'V' in relation to the E of b. 36, clearly demonstrating that he concurred with Schoenberg's view that whole-tone chords can function as altered dominants. Trezise examines in some depth whether the [11, 5, 9, 1] chord at b. 48 can be said to function as V of E, concluding that it is 'heard as a lone relic of a harmonic order that has yet to define a dominant-tonic relationship'.[160] Janáček too appears to view the I–V progression outlined by bb. 36–57 as in no sense definitive: he withholds the *nadřazení* symbol from the tag representing E major ('d') until the 'Coda'.

All of Janáček's annotations in the 'smooth-sailing' section (bb. 60–71) are restricted to the level of the 'harmonic motive', with exception of the '?' (b. 68). Bars 60–3 and 66–7 are centred on '$E\flat^9$', bb. 64–5 on '[♭] III^7' in E♭ (i. e. F#$^6_5$). At b. 68 the bass moves to the expected G#. The principal chord above this, G#^{13} ('II^7' of F# to Janáček), is also of dominant quality. But the implied cycle-of-fifths progression is abruptly terminated by the sudden shift of orientation to the F scale on F at b. 72. Janáček's '?' thus suggests that the potential functionality of the progression in bb. 60–71 is thwarted by the harmonic lacuna between b. 71 and b. 72, not that tonality is 'suspended' at this point. The next section, much of which Janáček writes out in harmonic reduction, culminates in a second important $B\flat^9$ chord (bb. 90–1). This time it is the F that occurs on the first beat of the bar in the bass,

---

[159] Trezise, *Debussy: La mer*, p. 93.   [160] Ibid., pp. 63–4 (p. 64).

and a last-minute modification to B^{07} is followed by a deflection to A^7 instead of E.

As previously remarked, Janáček's harmonic analysis of bb. 92–162 is cursory. However, only bb. 130–51 receive no elucidation whatsoever. The chromatic interpolation in bb. 97–9 leads to E^9, which has a straightforward relationship with the preceding $A^{(7)}$ in bb. 92–6, as does the G^9 in bb. 102–3 with the ensuing C^9 (bb. 104–11). Similarly, bb. 112–24^2 are centred on A (E^7–D–A–A^7). Janáček next interprets the $C\sharp^{13}$ in bb. 126^2–9 – approached via a strong D$\sharp$–G$\sharp$ bass progression – as 'V of F$\sharp$', apparently seeing this chord (marking the half-way point of the movement) as the goal of the two earlier $G\sharp^{9/13}$ sonorities (bb. 18 and 68). He omits the subsequent tritonal shift to a G minor triad with an added sixth (b. 130). This sonority is reordered as $E^{\varnothing7}$ at b. 147, leading to the movement's third important $B\flat^9$ chord (b. 155), which he does single out. Janáček's priorities seem clear: his annotations relating to tonality and harmony are most detailed with reference to build-ups and structural highpoints.

At b. 163 the resolution of $B\flat^9$ is once again inconclusive, an unstable $E^{7\sharp}_{5\sharp}$ chord ceding to i–V^9 in C$\sharp$ minor (see p. 253 above). The movement's main build-up now takes place over the G$\sharp$ pedal. Janáček isolates the final stage of this (bb. 211–14) by means of a harmonic reduction, ostensibly because, although there is still a G$\sharp$ pedal here, the $B\flat^9$ returns in anticipation of its root-position statement in bb. 215–18. Crucially, the latter – the last of the four major $B\flat^9$ chords in the movement – is elaborated contrapuntally for the only time by the entire [10, 0, 2, 4, 5, 7, 8] acoustic scale on B$\flat$. As Janáček shows in harmonic reduction, the bass E that follows (b. 225) now initiates an altered V^9–I progression (bb. 237–45), after which the 'thickened' E chord is gradually reduced to its triadic 'kernel' (b. 258); and so, E major at last achieves *nadřazení*. Trezise describes the whole procedure as follows: 'There is a cumulative, end-directed process, which begins with a vague idea of a tonic and ends with clear-cut cadences onto a tonic triad derived from a series of prototypes.'[161] Janáček's goal-directed outline differs from Trezise's only in its highlighting of the start of the final tonic-defining progression (b. 225) as opposed to the point where the final bass E arrives (b. 245).

[161] Ibid., p. 93.

At a more detailed level, Janáček's conception seems to have much in common with Schoenberg's notion of 'extended tonality' as fleshed out by Pople. The harmonic language of 'Jeux de vagues' is centred on 'schemata' of functional or altered functional progression (especially root progression by a fourth), 'the contrapuntal motion within the duration of each chord' frequently referring to an 'established linear resource'. At the movement's core is a Bb^7–E 'vagrant' harmonic complex. This derives from the Bb–D–Ab dominant seventh outline, whose V^{13} expansion (Bb–D–F–Ab–C–E–G) exhausts the acoustic scale on Bb (Bb–C–D–E–F–G–Ab). That acoustic collection does not contain the tonic it implies (Eb), but is instead centred on a Bb–E polarity, as is the F scale on E, the other major diatonic scale associated with the complex (E–F#–G#–A#–B–C#–D#). Hence Bb^9–E is the main progression in the movement. In addition, the opening trichords of the two principal scales can be combined to produce a complete whole-tone collection, Bb–C–D–E–F#–G#, which, together with its other transposition, becomes an important subsidiary linear resource. Furthermore, the acoustic scale on Bb and the F scale on E share the whole-tone subset E–G#–Bb. The two key progressions in the movement are thus $G#^9$–Bb^9–E (bb. 18–36 and 171–225). The first of these follows up with B^9, the bass line then moving back to G# (and thereafter to D#) instead of resolving (bb. 48–60). In contrast, the second one does lead to B^9–E (bb. 237–45); and because B belongs only to the F scale on E and not to the acoustic scale on Bb, E finally establishes its 'superiority'.

Of course, unlike Pople, Janáček is firmly wedded to the notion of organic coherence. This is hardly surprising in historical terms. Also, as Trezise's analysis evidences, the 'illusion' of unity is much more compelling with regard to 'Jeux de vagues' (1905) than to Berg's Violin Concerto, composed thirty years later (1935). Nor should such considerations be allowed to obscure the fact that Janáček's actual approach to analysing 'extended tonality' is entirely 'mainstream'.

Analysis B

In Analysis B the columns are once more laid out horizontally. The top one is reduced to segmental timings and a total duration for the movement. There are a few refinements, of which the additional brackets above the durations for bb. 92–162 and 163–261 are the only significant ones. These affirm two of the major structural divisions and the process of increasing continuity implied in Analysis A. In the second column, the 'tonal motives' are emended, partly for the sake of conciseness (the reiteration of 'g' at b. 187 is deemed unnecessary), but mainly to resolve the initial anomalous overlaps between these and and the 'harmonic motives' on the first system of Analysis A. The 'harmonic motives' at b. 1 (C♯), b. 8 (C) and b. 9 (C⁴♯) become 'tonal motives' 'a' to 'c', and the 'tonal motives' at b. 18 and bb. 28 and 36 are conflated as 'd̄ (F♯–E)'. The last of these modifications is noteworthy. Now the important $G\sharp^9–B\flat^9–E–B^9$ progression spanning bb. 18–57 is seen as an indissoluble tonal unit. In keeping with this, Janáček inserts a '+' sign between the 'tonal motive' 'g' (b. 163) and the return of 'd' (b. 225): bb. 171–245 outline a large-scale $G\sharp^9–B\flat^9–E–B^9–E$ progression. The *výběr* symbol above the first 'd' thus appears to signify that the inconclusive tonal progression here is reiterated and completed in the closing stages of the movement. The total of ten tonal segments excludes the '?' (bb. 68–71). The 'harmonic motive' column, now the bottom one of the four, is left blank: Analysis B focusses on higher-order issues.

The 'melodic motives' in column 3 are also pruned: Janáček retains the same ten lower-case letters, but he leaves out the repetitions of 'a' at b. 28, 'd' at bb. 50, 54 and 68, 'ch' at b. 215, and 'c' at b. 237. The last of these omissions removes a dubious analytical proposition. Overall, the composer retains only the primary motivic statements within each of the ten principal tonal segments. A further condensation of the motivic dimension is introduced by the additional circles around some of the motivic labels and the curved line connecting the first statements of 'b' and 'c'. Janáček continues his distillation of the movement's motivic structure on fol. 2v.

Analysis C

C3 and C4: motivic process

In Analysis C3 (Appendix 10.3), Janáček originally reduced the motivic dimension of 'Jeux de vagues' to just four paradigms: cor anglais, b. 9; violins, bb. 36–9; cor anglais, bb. 62–3; violas and first clarinet, bb. 134–5. He later added a fifth (harps, bb. 48–9). He writes out each of his five 'pivotal motives', numbered '1' to '5', emblemising the 'miniature rondo' structure of bb. 62–7 and 163–86 through bracketed quasi-mathematical formulae. For motives '1', '2', '4' and '5', their principal modes of transformation are specified verbally. Motives '1', '4' and '5' also all bear the additional label 'a^2', while motive '2' – the only one to be assigned the label 'vyspělost' (maturity) – is allotted the extra tag 'a^3'. Janáček appears to be suggesting that these four core motives are not only related to one another, but that together they outline the evolutionary process of birth, growth, maturity and decay that can normally be traced in relation to individual motives. Naturally, Janáček is proposing diachronic rather than synchronic relationships between the four paradigms. The way in which the 'smooth-sailing' motive ('4') ultimately cedes its identity to the cor anglais motive ('1') in bb. 112–18 is examined on p. 240 above. Similarly, it is a variant of '1' based only on the attached arabesque (oboes, bb. 24–5 and 26–7) that is most closely related to the first appearance of '2': bb. 25, 27 and 36 are essentially identical rhythmically, and all three of these bars are based exclusively on the trichord D♯–E♯–F♯. To detail every one of the other such connections would be otiose. Noteworthy is the fact that motive '3' is even incorporated into this process: its whole-tone glissandos expand the the opening tetrachord of '1' (which is itself inverted at the end of the second statement of '2' in b. 43), and they also provide the gestural and harmonic basis of the prototype for the 'smooth-sailing' motive introduced at b. 50.

Janáček expands Analysis C3 in a table headed 'Their order (Architectonics)' (Analysis C4). This table's structural divisions vary little from those implied in Analysis A, as presented in Table 10.2, column 1b – of the twelve main segments identified there, only the sixth (bb. 72–91) is not marked out in Analysis C4. The other modifications are the subdivision of the third segment at b. 54 and of the eleventh at bb. 187 and 215. Analysis C4 confirms conclusively that Janáček is proposing an overlying motivic process. To begin with, motivic interconnections become increasingly intricate ('complication'). The horizontal line Janáček draws above bb. 104–63 indicates a tightening of the motivic web and concurs with his insertion of 'most homogeneous part' beneath the equivalent section of Analysis A. He seemingly posits an additional motivic connection by ringing the return of motive '2' (bb. 104–17) and writing 'hm' (harmonic motive) with a *výběr* symbol on top above b. 134 (motive '5'). Bars 104–11 and 134–5 (as well as bb. 140–1) are both centred on C^9 but refer respectively to the acoustic and to the whole-tone scale on C (i.e. harmonic *výběr* occurs). Janáček draws into his tonal scheme for the movement a passage he ignored in Analysis A: he views bb. 130–41 as relating to both bb. 104–11 and bb. 72–3.

The movement's progressive 'complication' reaches a preliminary highpoint with the reprise of motive '2' in bb. 163–70, which incorporates a clear reference to motive '5' (cf. b. 134 and the second violin part of b. 163) in addition to the connections already established with '1' and '4'. Trezise states that, while the first statement of '2' (bb. 36–43) 'emphasises . . . the individual bar', the return accentuates the larger four-bar unit, leading to the greater flow of bb. 171–214.[162] Such considerations probably lie partly behind Janáček's writing 'vyspělost' at this point. Another significant factor seems to be that the return of '2' contains the seeds of this motive's destruction. In particular, the E pedal is undermined then dismissed in both four-bar units, Janáček representing the reorientation to C♯ minor by 'tm' (key motive) with a *výběr* symbol on top. The result is that at b. 171 '2' is brushed aside; its final appearance (bb. 179–86) is then demoted to the status of counter-motive. The apparently new motive at b. 171 'selects' the D♯–F♯ outline of bb. 163–5, inaugurating the movement's final phase ('výběr') of increasing motivic 'complication'. The protracted build-up to the final dynamic highpoint (bb. 215–18) witnesses the combination, and textural subjugation, of earlier motivic profiles within the succession of variants of the four-bar model introduced in bb. 171–4. (The 'd e = d' above this part of the analysis appears to relate to the 'great rondo' originally proposed then later deleted in Analysis A.) A turning-point is reached at b. 215, where the 'complication' process is brutally terminated by the return of motive '5'. There ensues a precipitous descent into motivic fragmentation followed by extinction. Janáček summarises the entire plan beneath Analysis C4 with a crescendo mark that extends up to b. 215 and a diminuendo mark encompassing bb. 225–61.

Analyses C3–4 thus shed valuable light on two of Janáček's commonly used terms: 'complex reactions', and the 'complicated work'. In Analysis C3,

[162] Ibid., p. 77.

beneath 'Pivotal motives' he writes 'they stand out through complex reactions. Not to belittle simple reactions'. Further information is provided by the ink text of fol. 3v of the *La mer* analysis, which reads: 'Progressive work; inasmuch as there are complex reactions: always under the influence of precursors, to follow / the advice: do not complete closure! / Living "cutting" / Time and *object*... (complicated work) / Idea and maturity (complex reactions) / Material and affective newness'.[163] On a technical level, 'complex reactions' thus seem to be intricate syntagmic connections between the motives in a piece. Analyses C3–4 are a detailed exemplification of this with reference to 'Jeux de vagues', a particularly complex specimen. Also implied by Analyses A–C overall is that the movement is a 'complicated work' because it unfolds a dual process: its motivic dimension is cyclic, its tonal one end-weighted.

An insertion in Analysis C1 explains 'jednoduché reakce' (simple reactions), the counterpart of 'complex reactions'. In isolation, motive '3' embodies 'simple reactions' because, despite its connections with bb. 50–1 etc., it is not varied in the course of the movement. Rather, it twice occurs in the same form at points (at b. 48 and b. 225) where thematic momentum is disrupted regardless of a progression towards tonal clarification ($B\flat^9$–E–B^9 in bb. 28–57, $B\flat^9$–E–B^9–E in bb. 215–45). In short, the 'simple reactions' mark points of bifurcation in the dual motivic and harmonic process unfolded by 'Jeux de vagues'. Finally, another definition of the 'complicated work' explains the presence of Analysis C1. A Janáček pupil, Osvald Chlubna, transcribed the following from one of the composer's 1922–3 lectures: 'If there is connected to a tone yet another sensual image, for example something I hear, see etc., then such a connection is the essence of a complicated work.'[164] This statement brings the referential dimension of music into play. To Janáček, Debussy's complex motivic workings in 'Jeux de vagues' must have extra-musical significance.

---

163 ('Práce postupná; jelikož jsou to slož[ité] reakce: vždy pod dojmem předcházející pokračovat / rada: neukončuj závěrem! / "Výsek" životní / Čas a *věc* ... (Komplikační skladba) / Idea – a vyspělost (slož[ité] reakce) / Novost věcná a citová.')

164 ('Je-li s tónem spojena i jiná smyslová představa, na př. něco, co slyším, co vidím atd., pak takové spojování je podstatou komplikační skladby.') Quoted in Racek and Vysloužil, eds., *Leoš Janáček: O lidové písni a lidové hudbě*, p. 435.

C1 and C2: narrative

> Yesterday, 1 October 1924, it occurred to me that Insarov's Lola will certainly
> drown in [the Danube].
>
> (Janáček)[165]

Analysis C1 is Janáček's proposed narrative. Some prefatory theoretical remarks will be useful. In the nineteenth century the composition of instrumental works connected in various ways with literary models was commonly practised until after 1900. During the same period, the semantic potential of music was widely debated in discourse about music until, as Jim Samson observes, 'This issue was suppressed to an extent by the Formalism of our own century.'[166] In the last dozen years or so the topic has regained prominence, albeit with a new cast. Modern narrativisers tend to exhibit a quasi-scientific restraint, drawing their analogies from structuralist models such as Vladimir Propp's 'plot archetypes'. From this point of view, any instrumental work can constitute a narrative – even the finale of a Schumann string quartet.[167] The goal is to recreate the musical experience of a nineteenth-century listener in order to inform our own responses. One of this approach's most enthusiastic advocates has been Anthony Newcomb.

In an article about Schumann's Second Symphony, Newcomb proceeds from the plausible notion that the Finale begins as a *lieto fine* rondo, which is transformed into a sonata-form 'weighty, reflective summary'.[168] This transitional structure involves several intertextual references (notably to Beethoven's Fifth Symphony), signalling a minimal, two-stage 'plot archetype': 'struggle' leading to 'victory and resolution'. In a more recent article about Mahler's Ninth Symphony, Newcomb proposes as his plot archetype the 'spiral quest', which is found in the *Bildungsroman* (the

---

[165] ('Včera 1. října 1924 mi napadlo, že *Lola Insarova* jistě v něm utone.') Quoted from Adolf Veselý, ed., *Leoš Janáček: Pohled do života i díla* [Leoš Janáček: A View of the Life and Works] (Prague, 1924), p. 98 [Janáček's autobiography].

[166] Jim Samson, *Chopin: The Four Ballades* (Cambridge: Cambridge University Press, 1992), p. 81.

[167] See Anthony Newcomb, 'Schumann and Late Eighteenth-Century Narrative Strategies', *Nineteenth-century Music*, 11 (1987–8), pp. 164–74.

[168] Anthony Newcomb, 'Once More "Between Absolute and Programme Music"': Schumann's Second Symphony', *Nineteenth-century Music*, 7 (1983–4), pp. 233–50.

'Education of X Novel' – e.g. Dickens's *Great Expectations*).[169] Newcomb here invokes a greater variety of musical parameters (texture, disjunctions between 'characteristic styles' etc.) than in his analysis of Schumann's Second Symphony. He draws in poietic evidence (a verbal insertion by Mahler in the autograph) and the cultural context (Freud's ideas). All in all, his analysis certainly does not lack musical insight. Whether narrative is the most convincing vehicle for his analytical results is another matter.

Newcomb has come under sustained attack. To his most influential critic, Jean-Jacques Nattiez, it is not 'within the semiological possibilities of music to link a subject to a predicate'; hence 'music is not narrative and any description of its formal structure in terms of narrativity is nothing but superfluous metaphor'.[170] Carolyn Abbate attacks narrative strategies such as Newcomb's for their slavish adherence to 'what may be called a *miming model*' – deprived of her own voice, 'music dances to plots given to her from elsewhere'.[171] In Abbate's view, a 'defining mark' of narrative is a 'sense of the speaker's detachment, a particular human and moral stance toward the referential object of one's speech'; since 'Musical works . . . rarely have the capacity to present themselves as the voice of the teller', musical narrative is an exceptional and disruptive phenomenon.[172] More recently, the 'wrong turns by which . . . the case for musical narrative declines from metaphor into ontological illusion' are compellingly illustrated by Alan Street with reference to three potential narrative readings of Schoenberg's Five Orchestral Pieces, Op. 16.[173]

Robert Samuels proposes a partial rehabilitation of the plot archetype in relation to Mahler's Sixth Symphony.[174] He has his reservations about

---

169 Anthony Newcomb, 'Narrative Archetypes and Mahler's Ninth Symphony', in Steven Scher, ed., *Music and Text: Critical Inquiries* (Cambridge: Cambridge University Press, 1992), pp. 118–36.

170 Jean-Jacques Nattiez, 'Can One Speak of Narrativity in Music?' *Journal of the Royal Musical Association*, 115 (1990), pp. 240–57 (p. 257).

171 Carolyn Abbate, *Unsung Voices: Opera and Musical Narrative in the Nineteenth Century* (Princeton: Princeton University Press, 1991), p. 27.

172 Ibid., pp. 53 and 19.

173 Alan Street, 'The Obbligato Recitative: Narrative in Schoenberg's *Five Orchestral Pieces* Op. 16', in Pople, ed., *Theory, Analysis and Meaning in Music* (see note 7), pp. 164–83 (p. 182).

174 Robert Samuels, *Mahler's Sixth Symphony: A Study in Musical Semiotics* (Cambridge: Cambridge University Press, 1995), pp. 133–65.

Newcomb, but at least Newcomb's avenue of approach 'envisages a semiotic code by which the listener engages with the musical text'. Samuels selects a plot archetype for Mahler's Sixth Symphony that takes into account the work's 'impulse towards negativity': 'The story of the protagonist struggling with forces that crush his or her individuality, promising and then denying freedom', which can be found in many nineteenth-century novels (e.g. *Madame Bovary* and *Anna Karenina*). This plot, which seen in terms of nineteenth-century culture and society 'virtually necessitates a female protagonist', runs as follows: 'adolescence and first realisation of social forces'; 'engagement with society, constraining personal choice'; 'the promise of freedom and attempted escape through personal fulfilment'; '*peripeteia* and ultimate extinction'. Samuels's musical analysis is markedly more sophisticated than that of Newcomb, paying notable attention to intertextuality and voice-leading. Also, he avoids Newcomb's 'biography in notes' tendency. His conclusion is that 'Mahler's Sixth Symphony represents the suicide of the Romantic symphony.' However, the reading has its limits. Most disturbingly, it compromises 'some of the narrative features which first suggested it' (e.g. 'the great dissimilarity of the individual movements'). Samuels has reached an aporia and now belatedly quotes Street.

This highly selective sketch of the theory of musical narrativity provides us with the most relevant context for Janáček's 'Jeux de vagues' narrative. We now need a brief outline of the reception history of the extra-musical dimension of *La mer*. Debussy's well-documented attitude to programme music does not encourage interpretation of the work in representational terms. Of Beethoven's 'Pastoral' Symphony he wrote that 'there is no attempt at direct imitation, but rather at capturing the *invisible* sentiments of nature'.[175] Trezise argues that a significant feature of the early reviews of *La mer* is the granting to the ocean of a 'voice'. He traces this to Jules Michelet's 'popular' *La mer* (published 1861). Trezise concludes that, to a certain extent, 'The main motifs of *La mer* are imbued with a quality of incantation, of ancient voices crying out from the depths of the oceans.'[176] This view neatly avoids the specific.

Recent writers on *La mer* tend to take Debussy's ambivalence about representation seriously. But even those who propose a connection with

---

[175] Quoted in Trezise, *Debussy: La mer*, p. 38.   [176] Ibid., p. 39.

Symbolism are very guarded.[177] Jonathan Dunsby articulates the dilemma in a recent article about *En blanc et noir* (1915). Drawing out some of the most striking resonances in the music of the poetic epigraphs to the three movements, he concludes:

> No degree of analysis of the purely musical structures of *En blanc et noir* can possibly reveal its historical moment ... Without the poetry, it is a denuded score. It is not, however, 'programme' music overall, not a 'depiction', but a work of high Symbolism in which the poetic and the musical intertwine in a way to which there is no 'solution' beyond the profound lure of interpretation.[178]

A few recent authors have nonetheless attempted to adopt a more straightforward narrative stance towards *La mer*. Three additional angles are explored by Trezise. The first is representational and is applied only to the opening bars of 'Jeux de vagues', which are described as 'a depiction of a gull diving into the water'.[179] The second has a psychobiographical slant.[180] Trezise uncovers a number of intertextual signifiers in 'Dialogue du vent et de la mer': the violent ' "Romantic" false climax' at the end, an overt connection between the start of the movement and a sketch for the closing stages of Debussy's unfinished opera *La chute de la maison Usher*, and an allusion in bb. 127–35 to the last act of *Götterdämmerung*. These references can be connected with various external factors: e.g. some of the material in *La mer* was probably taken from an abandoned 'Poe' Symphony of 1890. Out of all this emerges a narrative centred on the 'upheaval' and 'guilt' that Debussy experienced on leaving his wife Lilly for Emma Bardac in 1904: premonition of disaster (the first two movements), and terrifying turmoil and ultimately redemption through love (third movement). Based on rather scant musical evidence, this reading explains little of the first two movements and flirts perilously with the old-fashioned 'biography in notes' strategy. Trezise's third narrative approach is pure Newcomb in essence. This is his suggestion

---

[177] See, for example, Arnold Whittall, 'Impressionism', in *The New Grove: Dictionary of Music and Musicians*, ed. Stanley Sadie (London: Macmillan, 1980), vol. IX, pp. 30–1 (p. 31).

[178] Jonathan Dunsby, 'The Poetry of Debussy's *En blanc et noir*', in Craig Ayrey and Mark Everist, eds., *Analytical Strategies and Musical Interpretation: Essays on Nineteenth- and Twentieth-century Music* (Cambridge: Cambridge University Press, 1996), pp. 149–68 (p. 168).   [179] Trezise, *Debussy: La mer*, p. 62.

[180] Ibid., pp. 41–4.

that there are rhythmic, melodic and tonal 'narratives' spanning all three movements. His justification of such an analytical strategy is an open invitation to criticism:

> There is no evidence that Debussy's 'symphonic poem' tells a story ... But what *La mer* does have in common with a literary story is a sequence of musical events that echoes narrative devices such as an introductory paragraph or the speeding up of events as one reaches a climax ... These narratives account for the deep-seated sense of unity many have admired in *La mer*.[181]

Janáček's plot for 'Jeux de vagues' is rather different. He suggests that the movement's title, which he renders as 'Hra vln' (NB 'hra' is a singular noun), is a metaphor for a human drama, 'Hra života' (Play of Life). The scenario is crushingly deterministic. The movement's main theme, 'a flung-about wavelet' ('1'), is a metaphor for a human being buffeted by 'Fate'. Janáček's four other principal themes complete the story. First, the protagonist tries to engage in normal human pursuits (2 – 'cheerfulness, association [i.e. social interaction]'), attempts which are thwarted (3 – 'heavy black clouds'). This leads to dissolution, 'depression and isolation' (4), and ultimately death – a 'stroke of Fate' (5). This plot is in fact virtually identical with Samuels's for Mahler's Sixth Symphony.

Nevertheless, Janáček's programme seems an unlikely choice for a 'scherzo' middle movement, especially bearing in mind Debussy's comment that its ending is 'neither open nor closed'. One explanation is afforded by fol. 1v of Janáček's analysis (Appendix 10.2), the third column of which addresses the relationship between music and text in the 'symphonic poem'. Perhaps, then, Janáček viewed *La mer* as a cycle of three closely related symphonic poems, similar (if not identical) in format to his own *Taras Bulba* and *The Danube* (see p. 207 above). And, of course, Debussy's 'symphonic sketches' does raise significant difficulties as to the degree of connection between the movements. Be that as it may, many writers since 1945 have taken symphonic teleology in *La mer* for granted. Other commentators exude indecision. Having explored potential generic models including Schumann's *Overture, Scherzo and Finale*, Trezise concludes: 'If one did not know *La mer*, one might believe that the three move-

---

[181] Ibid., p. 76.

ments were separate works'.[182] However, this pronouncement does not prevent him from immediately launching into a detailed exposition of narratives embracing all the movements. All in all, Janáček's apparent equanimity in treating 'Jeux de vagues' as to some extent 'a separate work' is not entirely unreasonable.

It is extremely profitable to pursue Janáček's plot archetype from another angle: its cultural context. Janáček's metaphor of the hostile forces of Nature controlling human destiny is a standard nineteenth-century trope. We already know from Samuels's work that it is decidedly common in nineteenth-century (especially realist) novels. One might add that it is also frequently encountered in Russian (and Czech) realist dramas, notably Ostrovsky's *The Storm* (1859). The central protagonists in *Anna Karenina*, *Madame Bovary* and *The Storm* are women; all three commit suicide. As Margaret Higonnet remarks, 'In the nineteenth century, women's suicide becomes a cultural obsession.'[183] Nineteenth-century literature feminises suicide, treating it as a 'malady' – a result of mental breakdown, frequently caused by a woman's abandonment by a lover.

We do not know the gender or manner of death of Janáček's fictitious protagonist. Or do we? There is strong circumstantial evidence that she is in fact female, and that she kills herself. Janáček was completing *Káťa Kabanová* when he wrote his *La mer* analysis (see p. 204 above). That opera's libretto, based on Ostrovsky's *The Storm*, contains all the characteristic elements of the stereotypical female suicide plot. Káťa is subjected to intense bullying by her mother-in-law, and to beatings by her weak drunkard of a husband. She takes Boris as her lover and is driven to confess publicly. Boris abandons her, and she sinks into crazed despair, finally throwing herself into the Volga, whose primal, unintelligible voice (represented by an offstage wordless chorus) lures her to her inevitable demise. Contributing to her downfall are social forces, religion, Nature and her own inclinations. She is powerless, as Janáček's famous pervasive timpani motive reminds us. The protagonist of the 'Jeux de vagues' plot could easily be Káťa.

There is more. Janáček's output as a whole is strikingly preoccupied with the death of female characters: e.g. *Věc Makropulos* (The Makropulos

---

[182]   Ibid.
[183]   Margaret Higonnet, 'Suicide: Representations of the Feminine in the Nineteenth Century', *Poetics Today*, 6, nos. 1–2, (1985), pp. 103–18 (p. 103).

Affair; 1923–5), the *Vixen* (where the heroine's death is his own invention), and the First String Quartet 'inspired' by Tolstoy's novella *The Kreutzer Sonata* (1923, adapted from the Piano Trio of 1908; rev. 1909). More particularly, Janáček displays an enthusiasm for suicide. As regards opera, in addition to *Kát'a* there are sketches for an unfinished *Anna Karenina* (1907). Even *Její pastorkyňa* (Her Stepdaughter; 1894–1903; rev. 1906–7), although containing an actual body count of only one baby boy, merits closer inspection. Nancy Miller argues that the 'myth of the problematic heroine' is integral to the development of the novel, adapting to her purpose Greimas's distinction between 'dysphoric' and 'euphoric' plots. In the former plot type, the heroine is driven to a premature death (e.g. *Clarissa*); in the latter, she submits to a sterile marriage without describable future – in effect, another form of suicide (*Moll Flanders*).[184] The 1890 Gabriela Preissová play on which Janáček's opera is based is a classic 'euphoric' plot: abandoned by a spineless lover, Jenůfa is driven into an unpromising marriage. Significantly, Preissová's other play (originally a short story) that was used for an opera libretto – *Gazdina roba* (The Farmer's Woman; 1889), set to music with the title *Eva* by Josef Foerster (1899) – is a 'dysphoric' counterpart to *Her Stepdaughter*: Eva commits suicide by casting herself into the Danube.

Another of Janáček's female suicide works is the male-voice chorus *Maryčka Magdónova* (1906; rev. 1907). The young working-class heroine, assailed by a series of appalling personal disasters and then arrested for a trivial offence, throws herself into the river Ostravice. This brings us to Janáček's overriding obsession: female death by inundation – one of the most resonant tropes of all the nineteenth-century arts, the iconographic *locus classicus* of which is John Everett Millais's *Ophelia* (1852). Janáček's women are prone to an 'Ophelia complex'. Even Emilia Marty, voluntarily surrendering herself to death as the lesser of two evils, is, like Isolde, 'drowned' by the orchestra. Of course, many musical heroines drown themselves (Senta in *Der fliegende Holländer* is a particularly spectacular example); and the heroines of works by Slavic composers are particularly likely to do so: Lisa in Tchaikovsky's *The Queen of Spades* (reviewed most

---

[184] Nancy Miller, *The Heroine's Text: Readings in the French and English Novel* (New York: Columbia University Press, 1985).

warmly by Janáček in 1896)[185] is yet another example; and indeed, at the end of Shostakovich's *Lady Macbeth of the Mtsensk District*, Katerina drags her rival Sonyetka with her into the water. But to no other composer was the drowning woman such an irresistible topic as it was to Janáček. The protagonist in his 'Jeux de vagues' narrative might well commit suicide by flinging herself into the sea.

Inevitably, then, Janáček's *The Danube* is connected with at least two drowned women. A cutting from the Brno daily *Lidové noviny* preserved with the autograph score is wholly predictable. This is of *Lola*, a poem by Alexander Insarov (the pen name of Soňa Špálová). Its three verses tell of a prostitute who has fallen on hard times. At the end of it Janáček has scribbled: 'She jumps into the Danube'. This emendation is confirmed publicly in his autobiography (see the epigraph to this section). It is not clear in which movement(s) Lola's demise is depicted, although Vogel suggests the fourth. Vogel further notes that there are in the autograph of the second movement quotations from Pavla Křičková's *Utonula* (The Drowned Girl).[186] The protagonist of this poem is a curious hybrid of Lucretia and Ophelia, drowning herself when she discovers that a youth has been watching her preparing to bathe naked. At least one of the quotations is attached to a viola motive that is 'a rudimentary setting of the words'.[187] Janáček's manuscript calls to mind Dvořák's autograph of his 'symphonic poem' *Holoubek* (The Wild Dove; 1896), a piece about which Janáček published an analysis.[188] Here too Dvořák inserted text, some of which he seems actually to have set in order to create instrumental motives. Needless to say, that work's programme involves yet another female suicide by drowning. All this sheds light on the scherzo-like third movement of *The Danube*, with its exhilarating vocalise for solo soprano. The implication seems to be that Křičková's drowned girl – now part Lorelei, part water nymph – has merged with the water's fatally alluring voice and is 'singing' from the bottom of the Danube, an implication strengthened by the fact that at the end of this 'scherzo' the soprano pertinently quotes from/pre-echoes a motive from the finale (bb. 175–81 etc.) of the Wind Sextet *Mládí* (Youth; 1924).

The idea of women who drown themselves becoming mermaids is

---

[185] See note 136.   [186] Vogel, *Leoš Janáček: A Biography* (see note 3), pp. 288–9.
[187] Ibid., p. 289.   [188] See note 9.

another powerful nineteenth-century trope with a long historical pedigree. It is the Slavonic Rusalka who most potently combines the 'mermaid' and 'female suicide by drowning' tropes. In Dargomyzhsky's *Rusalka* (1856, given at the Prague National Theatre in 1889) the heroine is a human girl who becomes a water nymph when she drowns herself, betrayed by her aristocratic lover. Also, Jaroslav Kvapil's libretto for Dvořák's *Rusalka* (1900) can be mapped on to Janáček's 'Jeux de vagues' narrative. Rusalka is granted human attributes by a witch so that she can pursue the young Prince. Unfortunately, she is denied powers of speech and is warned that, should the Prince prove false, they will both be damned forever ('human being into Fate'). She initially enchants the Prince, who introduces her into court society ('cheerfulness, association'). However, his attention wanders to a foreign Princess ('heavy black clouds'), which results in Rusalka being condemned to wander as 'will-o'-the wisp' ('isolation'). The Prince's 'stroke of Fate' is administered by Rusalka herself in the form of a kiss, after which she, unsuccessful as a human, sinks alone into the water – her 'stroke of Fate'.

This brief examination of the network of associations raised by Janáček's 'Jeux de vagues' programme shows that his response to the movement was over-determined. Even so, in our gender-conscious era one cannot help feeling squeamish about all this. Superficially, Janáček is sympathetic towards his heroines: he describes Kát'a in a letter to Kamila Stösslová as 'a young woman ... of such a soft nature that I'm frightened that if the sun shone fully on her, she would melt, yes even dissolve'.[189] But Janáček's very reliance on social victimisation, his paternalistic attitude towards Kát'a, as well as his emphasis on Kát'a's fragile passivity, are all disquieting. Yet more distasteful is his penchant for violence: his women *hurl* themselves into the water. In contrast, the heroines of some nineteenth-century women writers – notably Maggie Tulliver in *The Mill on the Floss* and Edna Pontellier in Kate Chopin's *The Awakening* – are gently 'embraced' and carried away by the water.

It is dangerous to review the past through the filter of our own cultural agenda. However, one important point needs to be made. The reception of much of Janáček's music is today still dominated by the sentimental

---

[189] Tyrrell, *Intimate Letters*, p. 30.

notion of Kamila Stösslová as muse. This puzzling manifestation of the psychobiographical hermeneutic impulse run amok is enshrined in John Tyrrell's translation of a substantial proportion of the correspondence between Janáček and Stösslová. In his preface, Tyrrell asserts effusively that these letters are 'by far the most important source for the understanding of Janáček's emotional and creative life in the last twelve years of his life', adding that 'they contain a great love story'.[190] If nothing else, it may be a useful corrective to this, the most enduring of all Janáček myths, for us to remember that Janáček's obsession with Stösslová has its darker side.

Returning to 'Jeux de vagues', Janáček's analytical basis for his plot archetype concerns a respectably wide range of musical dimensions. He seems to have drawn his image of the wave mercilessly tossed around by deeper forces and hence of the human battered by Fate from what he perceives as the relationship between motive and other structural elements in the movement: dynamic 'waves' and goal-directed rhythmic and tonal processes are the primary factors, not the evolutionary motivic transformations. More specifically, in bb. 1–163 the motivic domain in general (representing the protagonist) focusses increasingly on motive '2', whose grace notes, trills and arabesques imply 'cheerfulness' and attempts at social integration. The emphatic expulsion of this motive by the build-up to the final highpoint and the movement's subsequent collapse into motivic fragmentation are seemingly analogous in Janáček's opinion to the descent of his female protagonist into madness and suicide. The last statement of motive '1' is symptomatic: in bb. 257–8 its defining whole-tone tetrachord is ultimately extinguished, as it is absorbed into diatonic harp arpeggios. The entire plot is summed up in Analysis C2, where the motivic essence of bb. 1–214 in C4 is summed up by a pseudo-mathematical formula and the caption 'argument' (i.e. resistance), that of bb. 225–61 by a few motivic labels, a decrescendo mark and the caption 'resignation' (i.e. capitulation). Strangely, there is some support for Janáček's interpretation in Debussy's 'Coda', in the form of an unlikely intertextual reference in bb. 231–6, which are, in the words of Trezise, 'remarkably similar to the off-stage chorus that evokes the storm and Gilda's impending murder in Act III of [Verdi's

---

190 Ibid., p. xi.

Rigoletto]'.[191] Gilda gives herself up passively to murder, thus in effect committing suicide, and we know that the sack containing the body is ultimately destined for the river.

To Janáček, without a narrative 'Jeux de vagues' is thus (to quote Dunsby) a 'denuded score', in spite of all his detailed 'analysis of purely musical structures'. Significantly, he also feels compelled to sketch a narrative for 'Dialogue du vent et de la mer' on fol. 3r of his *La mer* analysis, this time a more literal affair involving a conflict between the 'prosebné' (plaintive) wind and the sea, which prevails, thereby ensuring the wind's 'zánik' (extinction) – obviously a reference to the 'grand slam conclusion'. The comments on fol. 1v (Appendix 10.2) amplify this viewpoint, implying that although music has 'deeper roots in *things* and their affectivity' than words, the 'complex reactions' in a 'programmatic symphonic poem' create a 'logical' structure that is only apparently self-referential: these 'complex reactions' demand (and defy) interpretation. The positioning of the 'Jeux de vagues' narrative in the manuscript is revealing. Everything suggests that it is a late addition, squashed in on a verso; an addendum to Janáček's argument. The necessity *and* inadequacy of his plot archetype are laid bare. What Janáček is doing is narrativising his purely musical analysis rather than the actual music. This is what all narratively inclined musical analysts do at the draft stage, often presenting their thought processes in reverse order in the printed product to imbue their narrative plots with immediacy. Janáček's *La mer* analysis reminds us that, if any work invites a narrative analytical strategy, the invitation is booby-trapped.

Conclusion

This bottom-up examination of Janáček as musical theorist and analyst suggests strongly that little he has to say can justifiably be regarded as incoherent, or even idiosyncratic. It also indicates that those who feel compelled to justify his theoretical work on tangential grounds are misguided. Janáček's principal ideas in fact intersect with, and contribute to, the major trends of twentieth-century thought about music. Moreover, much of his 'home-made' terminology (Tyrrell's description)[192] actually proves to be

---

[191] Trezise, *Debussy: La mer*, p. 48.   [192] Tyrrell, 'Janáček', p. 48.

eclectic, merely requiring his reader to be well acquainted with the important musico-theoretical, philosophical and scientific texts of his time. His analysis of 'Jeux de vagues', probably the first ever to be written, is penetrating in its own right, and it adumbrates many of the concerns of later analysts. The supposedly abstruse 'metaphysical' element of his theory of *sčasování* turns out in analytical practice to consist of perfectly comprehensible ideas about narrativity that are of considerable relevance today. Quite simply, Janáček's achievements in the field of music theory and analysis have not received the acknowledgement they deserve.

Appendix 10.1 Janáček's *La mer* analysis, fols 1r and 2r; 'Jeux de vagues', Analyses A and B

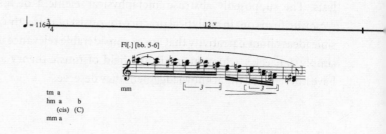

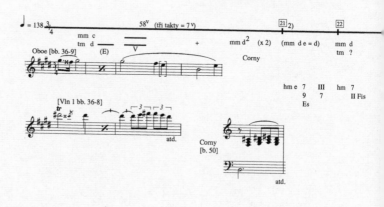

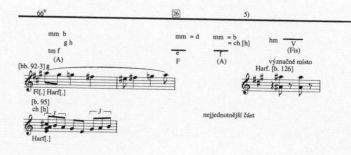

La mer

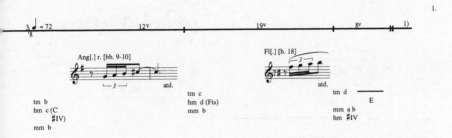

275

Appendix 10.1 *(cont.)*

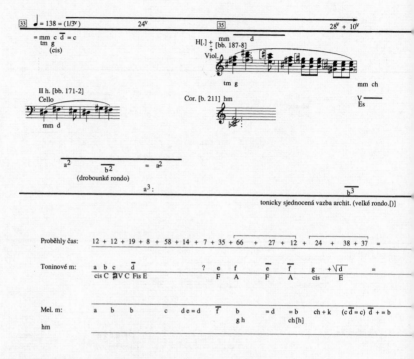

Amplifications/Translations for fols. 1r and 2r

Instruments

Ang[lický] r[oh]	English horn
Cl[arinetto in] A	
[Contra] bass[o]/Cont[rabasso]	
Cor[no in] F/Corny	Horn/Horns
Fl[étna]/Fl[étny]	Flute/Flutes
Harf[a]/Harf[y]	Harp/Harps
H[ousle]	Violin(s)
Tymp[ány]	Timpani
Vio[ly]/Viol[y]	Violas

Verbal insertions

a t[ak] d[ále]	et cetera
deset	ten
drobounké rondo	miniature rondo

276